COMPUTER PROGRAMMING
LANGUAGES MADE SIMPLE

COMPUTER PROGRAMMING LANGUAGES MADE SIMPLE

Calvin A. Hofeditz

MADE SIMPLE BOOKS
DOUBLEDAY & COMPANY. INC.
GARDEN CITY. NEW YORK
1984

Library of Congress Cataloging in Publication Data
Hofeditz, Calvin A.
     Computer programming languages made simple.
     (Made simple books)
     Includes index.
     1. Programming languages (Electronic computers)
I. Title.   II. Series.
QA76.7.H63   1984   001.64'24
ISBN: 0-385-18087-X
Library of Congress Catalog Card Number 82-45326

Contents

Contents

Introduction

WHY LEARN TO PROGRAM?

Despite the simplification of computer systems in the past few years, they are still complex tools. And there is a great difference between operating a machine and programming one. A *user* often has a tutorial display shown on the screen to guide him through a task. Even if such instructions are not provided, there is always an operator's manual to rely on for assistance.

On the other hand, the *programmer* has to create the displays on the screen, determine how the computer performs, and write the operating instructions. Quite a difference, indeed. Somewhat like the difference between using a lawn mower and building one.

It's not difficult to write simple programs in BASIC and Pascal. Within a week and using no more than ten of the instructions in either of these computer languages, the beginner can have his computer performing many calculations and other tasks.

Unfortunately, these tasks alone do not justify the cost of a computer and its software for they could be done with a calculator and basic instructions. Thus, the beginner is not likely to be satisfied with having developed only a rudimentary programming skill.

There are, of course, many reasons why people would want to develop the ability to use computers and the programming languages available with them. All are related to self-interest.

The Competition Will Use the New Tools

The computer is a new tool that is rapidly becoming available to millions of people who have never used sophisticated equipment before. With respect to small businesses, computers properly applied can greatly reduce operating costs. Small machines can be purchased or leased, and time on larger machines can be rented. These new tools and methods are available, and are being used by a great many small businesses now. Use of computers will spread even more quickly as prices continue to come down. The small businessman has no choice. He must learn to use these new tools to his advantage because the competition will.

To Organize Jobs for the Computer

But why does the computer user need to know anything about programming and programming languages? To organize jobs for the computer to process is one answer. There is much more involved in processing a stack of bills to be paid than sitting in front of a display screen and typing the information at the keyboard. Actually, the data entry at the machine is the last step in the organizing process. Before the power switch is turned on for the first time, the user must have determined which records are to be maintained and in what form, how the bill-paying process is to affect other records, and what the outputs are to be. The organizing of inputs, processing, and outputs for each task will always be required. The more the computer user knows about programming, the better he will be able to organize his jobs.

To Understand the Products Offered

Another good reason is to understand what you're buying. Differences in programs and programming languages have a dramatic effect on the performance of a computer. The sales sheets available to the prospective computer user aren't much help unless he is able to understand the material listed.

Many programs are often provided only as extra-cost options. Even the lowest-priced retailer is offering programming language packages at about $300 each. A poor choice of machine and programs can thus be very expensive to the owner of a small computer; not only in terms of actual cost but also in disappointing performance. It pays off, therefore, to understand the products being offered before buying them.

Do-It-Yourself Projects

The fourth reason for learning to program may be the most important. It is *the need to do it yourself*. Although there are hundreds of programs available for the most popular computers, it may be difficult to find one that fits your task perfectly. The alternatives in this case are to change your methods to match the capacity of the program, to hire a programmer to prepare a customized program, or finally to do it yourself.

As a Hobby and for Entertainment

We haven't said much about personal computers so far, having concentrated on business use. But let's assume that you are interested in a personal computer.

It's hard to define exactly what a personal computer is. We can say, however, that it is a small desktop unit, and if it has supporting equipment it is likely to be limited to a small printer and a tape unit. What does it do? Generally anything that a big machine does, only in smaller volumes and more slowly.

As of this writing, personal computers are offered for sale at prices as low as $100. These are incomplete machines, however. They rely on using a TV screen for display and a cassette tape recorder for storage, but they are unable to communicate with other machines without optional adapters. A complete personal computer with diskette storage and a display screen still costs $2,500 and up. At these prices, it is an expensive "toy," so we have to assume that the buyer uses it for tasks other than entertainment.

A wide variety of programs are available for the most popular personal computers. Most are optional, and they're not cheap. Therefore, one good way to get the most use out of a personal computer is to program it yourself. It should be an interesting hobby for those liking mathematics and electronics.

Most readers interested in programming their own machines are likely to prefer BASIC, particularly a modern version. This is a good selection because it is widely offered with personal computers, and the new versions have been developed fully to handle graphics and provide other features the novice programmer should find attractive.

And as a Profession

Skilled programmers are in great demand in the job market, and this should remain so for the foreseeable future. Many people in the computer industry believe that equipment development has outpaced the programs and considerable time will elapse before the programmers catch up.

In general, an applicant for a programmer's job should have a four-year degree in a field of learning that provides considerable training in mathematics. A good deal of the work involved in programming is similar to that necessary to lay out and solve a complex equation. In fact, the word "algorithm," which is seen in mathematics, is also frequently used to mean "the programming solution to a problem."

WHY ARE THERE SO MANY LANGUAGES?

The answer to this question is fairly simple. Computers have been used in business for over thirty years, while some models were used in engineering and scientific applications even before that. A great many models were developed during this time. As one would expect, programming groups were also busy providing languages for the various models, always trying to make the languages more powerful and easy to use. Logically then, many languages were produced.

Among the most commonly used high-level languages are BASIC, COBOL, FORTRAN, Pascal, and RPG. We cover all of them in this book but devote less attention to RPG, a language with a limited purpose and whose instructions are not in the same class as the others mentioned, and to FORTRAN, which is primarily intended for engineering and scientific applications. Any serious reader will have no difficulty in finding descriptions of at least five more high-level languages on a computer science bookshelf in a large bookstore.

WHAT YOU'LL
FIND IN EACH CHAPTER

When one reaches the computer science section in a bookstore, one finds that most of the reference books dealing with programming languages are fairly large. A typical reference book on BASIC alone has as many pages as this one. How then can we hope to discuss such complex subjects within these covers? We'll answer that question in the following paragraphs.

The largest portion of this book is devoted to three very popular languages—BASIC, Pascal, and COBOL. Each has a good deal in common with the others. Records, files, arithmetic operators, coding forms, and flowcharts, for example, are more alike than different from one language to another. Therefore, one general discussion of these subjects common to all languages is given in Chapter 2.

Next, we have concentrated on the "core" of each language, eliminating discussions of rarely used instructions and those that apply to only one brand of computer. Knowledge of uncommon instructions is of very little use to anyone other than a programmer of a specific model.

We've also limited the number of sample programs to one per language. A great many programming books have an excess of sample programs and only the most dedicated reader ever uses them.

These are some of the ways in which we've managed to "boil down" a great deal of material to a usable size. Now let's examine how the material is organized and what you can expect to find in each chapter.

There are six chapters, which are supplemented by a Glossary of Terms. Each chapter is followed by a self-test. The six chapters are:

Chapter 1. What Programming Is
      2. Components of a Programming Language
      3. BASIC, *Beginner's All-purpose Symbolic Instruction Code*
      4. Pascal
      5. COBOL, *Common Business Oriented Language*
      6. Other Languages, Old and New

Chapter 1, What Programming Is, provides the fundamentals: What programs are, how they are planned and organized, what elements of the computer the programmer controls, flowcharting, and how computer data is organized.

Chapter 2, Components of a Programming Language, covers material common to all languages. It shows that each language is really a system, consisting of a set of words the programmer may use and a group of complex programs that interpret and apply those words. The entry program, the compiler, and the run-time system are described, and their relationship to the programmer is shown.

This chapter also discusses syntax diagrams and coding forms, which establish the sentences that may be used and the form in which they are provided. Next covered are topics common to all languages, including character sets, operators, variables, constants, expressions, arrays, functions, and procedures.

Chapters 3, 4, and 5 each deal with a specific programming language, covering *BASIC, Pascal,* and *COBOL,* respectively. Each chapter provides the following information:

- A brief history of the language's development and use.
- A description of how the programming system is organized. Its major components, divisions of instructions, and a description of its instruction set (instruction-by-instruction).
- How a program is written, including a sample program.
- A self-test, including exercises in which programming statements must be written.

Chapter 6, Other Languages, Old and New, discusses those languages which the reader is less likely to use but should know about. Included are descriptions of FORTRAN and RPG II. This chapter does not provide programming examples but does show the instruction set and the appearance of a program. Also included in Chapter 6 are descriptions of recent additions to BASIC. And concluding this chapter is a description of a unique language called "Logo."

COMPUTER PROGRAMMING LANGUAGES MADE SIMPLE

1

What Programming Is

THE PURPOSE OF A PROGRAM

Many people think of a computer as an intelligent machine; it is not. All the "intelligence" is entered into the machine by man, either as part of the machine design or in the form of a program. The computers that we concern ourselves with in this book do no useful work without a program.

The question to be asked then is: What is a program? And the answer is a very simple one: It is a set of instructions that make the computer perform a specific task. The instructions chosen must all be within the capacity of the computer to perform them, and they must be arranged in the proper order.

Computer programmers originally had to choose from a set of instructions each of which executed a very small step. A great many instructions were necessary to perform even small jobs, and arranging the steps in order was a complex task, requiring a great deal of time and skill.

Fortunately, high-level programming languages have been available for many years. A high-level language is one in which each instruction performs a recognizable operation rather than one small step. For example, a PRINT instruction in the high-level language called BASIC causes information to be shown on the screen. Actually, the computer must execute many small steps to produce the display, but a programmer using the high-level language does not have to be concerned about them.

WHAT IS SOFTWARE?

For many years the term "software" has meant the programs that a computer executes. "Hardware" has become the commonly used term for the equipment—it being "hard" in the sense that it is not easily changed—and "software" is used to mean the programs and their supporting materials, such as instructions on how to use them.

A good way to visualize what software is is to use a home stereo system as an analogy. The stereo is the hardware, and while it may have some optional equipment, such as a cassette tape player, and several levels of performance, once the options are chosen, the stereo system is not easily or inexpensively changed. The same holds true for computer hardware.

If we now extend this comparison, the tape cassette, the phonograph record, and the eight-track cartridge are the "software" for the stereo system. They are easily changed and make the machine play what the user wants it to.

Although the media on which music is supplied and the methods for playing it have become standardized, computer software has not. What will "play" on one computer may be totally useless on another. Some software can be transferred from one type of machine to another, but the process is not yet a simple one. As computers come into very widespread use we can expect to see great improve-

1

ments in the ability to transfer and convert programs. As yet, however, many computer users can expect to find that they have to shop around, write their own programs, or be satisfied with "rock music" when they really want to hear Beethoven.

TYPES OF PROGRAMS

The next subject we'll discuss is the types of programs. First to come to mind are the programs that make the computer perform useful work, such as printing a telephone bill. These are called "application programs." To look at it from another point of view: Application programs are those that make the computer do the things that the user bought or leased it for. Of course, these "applications" cover a very wide range of tasks.

A second type of program is one that does the "housekeeping chores" associated with the application of the computer. These "housekeepers" are called utility programs. Although they are application programs themselves, they are thought of as a separate category because they support the main tasks rather than perform them themselves. Copying files of data and purging outdated files are examples of "utility" functions.

So, application programs and their subdivision, utility programs, are the ones that the operator of the computer uses every day, and they may be the only programs the operator ever sees producing results. There are other types, however, that are of equal importance.

Diagnostic programs are the ones used to isolate failures when problems arise. The nature of computer design, function, and construction make it difficult to find a failing part by simply observing the failure symptoms. An exercise of the machine's functions is necessary. This is the purpose of diagnostic programs. They try all the functions that the computer is designed to perform, and they summarize the results for a repairman.

Now we'll get to the programming languages that are the subject of this book. A programming language is a set of commands that a programmer can give the computer, but there is much more to it than that. It is really a "programming system," which is made up of several complex programs. The system is loaded into the computer before the language is used. In later chapters, we'll discuss the details of a programming system, but for now, we'll say only

that it consists of entry programs, listing programs, assembler and compiler programs, interpreter programs, and aids that make it possible to use the language.

Last on our list is a type of program that computer users seldom see, and most users may not even be aware of its presence. It is called an operating system. It is a link between the computer equipment and most types of programs we've discussed up to now. An operating system is provided to get the computer started and establish the initial operating conditions. It then manages loading of other programs, organizes storage media, and handles access to the storage media.

ELEMENTS THAT CAN BE PROGRAMMED

One of the first questions that should come to mind is: What components of the computer can actually be given instructions? The answer to that is that there are several, some of which produce visible results and others of which appear to do nothing at all. There are five basic things that the programmer of a small machine can control:

a. The output on a printer or typewriter.
b. Acceptance of inputs from a keyboard.
c. The display of information on a screen.
d. The storage of information on storage media such as diskettes, disks, and tapes.
e. The internal functions that the computer is capable of performing.

In the case of a printer or typewriter, the programmer selects the information to be printed and positions it on the paper.

In the case of inputs from a keyboard, the programmer determines when the computer will accept the inputs and, in some cases, what kind of information may be entered.

When programming the display screen, the programmer selects the information to be shown and determines where it will appear on the screen.

Storage of information requires the programmer to select the storage medium, to name and organize the stored information, and determine when it will be stored or read.

Finally, each computer has a limited number of functions it can perform. Selecting from these functions, the programmer tells the computer which functions to perform and the order in which they are to be performed.

Programming a Printer

What can be chosen on a printer? The characters to be printed is the obvious answer, but there are other answers as well. First, the programmer may choose either the character to be printed or a variable. To illustrate: The programmer may say print the letter "A," or he may say print whatever character is held in location 5. The former is used when a specific message is to be printed, and the latter is used when there is no way to know in advance what this information will be.

The programmer can also choose the position on the paper in which the information is printed. He can specify the number of the line on which printing is to begin and the column in which the first character is to be placed. Some programming systems also permit the use of the "tab" feature, which is used in generally the same way as it is on a typewriter.

Now let's examine the type of instructions that the programmer uses to make the printer operate. The words available depend upon the language, but PRINT, WRITE, and WRITELN (write a line) are typical. The action they produce is shown in Figure 1-1. Information is taken from the computer and printed on a form in the printer. Directions to place this information in a specific location on the page are either provided along with the information or are given separately prior to printing.

Programming a Keyboard

Controlling inputs from the keyboard is another important function that the programmer must consider. When programs are being executed by the computer, they pay no attention to the keyboard unless specifically instructed to do so. Therefore, the programmer must provide a statement that causes the computer to pause, accept the typed entry, and then proceed.

Again we'll use a figure (Figure 1-2) to show the movement of information. Typical instructions available to do this job are ACCEPT, INPUT, READ, and READLN (read a line). Each takes data typed at the keyboard and places it in a specific storage location in the computer; the location is selected by the same instruction that gets the data. The instructions we've listed don't process the information or take action based on its contents; they simply read it.

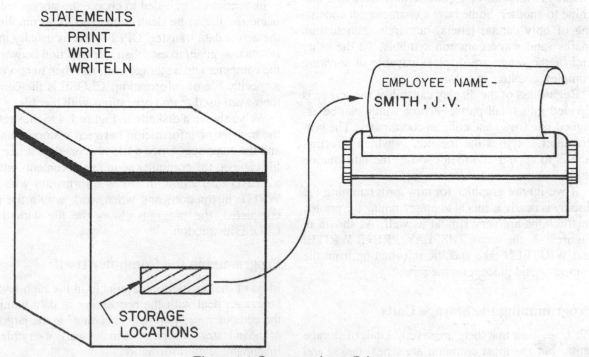

Figure 1-1 Programming a Printer

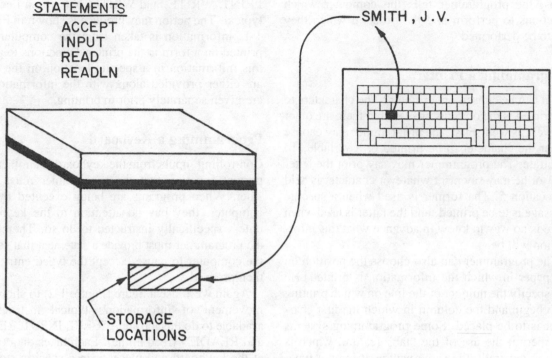

STATEMENTS
ACCEPT
INPUT
READ
READLN

SMITH, J.V.

STORAGE
LOCATIONS

Figure 1-2 Acquiring Data from a Keyboard

Programming a Display

Displays available vary considerably from one machine to another. Some have a character set consisting of only capital letters, numerals, punctuation marks, and some common symbols. At the other end of the range are displays capable of showing complex graphics in color.

Regardless of the display capability, the screen is divided into small parts, each of which can be assigned line (row) and column coordinates. The programmer specifies the location in which information is to appear and then chooses the information itself.

If we ignore graphics for now, programming the display is nearly identical to programming the printer. Instructions are very similar as well. As shown in Figure 1-3, the words DISPLAY, PRINT, WRITE, and WRITELN take specific information from the computer and place it on the screen.

Programming the Storage Units

We'll see later that there are several kinds of storage units, but the most common are tapes, disks, and diskettes. They hold files of information that the program is to process, and they store the results in either new or existing files.

Instructions are needed to choose the storage unit, name the file to be dealt with, and to accomplish the actual data transfer. OPEN-a-file is usually the instruction given to establish a connection between the computer and a storage unit, and then to choose a specific file of information. CLOSE is the common word used to end operations with that file.

We've shown a diskette in Figure 1-4 to illustrate the transfer of information between a storage unit and the computer. Once a file is opened, just like a file cabinet, the computer acquires its contents with a READ instruction. It stores information with a WRITE instruction, and when work with a file is completed, the program closes the file with the CLOSE instruction.

Programming the Computer Itself

Most of the instructions available in the high-level languages deal with the processing of data within the computer, or "number crunching" in the jargon of the industry. Computers can do nearly everything imaginable with information.

Of course, the word "computer" makes most

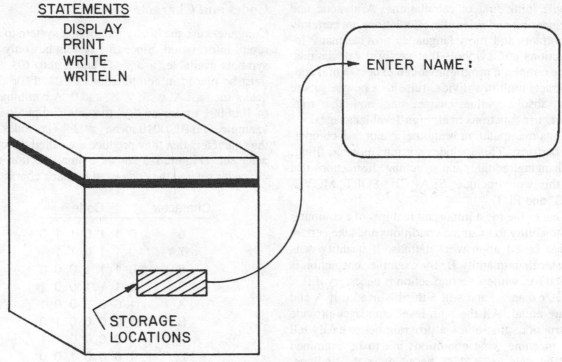

STATEMENTS
   DISPLAY
   PRINT
   WRITE
   WRITELN

STORAGE
LOCATIONS

ENTER NAME:

Figure 1-3 Displaying Information

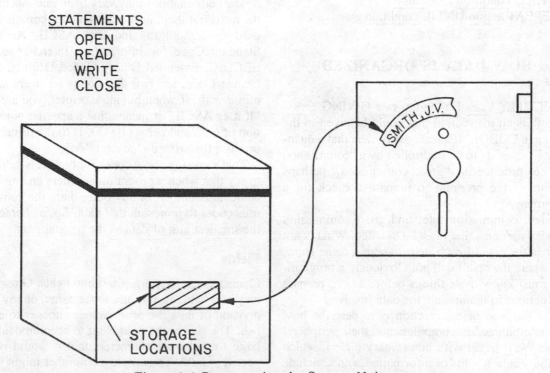

STATEMENTS
   OPEN
   READ
   WRITE
   CLOSE

STORAGE
LOCATIONS

SMITH, J.V.

Figure 1-4 Programming the Storage Units

people think first of calculations. Arithmetic and engineering and scientific calculations are certainly important, and most languages provide many instructions and symbols that perform calculations. For example, a programmer can expect to find add, subtract, multiply, divide, raise to a power, square root, absolute value, cosine, sine, and other trigonometric functions in all high-level languages.

Data manipulation is another major task computers perform. This includes sorting, moving, filing, exchanging, editing, and searching. Instructions that do this work include: SEARCH, SORT, MOVE, GET, and PUT.

One of the most important features of a computer is the ability to examine conditions and take certain action based upon what it finds. If quantity A is greater than quantity B, for example, one action is called for, while a second action is necessary if B is greater than A, and still a third is needed if A and B are equal. All the high-level languages provide instructions that allow a programmer to easily tell the machine what conditions are to be examined and what is to be done based upon the findings. Among the instructions available are:

IF condition THEN action 1 ELSE action 2
ON condition GOTO part of program
WHILE condition DO action
REPEAT action UNTIL condition

HOW DATA IS ORGANIZED

"MULTIPLY sales BY comm-rate GIVING gross-comm" is an instruction that could be given in the language COBOL. It's reasonably clear that a quantity of "sales" is to be multiplied by a "commission rate" to produce the "gross commission," perhaps as part of the program to prepare a check for a salesman.

Sales, commission rate, and gross commission are all data items that must be handled. What is not clear is the size of each item, where it came from, and where the result will go. Obviously, a programmer must know these things before he can prepare instructions to manipulate the data involved.

The purpose of this section is to describe how data is organized in computers and their peripheral units. We'll begin with bits (*bi*nary digi*ts*), which are the smallest units of information, and conclude with data bases, which are often giant collections.

Codes and Characters

Computers use the binary numbering system to represent information. Since this system has only two symbols available, a one (1) and a zero (0), they must be placed in combinations to stand for characters such as: A, ¢, 3, 7, Z, and 0. A combination of 1000001 means an "A" to some computers, for example, and 0110010 means a "2." The codes and the characters that they produce are called the character set. (Figure 1-5 shows a small section of a character set and the code used for each character.)

Character	Code
6	0 1 1 0 1 1 0
7	0 1 1 0 1 1 1
8	0 1 1 1 0 0 0
9	0 1 1 1 0 0 1
A	1 0 0 0 0 0 1
B	1 0 0 0 0 1 0
C	1 0 0 0 0 1 1
D	1 0 0 0 1 0 0
E	1 0 0 0 1 0 1

Figure 1-5 Codes and a
Character Set

The combinations may vary from one machine to the next, but there are some standard combinations used throughout the industry. ASCII, American Standard Code for Information Interchange, and EBCDIC, Extended Binary Coded Decimal Interchange Code, are two that computer users are familiar with. If when buying a printer, you are told, "It uses ASCII," it means that a specific combination of ones and zeros (1000001) to the printer will produce the printed character "A."

That's enough about codes for now. It is sufficient to say that when a programmer enters an employee name and number, or any other data, the computer uses codes to represent that data. So, a character is the smallest unit of data as the programmer sees it.

Fields

Characters are then organized into fields. Gross sales may be a field, as may employee name, or any other division of data the programmer chooses to establish. The size of the field is set to accommodate the largest number of characters that it would be expected to hold. The employee number might be set to seven characters, social security number to eleven characters, and employee name to twenty-one characters. A simple example of this is shown in Figure 1-6.

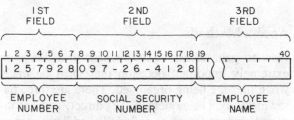

Figure 1-6 Fields in an Employee Record

Types of Fields

In Figure 1-6 we've shown three fields: employee number, social security number, and employee name. How are they used, and what characters may they hold? Well, they're certainly not added, subtracted, multiplied, or divided; the results would be nonsense. These then are alphanumeric fields, and they may hold any of the characters in the character set.

Suppose we added the employee pay rate field to our figure. It is intended to be used in arithmetic and thus may hold only numbers. The pay rate field, therefore, is a numeric field.

The distinction between numeric and alphanumeric fields is an important one because the fields are treated differently. High-level languages provide a way for the programmer to state the size of a field and whether it is numeric or alphanumeric. Within the computer itself, the fields are often represented differently.

Records

The next level of organization is usually the record,

in which fields of information related to one another are handled as a group. Record length depends upon the type of information.

A typical record is shown in Figure 1-7. It is moved between storage media as a unit, although the fields within it are used by themselves in calculations.

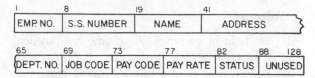

Figure 1-7 A Typical Record Format

A record can be identified and located in different ways. Each may include information that distinguishes it from all others (a label of some kind), or records may simply be numbered in sequential order so the fourth record in sequence is identified as record 4.

Files

Records organized into groups are called files. Normally, all the records in a file have the same format and pertain to the same subject. A file called PARTS LIST would contain many records each of which give the number, description, and price of a part. The fields holding these entries would be the same length in each record and appear in the same position. A simple example of such a file is shown in Figure 1-8.

Files have names and control information associated with them; this is stored on the recording medium along with data so that a file can be transported from one computer to another.

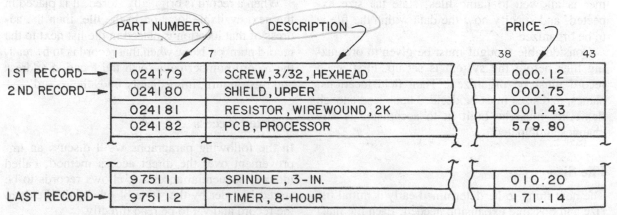

Figure 1-8 A Parts List File

Up to now, we haven't mentioned how records and files are held physically. Recording media consist of the tapes, diskettes, and disks mentioned earlier. There are other forms as well, cards for instance, but let's concentrate on the magnetic recording media.

A Volume

Files are held in volumes. A volume is a physical unit of storage: a disk, a diskette, a reel of tape. Files occupy less than a full volume in most systems but this is not always true. Volumes include labels and control information, such as the names of the files present, the space occupied by each, and the remaining space available. Programs that control the recording of information examine this information to determine if there is space available before recording new data.

PLANNING A DATA FILE

We now know that a file is a group of related data, that each entry is organized in the same way as the others, and that the file is known by one name. An example would be a file named CURRENT EMPLOYEES. In this case, the information pertaining to each employee is organized in the same way as that for every other employee. Last name may occupy the first twenty spaces of every employee record, and current salary may occupy positions forty-five through fifty of each record.

Of course, file size and the format of entries differ greatly from one file to another. The programmer is allowed to name files, state the size expected, and specify how the data within the file is to be organized.

Considerable thought must be given to organizing files before the system is set up. First, each record must be organized. Then field locations, names, and sizes must be decided upon, and enough flexibility must be built in to accommodate any changes anticipated.

File Size

The next thing to be determined early is initial file size and possible expansion needed. Each file must bear a unique name, so it is awkward to start a

second file when the first is full. It is common practice, however, to open a new larger file and copy the existing information into it.

Access Methods

How to gain access to the records in a file is an extremely important decision that must be made when files are being organized. There are three basic methods: (1) sequential, (2) direct, and (3) indexed. Indexed is often called "keyed," both terms meaning that each record contains information that allows it to be located and identified. For the purpose of this description, we'll call one type of file "sequential access," the second "direct access," and the third "indexed" or "keyed" access.

Sequential Access

As its name implies, a sequential access file has records entered into it in the order in which they are received. Each new record is added to the end of the file. It is not possible to insert records nor is it possible to delete them. (Of course, a special program could be prepared to edit the files.)

Direct Access

As strongly implied by its name, a direct access file allows the user to select any record in the file without reading through others. This type of file can be stored only on units having the proper mechanical characteristics, as disks have. Records are numbered, and a list of the record numbers and their storage location is maintained by the storage manager program.

When a record is originally stored, it is placed in the next available location in the file, then the address of that location is placed in the list next to the record number. Now, when that record is to be read, the record number calls forth the location address and this, in turn, immediately finds the record.

Indexed Access

In the following paragraphs we'll discuss an improvement over the direct access method, called indexed sequential access. It allows records to be stored in order by the value of one of the fields in the record and yet to be read directly.

Assume that a file of employee records was to be

established and maintained. This would usually require that an employee's record be chosen by name, employee number, or social security number and brought into the computer. After the record is revised, it would be returned to the file in exactly the same place so that there would not be two records in the file for the same employee.

The programming task is greatly simplified if a "keyed" file is used. The "key" in this case would be one of the items mentioned above, name or number. Usually number is the best choice because its length can be predetermined and there is no chance of duplication. So, the file is established as a "keyed access" file, and the key length and position in each record are decided upon. All records are placed in order by the value of the key and the programmer can insert, update, or delete as he sees fit.

THE NEED FOR A DATA BASE

Organizing records and files is an important step, but the work doesn't stop there in most cases; files are often organized into data bases. A data base is a collection of related data, stored so that there is a minimum of redundancy. In other words, there is little duplication of information.

A data base does not require that one giant file be established, only that there be ways of linking and gaining access to the related information. In the case of employee data maintained by a major company, for example, there might be three separate files of employee information in the data base, but the only redundant information would be employee number, which appeared in all three files and served as a link between them.

STEPS INVOLVED IN PREPARING A PROGRAM

This is a task that must be well organized from beginning to end if it is to be successful. What seems to be a simple program occasionally turns out to be very difficult, particularly if it must interact with others.

Five major steps are involved in program development: (1) preparation of the program specifications, (2) design of the program, (3) writing the program, (4) testing, and (5) documenting and releasing the program. Writing the program is often called "coding," and that is what we'll call it in the rest of this discussion.

Program Specifications

Program requirements, or specifications, are extremely important. If they are incorrect, misleading, or incomplete, the programmer may be forced to repeat a good deal of his work after the program is tested. Specifications state what the program must do, what the inputs are, and what the output must be. They frequently describe interaction with the operator, displays and printouts that must be produced, and the relationship to other programs and data. Record and file layouts may be stated as well. Finally, and most important, specifications define the overall processing that must be done and generally the order in which it must be done.

Program Design

Design is the next step. Through one method or another, the programmer must lay out the overall logic involved in meeting the program requirements. Flowcharts, pseudocode, and decision tables may be used singly or in various combinations to produce the program logic.

Coding the Program

Now the coding is started. Complex programs may be subdivided, allowing many programmers to work simultaneously. How the divisions are made depend on the design of the program and the skill and specialties of the programmers. Of course, their activities must be well coordinated.

As to the language used, the programmer may not have a choice. Perhaps the entire system of which the current program is only a part uses COBOL, and this makes it necessary to use COBOL despite the fact that a programmer may be more proficient in another language.

Regardless of the language chosen, the programmer must be very careful in using it. As we'll see in later chapters, words and punctuation differ considerably from one language to another. Even where the words appear to be identical, they may not produce exactly the same result. In addition, languages differ somewhat from one type of computer to another, and this may result in errors if the programmer is not fully aware of variations.

In some cases, the programmer can type in his source statements directly at a computer, while in others the program must be written out on a coding form and provided to a keypunch operator for the preparation of cards. Whatever method is used, the result is the same: Source statements are entered into the computer.

Source statements are the instructions the programmer prepares. They are the source of the program; hence, the name "source statements."

Some type of compilation is then done. The tools available and the results produced depend on the language and the system; however, the source statements are processed so that the program can be executed by the computer.

Testing

The testing that a programmer can do by himself may be limited. This depends to a large extent on whether he has a complete and independent program or only a section of a large and complex system. Of course, availability of the computer and data to be processed affect this as well.

Formal testing is a major step. After the originator has satisfied himself that the program is complete and accurate, it must undergo testing to determine that it meets specifications. This test is usually conducted by a separate group, and it requires good planning.

Releasing the Program

This brings us to the last step in program development, which is documentation and release. There are at least three program users that must be considered: (1) the operator, (2) the applications specialist, and (3) other programmers. The operator is the person who will actually be using the program to process data. Often this individual has limited technical training, so a description of the purpose of the program, its inputs and outputs, and in general what it does is required for the operator. Of course, a full set of operating instructions must be provided as well.

We've used the term "applications specialist" to mean the person that is responsible for the data processing installation in which the program will be used. He needs another level of documentation.

Record layouts, file organization, system and program flowcharts, a description of the processing done, and data used and produced are examples.

Finally, we must keep in mind that the program may be revised by other programmers in the future. This makes it necessary to provide still another level of documentation, which includes a list of source statements, test data, and detailed descriptions of the program logic.

The Finished Program and Its Documentation

Assuming that the programmer is finished and has a tested program, what materials can we expect to see? A typical package appears in Figure 1-9. The finished program (the object program) is most important; it will be stored, possibly along with others, on a disk, diskette, tape, or cards. This depends on the size of the program, its purpose, and the type of computer.

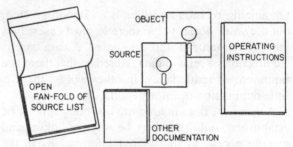

Figure 1-9 A Finished Program and Its Documentation

Also very important is the source program, since it is the source statements that will be revised if changes are required. It too will be held in one of the storage media mentioned above, but is likely to be kept by itself. Accompanying the source program is the source list, most often on printer paper stored in a binder especially designed to allow easy access to the pages.

If the program is at all complex, operator instructions and reference material is provided. This describes the purpose of the program, what it requires, and how to use it. Finally, the performance specifications, program description, flowcharts, and development materials are provided as required by company practices. The user of the program does not have access to this detailed material but it is available to programming and supervisory personnel.

FLOWCHARTS

We'll start with a broad definition of what a flowchart is: A set of symbols and notations that show how a program is organized to perform its intended functions. A simple chart is shown in Figure 1-10.

Rectangles, diamonds, parallelograms, circles, and several special symbols appear in this sample. Each represents an action that the program takes, and the order in which the actions are taken is indicated by the arrowheads on the lines that interconnect the symbols.

It's always important to carefully inspect the tools available before using them. So first we need to examine each symbol and its purpose.

There are nineteen basic symbols, shown in Figure 1-11, available for use in flowcharts. There are some variations of symbols. The meaning of each symbol is as follows:

a. *Punched-card Symbols*. The punched-card symbol is used to represent either inputs from cards or an output to be punched into cards. A card deck is a small group of cards, and a card file is generally a larger group.

b. *Magnetic-tape Symbol*. The magnetic-tape symbol represents either an input from magnetic tape or an output to magnetic tape.

c. *Manual Input Symbol*. This symbol represents a manual input from a typewriter linked to the computer or computer terminal equipped with a keyboard. (It could also represent switches or push buttons on a control panel.)

d. *Decision Symbol*. The decision symbol in which a question is asked represents a critical decision that affects the action that the program will take.

e. *Function Rectangle*. The rectangle is a box that holds a short statement of what process is to be accomplished or what action is to be taken. Often it is also used to hold comments.

f. *Flow Line*. A flow line and an arrowhead are used to show the path that the program will follow.

g. *Connector Symbol*. A connector symbol for flow lines shows more than one way of reaching the same point. More than one flow line may enter, but only one may leave.

h. *Display Symbol*. A display symbol, representing the display of information to an op-

erator, is used when the program provides an output for the operator to read on a screen.

i. *Document Symbol*. This symbol represents either an input or an output. An input might be an order form to be entered at the keyboard by an operator. An output might be a printed report at a printer.

j. *Disk and On-line Storage Symbols*. These symbols represent either an input from or an output to a magnetic disk or other type of on-line storage device.

k. *Communication-link Symbol*. A communication-link symbol represents a data link, such as voice-grade telephone lines, for transmitting information.

l. *Preparation Symbol*. A preparation symbol is used to define a manual action required, but it may also be used to show preparatory steps the computer takes.

m. *Terminal Symbol*. A terminal symbol indicates a point in the program at which the program allows a start, halt, or interrupt and end.

n. *Manual Operation Symbol*. The action required is listed inside this symbol, and it is usually an action performed by the operator.

o. *Input/Output Symbol*. This symbol would be used when there was no specific symbol, such as a tape symbol, to represent the I/O operation or when the programmer wanted to subdivide the I/O operation into two symbols: one specific symbol and one general I/O symbol.

p. *Off-line Storage Symbol*. An off-line storage symbol represents the storage of information that requires special action to obtain.

Now we can begin to put some of the symbols together to show some common functions that programs perform.

If the steps of a program were all performed in the sequence in which they appear, flowcharts would be of little use; a list of major functions in the order they are performed would be adequate. Because most programs are far more complex in their logic than a simple sequence, flowcharts are extremely useful in program development. There are other important tools, such as decision tables and pseudocode, but we'll discuss those later.

There are three basic functions that a flowchart can show. Of course, sequence of the program is the first. By providing the flow lines and arrowheads, a programmer can clearly show the order in which steps are executed. Next is repetition. Flow-

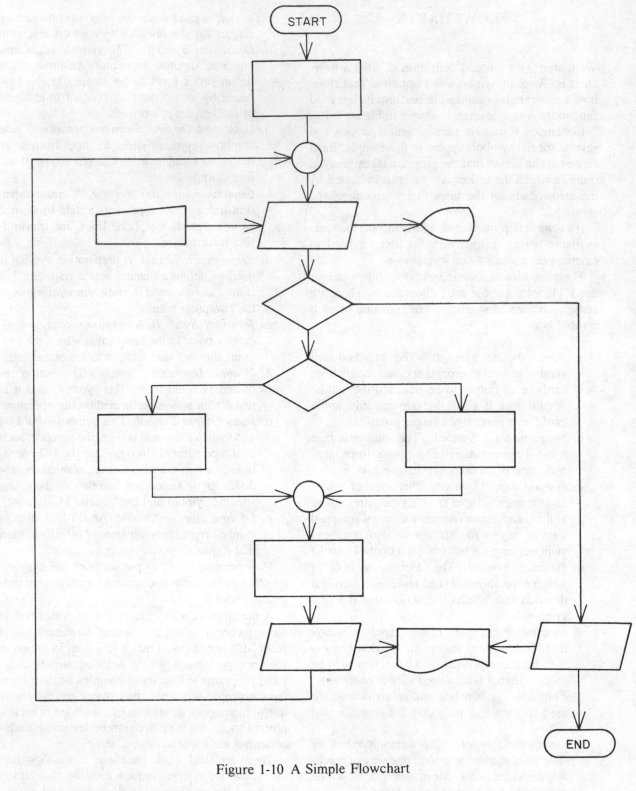

Figure 1-10 A Simple Flowchart

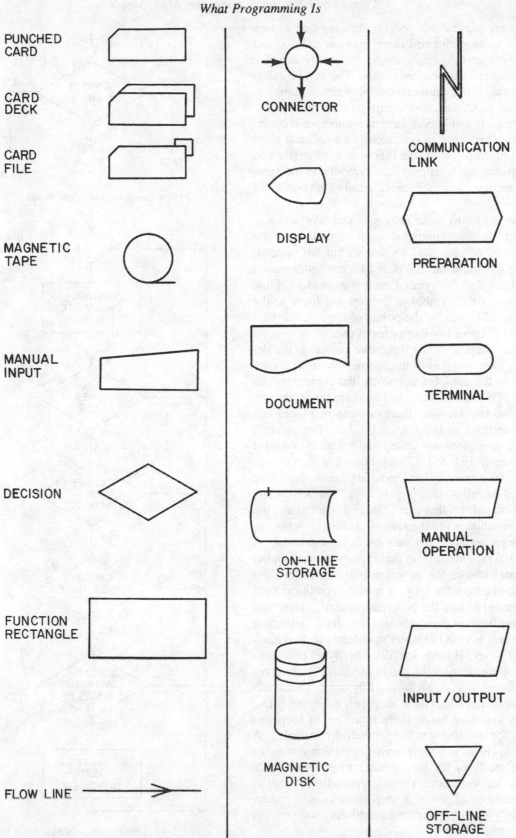

Figure 1-11 Most Common Flowchart Symbols

charts are particularly good at showing that a function is to be performed more than once. Last, and closely related to sequence, is the ability to make decisions and take multiple paths. This can be called selection. So, to summarize: Flowcharts show sequence, repetition, and selection of alternate paths.

Using the symbols is the next subject we'll cover. Showing sequence of operation is the simplest place to begin. In this case, the functions to be performed are written in the appropriate symbol and the symbols arranged in order from the top to the bottom of a page.

The ability to make decisions and take action is shown by the diamond-shaped symbol, with the condition being tested written within the symbol. There are some variations as to where information is written, but the symbol itself is a standard. Flow lines enter the symbol at the top and leave at the bottom and sides, at the points of the symbol. Figure 1-12 shows two examples of use.

Since there are only three exit points on the decision diamond it is limited somewhat in its ability to show the complex decisions that computers can make. Of course, these decisions are made one at a time, so the decision diamonds can be placed one after another in succession to show the order in which conditions are tested and the path taken for each result. Figure 1-12 (b.) shows just such a case. Here, four consecutive decisions are made. If the candidate fails—that is gets a "no" answer at any decision point—that candidate is discarded and the next is subjected to the same screening process.

Loops are the next subject to be discussed. A loop is a process, a task, that is performed a number of times before the program continues. Once the program enters the loop, a specific condition must be present before the program proceeds. That condition often involves checking a count to determine if the process has been performed the required number of times. If there are fifty employees in a company, for example, the group of steps that prepares W-2 forms must be performed fifty times. This would appear in flowchart form as shown in Figure 1-13.

On the other hand, there is a kind of loop that waits for something to happen before continuing. A loop such as this may wait for equipment to be made ready or for the operator to press a certain key at the keyboard. There is generally no limit to the number of times a loop such as this is performed—it simply continues until the condition that it requires is present.

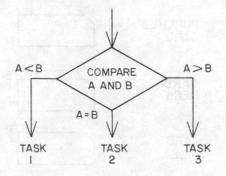

a. One Decision – Multiple Paths

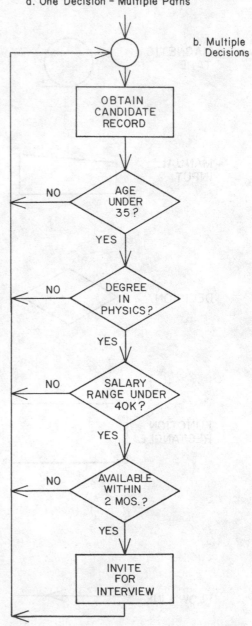

Figure 1-12 Decisions Shown by Flowcharts

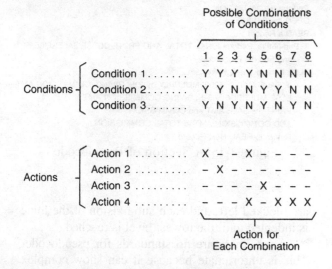

Y—Condition Exists.   N—Condition Does Not Exist.

Figure 1-14 A Decision Table

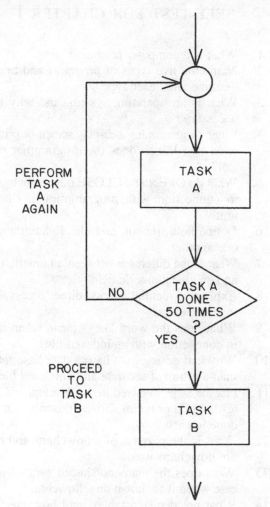

Figure 1-13 A Loop Shown by a Flowchart

Decision Tables

Decision tables are often helpful when the selection process becomes complex and difficult to keep in mind. Tables are suggested because they force the information into a matrix form. (It's very easy to overlook all the possibilities, otherwise.) And, naturally, they are easy to read when one has to go back to revise the program.

A decision table is shown in Figure 1-14. Notice that it requires the programmer to consider what action he must take in eight different situations. Although this is a very simple example, it does serve to illustrate that a programmer might overlook some of the possible combinations and not include them in his program unless he uses a decision table.

Pseudocode

Last among the three methods commonly used to organize programs is one called pseudocode. It provides English statements of what is to be done, and it often uses words that become part of the source statements in the programs themselves.

Earlier in this chapter, we used several examples of instructions needed to make decisions in a computer. Among them were:

IF <u>condition</u> THEN <u>action 1</u> ELSE <u>action 2</u>

REPEAT <u>action</u> UNTIL <u>condition</u>

It should be obvious that the capitalized words, which become part of the program, can also be used in full English sentences that express the logic of the program. For example:

IF the applicant is under 35, THEN use table 1 for rates.
ELSE use table 2.

REPEAT payroll procedure UNTIL employee count reaches 50.

This is the nature of pseudocode. Usually an indentation scheme shows the relationship between the lines. In other words, decisions and actions are indented to show subordination as in Figure 1-15. Statements expressing the main flow of the logic

```
Perform INITIALIZATION
OPEN the SALESFILE
READ a Record
IF End-of-File, Perform FINAL TOTAL AND PRINT, CLOSE SALESFILE,
    and End the Program
ELSE Perform the Following:
    IF SALE AMT  > $200, MULTIPLY by 2%, GIVING COMMISSION AMT
    ELSE MULTIPLY by 3%, GIVING COMMISSION AMT
    PRINT the SALE AMT and COMMISSION AMT
    ADD COMMISSION AMT to TOTAL COMMISSION
    Return to READ Next Record
```

Figure 1-15 A Section of Pseudocode

are blocked left, and each subdivision of the logic is indented until the lowest level is reached.

As yet, there are no standards for pseudocode. This is unfortunate because it can show complex logic better than flowcharts in many cases. Alone, the physical limitations of the flowchart symbols for decisions prevent the expression of many relationships, and a programmer may oversimplify the decision in order to make it fit.

Figure 1-15 is a case of reading the sales records for a salesman from a file and calculating total commission due. We've assumed only one salesman and one file. The pseudocode opens the sales file and reads one record at a time. For each sale, it calculates the amount due the salesman. It prints a line showing results and maintains a running total. When the last record is read, it prints the final total, closes the file and ends the program. When most readers reach the COBOL chapter, they'll recognize that this pseudocode is remarkably close to the final code needed to program this problem in COBOL.

SELF-TEST FOR CHAPTER 1

1. What is a computer program?
2. Name the five types of programs and briefly describe what each type does.
3. What is an operating system, and why is it necessary?
4. When programming a display screen or printer, what two things does the programmer control?
5. What do OPEN and CLOSE mean when used in connection with programming a storage unit?
6. Define field, record, and file. Relate them to one another.
7. What is the difference between a numeric field and an alphanumeric field?
8. Explain sequential access, direct access, and indexed access.
9. What does the word "key" mean when used in connection with an indexed file?
10. Why is it desirable to have a data base rather than a group of separate and unrelated files?
11. List the steps involved in the development and testing of a program. Briefly describe what is done in each.
12. What is the purpose of a flowchart, and how are flowcharts used?
13. What does the diamond-shaped symbol indicate when it is shown on a flowchart?
14. What are decision tables, and how are they used?
15. What is pseudocode, and how is it used?

2

Components of a Programming Language

When one thinks of a programming language, the first thing that comes to mind are the words that comprise the language. Rightly so, because these are the key elements, but they are only the "tip of the iceberg." A programming language is really a complex system consisting of many components that make it possible for a programmer to use the words. In this chapter, we'll discuss all of those components and show how they work together.

PHASES OF OPERATION

Let's begin by examining a simple statement in a high-level language and see what must happen to that statement before a computer actually performs the action called for. The statement is:

READ (5,*) A, B, C

This statement, which is from FORTRAN, is intended to make the computer accept certain data (A, B, and C) from an input unit (number 5), perhaps typed in from a keyboard or read by a card reader. The programmer must give the statement, following certain rules for its construction. A section of the programming system, called an entry program, accepts the statement and places it in order with the others entered. This is shown in step 1 in Figure 2-1. So far, the statement is in the pro-

gramming system but the computer has not executed it.

After all the statements are entered, the next phase is started (step 2 in the figure). The programmer signals that his entries are complete and that he wishes to have them processed. This is done by another part of the programming system, which is called the compiler. Following certain rules, the compiler takes each of the statements and converts them to a form the machine can execute. When finished, the compiler signals the programmer that his program is now available to be executed.

If the programmer wishes, the programming system can provide him with a list of all the statements he entered. Also available with this list (step 3 in the figure) are notes that the compiler has made concerning errors the programmer may have made in using the language.

Assuming that there are no errors, the programmer is finally ready to execute the program he has written. This is called "run-time" or "execution time." Usually, the programmer enters the name of his finished program along with a command to run that program. At this point (step 4 in the figure), the machine begins to carry out each of the statements the programmer has entered.

Part of the programming system must remain in the computer to supervise the execution of the object program, but other portions of the programming system, such as the section that accepts source

17

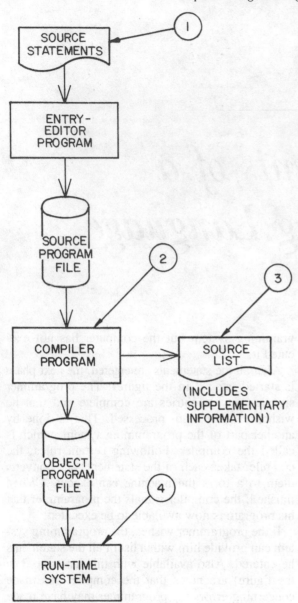

Figure 2-1 Components of a Programming System

statements, are not required during the "run-time" phase.

Thus, the major components of a programming language are an entry program, a compiler, and a run-time system. The source statements themselves do nothing without having been processed by these elements and converted to a form the computer can use.

Most programs have at least minor mistakes in them. So when a programmer executes his own object program for the first time, he is likely to be surprised by some of the results. Each mistake is called a "bug," and this brings us to another phase of operation, which is called "debugging."

Most of the programming systems provide aids to make debugging fairly easy. Step-by-step execution modes are usually available, and thus the programmer can cause the computer to stop after each source statement is executed so that he can see what each statement has done. After locating faults in the source statements or data, the programmer returns to the entry phase and "edits" the program by replacing, adding, deleting, or modifying the original source statements or data. Compilation is then done again, and a new object program is produced.

There are also variations of the usual steps—entry, compilation, and execution. One involves an intermediate code. In this case, the compiler converts the source statements to an intermediate code rather than machine language and an interpreter processes this code into machine language during program execution.

In another variation, the source statements go to the interpreter after only a limited amount of pre-processing and the interpreter converts them into machine language during execution of the program.

Thus, we have *three common arrangements:* (1) *compiler alone,* (2) *compiler and interpreter,* and (3) *interpreter alone.* In general, the first scheme results in the fastest execution of programs because the program is in machine language before execution begins.

THE STATEMENTS AVAILABLE IN A LANGUAGE

Each programming language has a set of statements that the programmer may issue. Most use words that are English or near-English and by themselves are fairly easy to understand. The keywords, or reserved words, as they are often called, have a specific meaning to the programming system and must be used in no other way.

In Figure 2-2, a section of the reserved word lists is shown for each of the three major languages, BASIC, Pascal, and COBOL. Notice that there is some similarity among the languages and that most of the words available are in English, not coded or abbreviated in any way. These are the tools the programmer has to work with.

BASIC

ACCESS	ELAPSED	MARGIN	RESET	UNTIL
AND	ELSE	MAT	REST	URGENCY
ARITHMETIC	ENABLE		RESTORE	USING
AT	END	NAME	RESUME	
	EOF	NATIVE	RETRY	VARIABLE
BASE	EVENT	NEXT	RETURN	VIEWPORT
BEGIN	EXIT	NONE	REWRITE	
BOUNDS		NOT		WHILE
BREAK	FILE		SAME	WINDOW
	FOR	OFF	SCRATCH	WITH
CALL	FROM	ON	SELECT	WRITE
CASE	FUNCTION	OPEN	SEQUENTIAL	
CAUSE		OPTION	SET	
CENTERING	GO	OR	SIGNAL	
CHAIN	GOSUB	ORGANIZATION	SKIP	
CLEAR	GOTO	OUT	STANDARD	

Pascal

		Data Types	Functions	Procedures
AND	MOD			
ARRAY		BOOLEAN	LN	GET
	NIL	CHAR	ODD	NEW
BEGIN	NOT	INTEGER	ORD	
		REAL	PRED	
CASE	OF		ROUND	
CONST	OR	**Constants**	SIN	
		FALSE	SQR	
DIV	PACKED	MAXINT	SQRT	
DO	PROCEDURE	TRUE	SUCC	
DOWNTO	PROGRAM		TRUNC	
		Files		
ELSE	RECORD	INPUT		
END	REPEAT	OUTPUT		

COBOL

ACCEPT	CORRESPONDING	EXTEND	LESS
ACCESS	COUNT		LIMIT
ADD	CURRENCY	FD	LIMITS
ADVANCING		FILE	LINAGE
AFTER	DATA	FILE-CONTROL	LINAGE-COUNTER
ALL	DATE	FILLER	LINE
ALPHABETIC	DATE-COMPILED	FINAL	LINE-COUNTER
ALSO	DATE-WRITTEN	FIRST	LINES
ALTER	DAY	FOOTING	LINKAGE
ALTERNATE	DE	FOR	LOCK
AND	DEBUG-CONTENTS	FROM	LOW-VALUE
ARE	DEBUG-ITEM		LOW-VALUES
AREA	DEBUG-LINE	GENERATE	
AREAS	DEBUG-NAME	GIVING	MEMORY
ASCENDING	DEBUG-SUB-1	GO	MERGE
ASSIGN	DEBUG-SUB-2	GREATER	MESSAGE
AT	DEBUG-SUB-3	GROUP	MODE
AUTHOR	DEBUGGING		MODULES
	DECIMAL-POINT	HEADING	MOVE
BEFORE	DECLARATIVES	HIGH-VALUE	MULTIPLE
BLANK	DELETE	HIGH-VALUES	MULTIPLY
BLOCK	DELIMITED		

Figure 2-2 Sections of Reserved Word Lists

SYNTAX DIAGRAMS

A statement given in a high-level language is like an English sentence in many respects. Proper construction conveys the information you wish to convey; improper construction produces nonsense. It is essential, therefore, that a programmer not only understand what each word does but also be familiar with the rules concerning statement construction.

This is not an easy task. There is a tool available that is of great value, however, and it is called a syntax diagram.

"Syntax" means the way in which words are put together to form phrases and sentences. Each language has very strict rules concerning its syntax and is "unforgiving"; it carries out the statement exactly as written, or rejects it if it cannot be executed.

Syntax diagrams are basically a way of summarizing the rules that apply to the construction of source statements. Pascal, which is a highly structured language, even provides syntax diagrams for the entire program organization.

Unfortunately, the style and symbols used for syntax diagrams differ from one language to another, although each style is easy to understand after some study. Standardization is also a problem. There are some differences in appearance of the syntax diagrams from one publication to another.

Figure 2-3 illustrates the same statement given in the three major languages we cover in this book. It is an "IF" statement, which determines whether or not a certain condition exists and then takes the action the programmer has specified.

Punctuation is often specified in syntax dia-

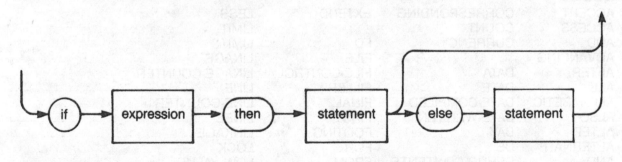

Figure 2-3 An IF Statement in Three Languages

grams. This is extremely important, because the systems act on punctuation in different ways. Pascal, for example, uses a semicolon (;) to denote the end of a statement, while BASIC uses no punctuation at the end. COBOL uses a period at the end of each sentence.

CODING FORMS

The process of writing out a program step-by-step is called "coding," which means that the programmer is giving instructions in the "code" or "code words" that the programming system can use. Not

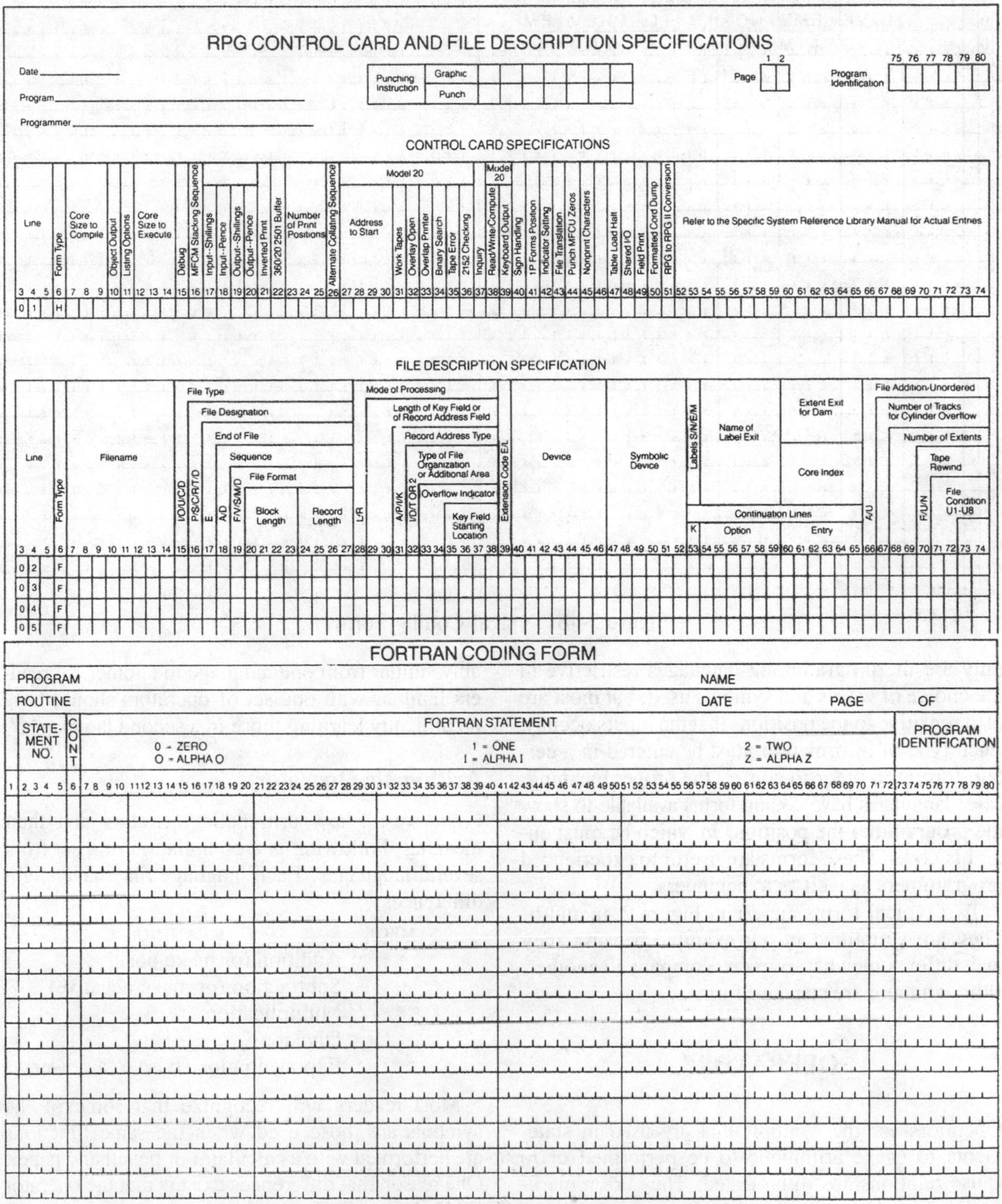

RPG CONTROL CARD AND FILE DESCRIPTION SPECIFICATIONS

Date _____
Program _____
Programmer _____

Punching Instruction: Graphic / Punch
Page
Program Identification (75 76 77 78 79 80)

CONTROL CARD SPECIFICATIONS

Line | Form Type | Core Size to Compile | Object Output | Listing Options | Core Size to Execute | Debug | MFCM Stacking Sequence | Input–Pence | Input–Shillings | Output–Shillings | Output–Pence | Inverted Print | 360/20 2501 Buffer | Number of Print Positions | Alternate Collating Sequence | Model 20 Address to Start | Work Tapes | Overlay Open | Overlay Printer | Binary Search | Tape Error | 2152 Checking | Model 20 Inquiry | Read/Write/Compute | Sign Handling | Keyboard Output | 1P Forms Position | Indicator Setting | File Translation | Punch MFCU Zeros | Nonprint Characters | Table Load Halt | Shared I/O | Field Print | Formatted Cord Dump | RPG to RPG II Conversion | Refer to the Specific System Reference Library Manual for Actual Entries

Line 01 — H

FILE DESCRIPTION SPECIFICATION

Line | Form Type | Filename | I/O/U/C/D | P/S/C/R/T/D | End of File (E) | A/D | F/V/S/M/D | File Format | Block Length | Record Length | L/R | Mode of Processing | A/P/I/K | I/O/T OR 2 | Overflow Indicator | Key Field Starting Location | Extension Code E/L | Device | Symbolic Device | Labels S/N/E/M | Name of Label Exit | K | Continuation Lines: Option / Entry | Core Index | A/U | Extent Exit for Dam | Number of Tracks for Cylinder Overflow | Number of Extents | Tape Rewind | F/UN | File Condition U1–U8

Lines 02 F, 03 F, 04 F, 05 F

FORTRAN CODING FORM

PROGRAM _____ NAME _____
ROUTINE _____ DATE ___ PAGE ___ OF ___

STATEMENT NO. | CONT | FORTRAN STATEMENT | PROGRAM IDENTIFICATION

0 – ZERO / O – ALPHA O 1 = ONE / I – ALPHA I 2 = TWO / Z – ALPHA Z

Figure 2-4a Typical Coding Form

COBOL CODING FORM

PAGE 1 NO3	PROGRAM								PAGE	OF	
0 0 3	PROGRAMMER					DATE			IDENT. 73		80

LINE NO									
4 6	7	8	12	16			40		72
01	0		ADD N-HOURS TO EMP-HOURS.						
02	0		ADD N-WAGE TO EMP-WAGE.						
03	0		MOVE EMP-NO-IN TO PREV-EMP.						
04	0		READ TIME-FILE. AT END MOVE			'EOF' TO EOF-FLAG.			
05									
06									
07									
08									
09									
10									
11									
12									
13									
14									
15									
16									
17									
18									
19									
20									
21									
22									
23									
24									
25									

Figure 2-4b Typical Coding Form

only are the programming languages restrictive in the choice of words and symbols used, but most are also sensitive to the positions that the inputs occupy. Each type of information must be entered in a certain format in order to convey the proper meaning. Most languages have coding forms available to show the programmer the positions in which he must enter his code. These forms are useful to experienced programmers as well as to beginners.

Two typical forms appear in Figure 2-4a and b. They are simplified in our example because they may differ somewhat from one company to another, although there are standard forms.

OPERATORS

Operators are the symbols that are used in statements to cause arithmetic to be performed or to cause relationships to be tested. They are remark-ably similar from one language to another, so readers familiar with one set of operators should have no difficulty learning those in a second language.

Arithmetic Operators

First, we'll show arithmetic operators and their meaning. Following is a compilation of a set from several languages. Each language may have slight differences.

SYMBOL	MEANING
+	Addition (or make positive)
−	Subtraction (or make negative)
*	Multiplication
/	Division
**	Exponentiation (raise to a power)

Most readers will recognize that some of the symbols are those used when the same functions are performed with a calculator or pencil and paper. One reason that differences exist is that the operator symbols must be chosen without any confusion from those available on a typewriter keyboard. For example, the superscript needed to show an exponent is not available on most keyboards.

Relational Operators

Next we'll show relational operators. These too should be familiar. There is a greater difference among languages in this case, however, so we've shown the symbols from three languages. In the case of COBOL, we've shown the full English form, although COBOL also allows symbol form, somewhat similar to BASIC, to be used.

BASIC	FORTRAN	COBOL	MEANING
=	.EQ.	IS EQUAL TO	Equal
<>	.NE.	IS NOT EQUAL TO	Not Equal
>	.GT.	IS GREATER THAN	Greater Than
<	.LT.	IS LESS THAN	Less Than
>=	.GE.	IS NOT LESS THAN	Equal or Greater Than
<=	.LE.	IS NOT GREATER THAN	Equal or Less Than

VARIABLES

Even in grade school nearly everyone used variables in simple equations. Area of a rectangle, for example, was $A = L \times W$. The length (L) and the width (W) were of course variable depending upon which rectangle was being considered. Therefore, the area (A) was also variable. Thus A, L, and W were the names of variables, and since the quantities involved were numbers, they were, specifically, the names of numeric variables.

Each of the programming languages has certain rules concerning how a programmer may name the numeric variables used. On one hand, simple BASIC allows a maximum of two characters in a numeric variable name. As long as we are dealing with only simple equations this is no problem, but most people find it too restrictive in other applications. FORTRAN allows names up to six characters long, while the other major languages (including modern BASIC) allow even more. Thus it is possible to be very English-like in naming numeric variables in some languages. "Interest rate," for example, might be named INT-RATE, a name whose meaning is easily recognized.

There is also another type of variable used in the high-level languages; it is not used as a number in arithmetic. Let's consider the case of a student name

in college records. Suppose that one student record after another is to be processed to determine whether or not tuition has been paid. The program to do this needs some way of acquiring student name without knowing it in advance. The student name is thus a variable that must be identified somehow. This variable is a character variable, which is commonly called a "string variable" in that it is made up of a string of characters. The name given to the variable is thus a string variable name. It would certainly be helpful if the string variable in our example could be called STUDENT-NAME, but again the languages have a wide range of sizes available to construct names.

CONSTANTS

There are also two types of constants: numeric and string. Logically, a numeric constant is a number written in a statement in its final form, exactly as it will be used in arithmetic. In using the equation to convert from Centigrade to Fahrenheit temperatures, for example, the constant "32" is written in the statement that does the arithmetic.

A string constant is a set of characters in the exact form it will be used. A statement might be written: PRINT "YOUR GRADE IS", X. In this case, the string constant is set off by quotation marks, which is a common method of showing that certain characters are a constant. Responding to this statement, the computer prints the words YOUR GRADE IS and follows them with the current value of the numeric variable X.

It may sound contradictory after we just explained that variables are named while constants are given in final form, *but constants can also be named in most languages*. The names must be declared to be names of constants and the value of the constant given. Once this is done, however, a programmer may use the name in his statement and thus write statements that may be easier to read. "PI," for example, has somewhat more meaning than 3.14 when someone is reading a program.

LITERALS

Included in some of the syntax diagrams for source statements is the word "literal." It means that the actual value to be used can be placed in the source statement. To illustrate, we'll use two source statements, one with only variables and the second using a literal:

ADD <u>Interest-Due</u> TO <u>Payment</u>
MULTIPLY <u>Payment</u> BY <u>36</u> GIVING <u>Total-Due</u>

In the first, the contents of the variables Interest-Due and Payment are added, whatever the actual values are. In the second, the contents of Payment is multiplied by the literal 36 to produce the contents of another variable, Total-Due.

ARRAYS

"Array" is another of the special words used in this chapter. However, an array is nothing more than a table of data. If it holds numbers, it is called a numeric array; if it holds string (character) data, it is called a string array.

Arrays that have only one row of entries, which are called "elements," are known as one-dimension arrays. Those that have two or more rows and columns are two-dimension arrays.

Arrays are named just as one would name a table. Naming rules vary from one language to another, but are often the same as the rules for naming variables. Thus, an array may be named for its contents, perhaps "INTEREST RATES." When the assigned name is used in a source statement, the statement gains access to the array.

Each element in an array is accessible individually. (Two simple arrays appear in Figure 2-5.) An element is the location at the intersection of a row and column. In the figure, 19 is an element, as is "EAGLE." Elements are identified by their row and column numbers. The 19 is element 1, and EAGLE is element 2, 3 (row 2, column 3).

There are source statements that establish an array and its size, others that enter the data in the elements, and still others that refer to and use the data held in these tables. Each language has certain rules for using arrays, which will be discussed in the appropriate chapter.

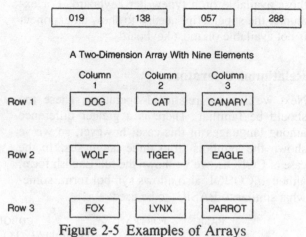

Figure 2-5 Examples of Arrays

We know so far that each element in an array is numbered (although some languages permit elements to be named). For example, RATES (2) selects the second entry in a one-dimension array named RATES, and A (5, 4) selects the element at the intersection of the fifth row and the fourth column of an array named A. The numbers in parentheses are called subscripts, and an array is also often called a "subscripted variable."

FUNCTIONS

Here's a word that has a broad meaning to the layman. In our high-level languages though, it has a very limited definition. A function is a certain preprogrammed operation offered by the language, or it is an operation that the programmer prepares and sets aside for use as if it was offered by the language. SQRT, square root, is a simple example of a function, and so are SIN and COS (sine and cosine).

If functions such as these are available, as they are in nearly all the languages, the programmer can use them by simply giving their name. Obviously, if they are not provided, he must perform the same operation in another way, using the limited statements available. We'll see how a function is called into action when we discuss the construction of expressions.

Most languages allow a programmer to create his own functions. It's a simple matter of declaring that a function by a certain name exists and then preparing the statements that will be called into action when that name is given.

EXPRESSIONS

Now that we know what operators, variables, constants, literals, array elements, and functions are, the next step is to see how they are put together to obtain results. When these components are placed in a source statement either singly or in complex combinations they make up an "expression." "A*B" is an expression, "C>D OR E>F" is an expression, as is "SQR(X)/Z."

When the arithmetic in the expression A*B is actually performed and the result obtained, the expression is said to have been "evaluated."

A*B is, of course, an arithmetic expression, but the term "evaluated" is also used to describe the resolution of relational expressions such as C>D that we gave in our examples. In this case, the evaluation produces a "yes" or "no" rather than a number.

A function, square root, was used in the fourth example, and when this expression is evaluated, the square root of X is found. In turn, it is divided by Z to complete the evaluation of the expression.

Now we confront two new subjects: (1) how expressions are written, and (2) the order in which the evaluation proceeds. In general, the same fundamental rules apply to all languages. First, expressions must be written on a line. Secondly, the evaluation proceeds in a certain predetermined order.

A few typical expressions are shown in Figure 2-6 to illustrate how the requirement to place all terms and operators on a single line affects the programmer. It takes some thought and care to convert the typical equation into a form acceptable to most programming languages.

Now let's examine the order in which all the activities involved in the evaluation of an expression proceed:

1. Functions are executed first. This is referred to as a "function call." The function call places a quantity in the expression.
2. Next, the arithmetic operators are applied, and they have the following priority from highest to lowest:
   Make positive or negative (+ and − signs with a single term)
   Raise to a power (exponentiation)
   Multiplication and division
   Addition and subtraction
3. Relational operators (less than, equal to, etc.)

Normally Written	On One Line
$A = \dfrac{bh}{2}$	A=B*H/2
$V = \pi x\, r^2 h$	V=PI*R**2*H
$A(-B)$	A*(-B)
$Z = \dfrac{a+b+c}{2}$	Z=(A+B+C)/2
$Y = d - \dfrac{a+b}{4c}$	Y=D-(A+B)/(4*C)
$X = \dfrac{\dfrac{a}{b+c}}{d-a}$	X=A/(B+C/(D-A))

Figure 2-6 Expressions Written in the One-Line Form

are applied next. Since the arithmetic has been done, quantities can now be compared.

4. Last, the logical operators (AND, OR, NOT, etc.), which we haven't discussed yet, are applied. These operators link conditions such as C>D *AND* A=B. Obviously, they can't be applied until it is known if C is greater than D and A is equal to B. Both of these conditions must be true if the expression using the AND operator is to return a "yes" when it is evaluated.

In closing this discussion on operator precedence we need to state one last rule: When operators of equal priority exist, they are applied in order from left to right in the expression.

Parentheses also play an important role in the order in which the components of an expression are evaluated. Whatever components are within parentheses are fully evaluated first, in the order discussed above, to result in a single quantity. Evaluation begins with the innermost parentheses and progresses outward until all parentheses have been removed.

PROCEDURES

A procedure is a "miniprogram" similar in construction to the "functions" we just discussed but generally considerably longer. Some programming languages allow these miniprograms to be constructed and called into use, while others do not. A procedure is given a name when it's constructed, and the overall program can cause that miniprogram to be performed whenever it wishes by simply entering the name of the procedure in a source statement. After the procedure is completed, the overall program continues from the point at which it called the procedure into action.

CONTROL STRUCTURES AND STRUCTURED PROGRAMMING

Structured programming is a term you may hear occasionally. What is structured programming, and how does it differ from unstructured programming? These are two questions we'll answer in this section. It's important to do this now because some languages we'll discuss later are much better suited to structured programming than others. If you have a good understanding of what structured programming is, you'll be able to recognize language features that aid in the preparation of structured programs.

Let's use an analogy to illustrate the difference between structured and unstructured programs. A pyramid of children's blocks placed alongside a bowl of cooked spaghetti should do. In the spaghetti, it is very difficult to follow an individual strand in the mass, and if the strand is removed, its place with respect to the whole is impossible to determine. Contrast this with the blocks. Each block is clearly identifiable and its place in the stack certain. When a block is removed, the place it occupied is left unfilled and the block can stand alone.

Admittedly, this analogy is severe, but it does serve to show the fundamental difference between structured programming, which allows parts to be clearly separated, and unstructured programming, which does not.

So the first language feature needed for structured programming is the ability to create the blocks. Logically then, the second feature is the ability to determine that a specific block should be used and for how long. Among the three major languages we cover, Pascal and COBOL are much better suited to structured programming than BASIC.

Structured programming generally requires that more planning be done. The program must be broken down into modules and, if necessary, submodules, somewhat like the organization shown in Figure 2-7. Each module (the "procedure" we spoke of earlier) consists of the steps needed to perform a specific task. In order to have that task performed, the program includes a statement that selects the desired procedure. After that specific procedure is completed, the program continues with the statement following the one that selected the procedure.

Procedures may also use other procedures by including statements to select them. When any procedure is complete, it returns to the statement following the one that called it into action. Figure 2-8 illustrates how procedures can be linked to one another.

Now let's discuss the features needed to create and use a procedure. There are some differences between languages, so we'll have to generalize. First, the language must have some way of saying that a group of statements are to be treated as a unit. Next, the language must have a way of choosing that procedure for execution. Some allow the procedure name to be given, and that's all that is needed.

Now we can return to Figure 2-7, which shows the difference between structured and unstructured programs. The unstructured example consists of a series of statements that are essentially inseparable. In contrast, we have the example of a structured program in Figure 2-8. The body consists of twelve statements that call procedures into action. Each time a procedure is finished, the program moves to the next statement.

There are more than twelve procedures in this program, however. In fact, there are thirty-one. We've simply numbered the procedures in our example; in practice, they would have names that indicated what task they performed.

To summarize what we've said: A programming language must have the ability to create and call procedures if it is to be well suited to structured programming. And structured programs are desirable because they are generally easier to prepare, test, and maintain.

There are, however, some other features that a language should have. For example, it may be necessary to call one procedure if a certain condition exists and a different procedure if it does not. It may be necessary to repeat a procedure a certain number of times or until a specific event occurs. Thus, there is much more to structured program-

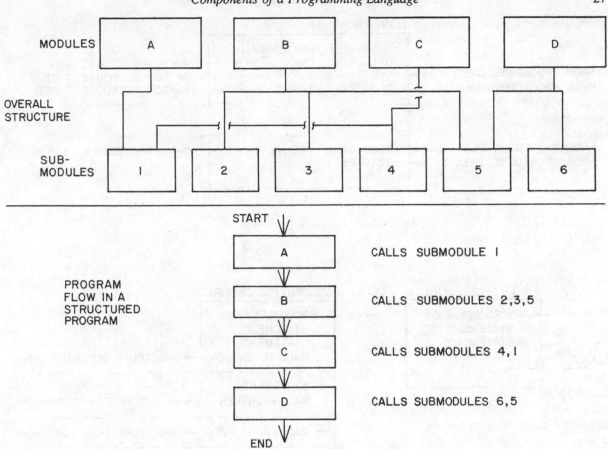

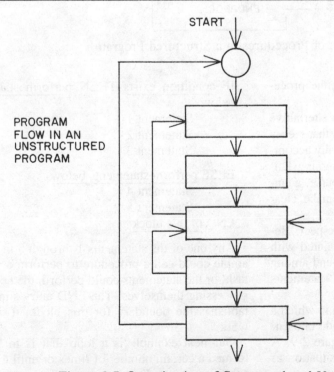

Figure 2-7 Organization of Structured and Unstructured Programs

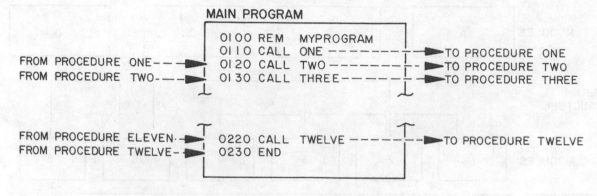

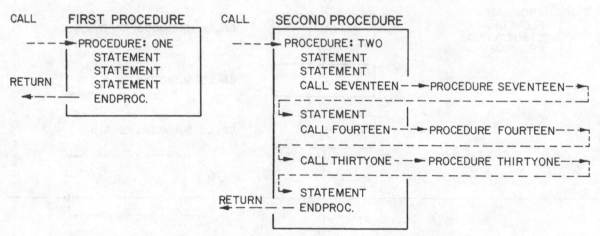

Figure 2-8 Use of Procedures in a Structured Program

ming than simply creating and calling the procedures.

The need to test conditions and take alternative actions based on the results is an idea that's easy enough to understand. How this is actually accomplished by the statements in a programming language is another matter, however. Of course, a language should provide statements that make clear the logic of the situation.

Some are better than others in this respect. Because we're just beginning to get acquainted with programming languages, we'll skip around among the three major languages and choose statements that are the easiest to explain.

First, we'll discuss the basic decision in which a condition is examined and one of two paths chosen. This is shown in flowchart form in Figure 2-9. A typical high-level language states this situation as follows:

IF <u>condition exists</u> THEN <u>perform statements below</u>
      Statement 1
      Statement 2
      Statement 3

ELSE <u>perform statements below</u>
      Statement 4
      Statement 5
END <u>of this block</u>

Any one of the statements 1 through 5 in the example could call a procedure to perform a specific task, or the statements could perform the necessary processing themselves. The END entry simply establishes the boundary for this block; it does no work.

Our next example is a loop that is to be performed a certain number of times or until a certain condition exists. One language offers a very clear

```
IF condition THEN
    statements 1,2,3
ELSE
    statements 4,5
ENDIF
```

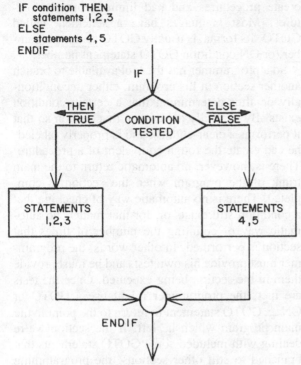

Figure 2-9 The IF/THEN/ELSE Control
Structure

```
FOR condition DO statements
PERFORM statements number TIMES
```

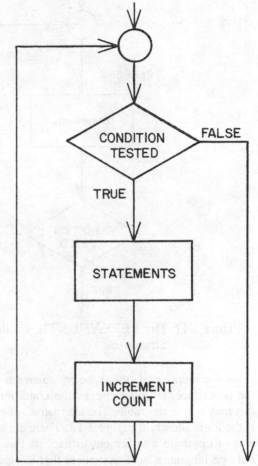

Figure 2-10 The FOR/DO and PERFORM
Number of TIMES Control
Structure

statement to handle this, while the others have statements that are slightly more difficult to use. Our easy statement is:

PERFORM procedure name number of TIMES

In this case, the programmer has only to give the name of the procedure to be performed and state the total number of times. This causes the logic shown in Figure 2-10 to be enacted.

Other languages offer a statement that is slightly more difficult to understand. It has some variation of this basic form:

FOR variable limit TO limit DO specified
(name of first — second — statements)

Each time the statements are executed, the variable named (which is called a control variable) is incremented to record that fact. As long as the variable is within the two limits set, this continues. The variable is thus a counter and the limits set determine how many times the loop is performed; when a limit is reached, the loop is stopped and the program goes on to the next operation to be performed. Of course, the programmer selects the name

assigned to the counter and its limits when he writes the statement.

Next we have the case in which a procedure (or a statement or group of statements) is to be performed until a certain event occurs. The logic of the situation is shown in Figure 2-11. Notice that the loop is entered unconditionally and thus the procedure is performed once before the occurrence of the event is checked. One language offers the following statement to handle this situation:

PERFORM procedure name UNTIL condition

and another offers:

REPEAT procedure name UNTIL condition

PERFORM statements UNTIL condition
REPEAT statements UNTIL condition

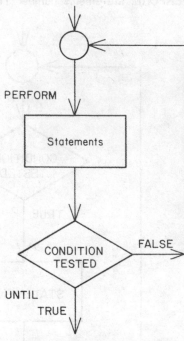

Figure 2-11 The REPEAT/UNTIL Control
Structure

As we mentioned, this type of statement enters the procedure before it checks the condition, and this may not be desirable. The alternative, of course, is the logic shown in Figure 2-12. There are several ways to prepare a statement to execute this logic, but one language has a statement that is especially easy to use:

WHILE condition exists DO procedure or statements

In this case, the condition is checked first. If it is not present, the loop is bypassed entirely; if it is present, the loop is performed until the event occurs that eliminates the condition.

The features discussed in the preceding paragraphs are called "control structures." All contribute to making structured programming easy, and they are also the elementary tools needed.

THE EFFECT OF
LIMITED CONTROL STRUCTURES

Let's examine some of the statements that a programmer might have to use if a language couldn't create procedures and had limited control structures. Most languages have a statement called GOTO. Its format is usually GOTO statement number, or ON condition GOTO statement number.

So a programmer has the tool available to branch another section of his program, either unconditionally or after determining that a certain condition exists. By carefully organizing that section so that it performs a clear-cut task and is properly labeled, he can create the rough equivalent of a procedure. There is, however, no automatic return to the main trunk of the program when the section is completed. There is no automatic way of checking that a condition still exists or, for that matter, no automatic way of counting the number of times that section is performed. In other words, the programmer must provide his own tests and he must provide them in the section being executed. Once the tests are met, the programmer might use a GOTO or ON __ GOTO statement to return to the point in the main program which he left. If the section we're dealing with included some GOTO statements that branched to still other sections, the programming logic becomes hard to follow and error prone.

WHILE condition DO statements

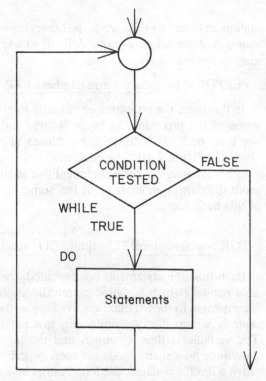

Figure 2-12 The WHILE/DO Control Structure

Some languages do include a pair of statements that help to control the return to the main program. That pair is GOSUB statement number and RETURN. An ON condition GOSUB statement number is usually available as well.

This pair of statements means "go to a subroutine and return automatically." A subroutine is the same as a section we spoke of above, and it too is the rough equivalent of a procedure. It is ended by the RETURN statement, which causes the program to go back to the main trunk at the point at which the branch took place. And there may be GOSUB statements within a subroutine, causing subbranches but automatically returning to the branch from which they came. This is the equivalent of a procedure calling another procedure.

Although the GOSUB/RETURN control structure helps some, the programmer must still provide, in the subroutine itself, his own tests for conditions or the number of iterations necessary to end the subroutine. Of course, once the RETURN statement is reached, the return is automatic; the programmer does not have to provide the number of the statement to which the program is to return.

The three high-level languages we cover in detail in this section have a variety of control structures available, some easier to use than others. It should be clear, however, that the IF/THEN/ELSE, REPEAT/UNTIL, WHILE/DO, and FOR/DO control structures do make programming easier than if only GOTO and GOSUB were available.

SELF-TEST FOR CHAPTER 2

1. Describe what takes place during each of the three basic phases (*entry, compilation,* and *execution*) involved in the preparation of a program.
2. What is a high-level language?
3. What is a compiler and, in general, what does it do?
4. What is a source program, source list, source file, an object program?
5. Describe what a syntax diagram is and why it is necessary.
6. Why are coding forms needed?
7. Two types of operators were mentioned in this chapter: relational and arithmetic. Use them to write $\frac{AB}{C}$, $(A^2)^B$, A is less than B, B is not equal to A.
8. Listed below in the left column are common arithmetic operators. Enter a number in the right column to show the order in which they are executed:

Operator	Order
+ (Add)	_____
*	_____
/	_____
− (Sub)	_____
**	_____
+ (Make positive)	_____
− (Make negative)	

9. Describe a one-dimensional array, a two-dimensional array.
10. Describe what a function is. When a function is used in an expression, what happens?
11. What does the word "evaluated" mean when used in connection with an expression?
12. Expressions must be written on one line in the programming languages we cover. What effect does this have on the programmer?
13. What is a procedure? What causes a procedure to be performed?
14. Structured programming has several advantages over unstructured programming. Name two and describe why they are important.
15. Several of the most common control structures available (WHILE/DO, IF/THEN/ELSE) were described in this chapter. Why is it important that they be available in a programming language?
16. When the programmer issues a GOTO statement to cause a branch to another part of a program, how is a return accomplished? (Assuming that one is necessary.)

3

BASIC
Beginner's All-purpose
Symbolic Instruction Code

INTRODUCTION

The acronym BASIC means "*Beginner's All-purpose Symbolic Instruction Code*." Developed in the 1960s at Dartmouth College, BASIC is the most popular language offered to users of small computers. It is easy to learn the meaning of each source statement because the keywords are English or near-English. PRINT, NEXT, RETURN, READ, and several more do exactly what their names suggest.

One of the first things that we must make clear is that there is not only one BASIC language; there are many. Most companies offering the language have "tailored" it in order to take full advantage of the strong points in their equipment and to meet its intended application. Although there is a standard for BASIC provided by the American National Standards Institute, it's unlikely that the reader will encounter a BASIC that is identical to the standard in all respects. Many are compatible with the standard, however, and, therefore, some programs written in BASIC can be moved from one machine to another after undergoing only minor changes.

WHAT DOES A BASIC PROGRAM LOOK LIKE?

Programs are as different as the people that prepare them. Some are very neat and well organized, while others are confusing and hard to follow. Some are very "wordy," while others restrict their comments to few or none. The liberal use of comments, titles, and blank lines can change a program's appearance dramatically, although not one line of the active statements is changed.

There are, however, some fundamental entries, the active source statements themselves, and these are what we're interested in. A good place to start is with two simple examples that solve very common problems: (1) conversion of temperature from Centigrade to Fahrenheit and (2) finding the length of the hypotenuse in a right triangle. These examples should make it easy for the reader to relate the work to be done to the steps that do it, although it's too early in this chapter to fully understand how each statement operates.

Our first example:

```
0010  * TEMPERATURE CONVERSION PRO-
      GRAM
0020  DISPLAY "TYPE IN TEMPERATURE IN
      DEGREES C."
0030  INPUT C
0040  LET F = (9/5) * C + 32
0050  DISPLAY "THE TEMPERATURE IN DE-
      GREES F IS:", F
0060  END
```

The first statement is a remark that titles the program; it does nothing else. The second statement gives an operator instruction that appears on the display screen, and the program waits for C, perhaps a + 17, to be typed in. It accepts C with the INPUT statement. C is then used in a calculation, the result of which becomes F. To conclude the program, statement 0050 displays a sentence on the screen and shows whatever value F turned out to be.

Next we have the case of solving for the hypotenuse of a right triangle when we know the leg sizes. It is to be done four times because we have four triangles. The problem is set up using the Pythagorean theorem $(C^2 = A^2 + B^2)$ and solving for C by writing the expression $C = \sqrt{A^2 + B^2}$. In BASIC the program takes the following form:

```
0010  REM RIGHT TRIANGLE SOLUTION
0020  FOR I = 1 TO 4
0030  READ A, B
0040  C = SQR (A**2 + B**2)
0050  DISPLAY "HYPOTENUSE = ", C
0060  DISPLAY           SPACES ONE LINE
0070  NEXT I
0080  DATA 10, 20, 30, 50, 60, 90, 100, 150
0090  END
```

The first line is a remark, a programmer comment, using the REM alternate instead of the * used in our first example. Next, line 0020 establishes that this program will be done four times. The instruction READ A, B takes the first two values (10, 20) in the DATA line (line 0080) and assigns these values to A and B, respectively. Now, the arithmetic is done by the expression. This line says "LET C equal the square root of the quantity A raised to the power of 2 plus B raised to the power of 2." (Notice that the word LET is not actually required.)

Now line 0050 shows on the screen the statement "HYPOTENUSE =" and follows it with whatever value C turned out to be. A blank DISPLAY instruction is then given, and the programmer has chosen to add a comment (SPACES ONE LINE) for himself; the comment does nothing.

At line 0070, the instruction NEXT I says "do it again if we haven't done it four times." So the program starts over at line 0020. This time through the READ instruction gets the values 30 and 50 from the DATA line and assigns those values to A and B. The calculation is done again; but A and B are 30 and 50, so the result is different. It is displayed, and the program runs a third time, now using 60 and 90 as the values for A and B, the triangle legs.

On the fourth pass, values 100 and 150 are used, and the result of the calculation displayed. When the line NEXT I is reached, it causes the FOR instruction to again check how many times the program has been run. This time, the FOR instruction finds that the program has been run four times and ends it by going to the END statement in line 0090.

Now that we've seen some very simple programs, let's examine a program complex enough to make buying a computer worthwhile. Our samples could be done easily with an inexpensive hand-held calculator, and while they are "real programs," they are not realistic examples of how computers are used.

In Figure 3-1, we've reproduced the first page of a five-page source listing to illustrate what an actual program looks like. The programmer has used remarks to title the program and record its history. Empty remarks lines are used for separation of sections and thus make the program easier to read.

Next comes a series of entries in which the format of the records to be used are laid out and other fields are defined. All the descriptive material on the right side consists of comments made by the programmer; it is not used by the program itself.

After thus establishing the format of the data with which the program will operate, the programmer provides the active statements, which are those that carry out the logic of the program. Some should be familiar. Line 02800, for example, displays an instruction on the screen "TYPE COMPANY CODE" and the following statement INPUT C$ takes what the operator typed in and assigns it to become the value of C$.

```
      LINE            TEXT                        COMMENTS

00100 * PRINT/DISPLAY INVENTORY
00200 * WRITTEN BY J. ALAM AUGUST 10, 1979. UPDATED AUG. 30, 1979.
00300 * UPDATED JAN. 8, 1980,FOR MULTIPLE COMPANIES IN INVNTRY.
00310 *
00400 * FOLLOWING DEFINES THE INVENTORY RECORD
00410 INCLUDE TRC
00500 FIELD C$=1                     COMPANY CODE - LOCATION 1
00600 *
00700 *                             SUBDIVIDE PRODUCT #
00800 FIELD P1=3.0                   PRODUCT CODE - LOCATION 2
00900 FIELD P$=10                    ITEM #        LOCATION 5
01000 FIELD P3=3.0                   NOT USED      LOCATION 15
01100 FIELD R=1.0                    RECORD TYPE - LOCATION 18
01200 *                             NOT USED      LOCATION 19
01300 FIELD W$=2                     WAREHOUSE CODE LOCATION 20
01400 FIELD D$=20                    DESCRIPTION  - LOCATION 22
01500 FIELD B=6.2                    BASE PRICE   - LOCATION 42
01600 FIELD U$=3                     UN/MEASURE   - LOCATION 50
01700 FIELD Q=8.0                    ON-HAND QTY  - LOCATION 53
01800 FIELD O=8.0                    ON-ORDER QTY - LOCATION 61
01900 FIELD R1=8.0                   REORDER QTY  - LOCATION 69
02000 FIELD R2=8.0                   REORDER POINT LOCATION 77
02100 FIELD C=8.0                    PHYS INV CNT - LOCATION 85
02200 * REST OF 128-BYTE RECORD IS SPACE-FILLED
02300 *
02310 * WORK FIELD DEFINED
02400 FIELD K$=18, X$=1, Y=1.0, J$=14, D=6.0, X=1.0
02410 FIELD N$=30, Y$=1
02500 *
02600 OPEN #3 "CONTROL"
02700 DISPLAY "PRINT/DISPLAY INVENTORY ITEMS"
02800 DISPLAY "TYPE COMPANY CODE"
02900 INPUT C$
02901 LET X=0
02902 GOSUB 16920
02904 READ #3 KEY J$ ERR 3400
02905 GET #3 16=N$
02910 LET X=1
03010 GOSUB 16920
03200 READ #3 KEY J$ ERR 3400
03300 GET #3 20=D
```

Figure 3-1 The Appearance of a BASIC Program

CHOOSING AN INSTRUCTION SET FOR EXPLANATION

We've chosen a set of thirty statements from the great many in use. In Figure 3-2 are shown the keywords from what is, as of this writing, a proposed new ANSI standard for BASIC. There are many words in this proposed standard, including some having to do with the construction of color graphics.

When we reach Chapter 6, we'll see another set of keywords, those for a popular modern version of BASIC, and we'll show how the graphics are programmed. Here, in Chapter 3 we'll stick with the fundamentals, however, and cover the statements that a reader must understand before he is ready for graphics.

ACCESS	ELAPSED	MARGIN	RESET	UNTIL
AND	ELSE	MAT	REST	URGENCY
ARITHMETIC	ENABLE		RESTORE	USING
AT	END	NAME	RESUME	
	EOF	NATIVE	RETRY	VARIABLE
BASE	EVENT	NEXT	RETURN	VIEWPORT
BEGIN	EXIT	NONE	REWRITE	
BOUNDS		NOT		WRITE
BREAK	FILE		SAME	WHILE
	FOR	OFF	SCRATCH	WINDOW
CALL	FROM	ON	SELECT	WITH
CASE	FUNCTION	OPEN	SEQUENTIAL	WRITE
CAUSE		OPTION	SET	
CENTERING	GO	OR	SIGNAL	
CHAIN	GOSUB	ORGANIZATION	SKIP	
CLEAR	GOTO	OUT	STANDARD	
CLIP	GRAPHIC	OUTIN	START	
CLOSE		OUTPUT	STATUS	
COLLATE	HANDLER		STEP	
CONNECT		PARACT	STOP	
CONTINUE	IF	PARSTOP	STREAM	
	IMAGE	PICTURE	STYLE	
DATA	IN	PLOT	SUB	
DATUM	INPUT	POINTER	SUBEXIT	
DEBUG	INQUIRE	POSITION		
DECIMAL	INTERNAL	PRINT	THEN	
DEF		PROCESS	THERE	
DELAY	KEY	PROMPT	TIME	
DELETE	KEYED		TIMEOUT	
DIM		RANDOMIZE	TO	
DISABLE	LENGTH	READ	TRACE	
DISCONNECT	LET	RECORD(s)	TYPE	
DISPLAY	LINE	RELATIVE		
DO	LOOP	REM		

Figure 3-2 Keywords in the Proposed New ANSI Standard for BASIC

OTHER COMPONENTS OF THE LANGUAGE

Source statements and keywords are, of course, very important components of any programming language. There are others, however, as we know. Operators, functions, arrays, variables, constants, and expressions are all important components as well. Since they usually differ somewhat from one language to another, it's necessary to examine each of these components early in a language description. Therefore we'll discuss BASIC's in the following paragraphs.

EXPRESSIONS IN BASIC

One word that the reader will undoubtedly tire of

seeing in this chapter is "expression." It has two dictionary definitions that apply here:

1. Mathematics—A designation of a symbolic mathematical form, such as an equation.
2. General—That which communicates, indicates, embodies, or symbolizes something; a symbol; a sign; a token.

These are broad definitions to be sure, but they are necessary because an expression can take many forms, ranging from a single number or letter to a complex equation.

Expressions are made up of one or more of the following components, which may appear in various combinations: constants, variables, operators, references to array elements, and references to functions.

Let's discuss what each component is and then show how they make up expressions. First is the variable.

A variable is an item subject to change during program execution, therefore, it must be named somehow. Think of the name as you would the letter assigned to the terms in a simple algebraic equation: $C = \pi d$. "C" and "d" are names for variables. Constants, of course, can appear in their final form because they do not change during program execution. π is the constant in this equation.

References to array elements are nothing more than the name assigned to a table of data and the number of the location in which a specific entry in that table appears.

References to functions are also very simple. There are several fundamental operations preprogrammed for the system user, and the user can cause them to be performed by simply calling them by name. For example, the operation "take square root" can be made to happen by giving its name, SQR, in an expression.

Last, the "operators" are nothing mysterious either. Arithmetic operators are the signs used to indicate what arithmetic is to be done, just as they are in pencil and paper methods. Relational operators are the greater than ($>$), less than ($<$), and similar signs with which most readers are already familiar.

STRING CONSTANTS AND STRING VARIABLES

Variables are basically one of two types: (1) numeric, pure numbers, and (2) "string," which is alphanumeric in that letters, numerals, and symbols may be used. Perhaps the definition that fits our use of the word "string" best is: "A series of related items arranged in a line." BASIC uses string constants and string variables. Constants are enclosed by quotation marks and may include any character in the character set except the quotation marks.

Because they may change during program execution, string variables can only be named, and the name they use must distinguish them from numeric variables. A two-character name is used.

In simple BASIC, the first character is a letter and the second a dollar sign ($). It is $ that distinguishes the name for a string variable from that of a numeric variable. Names used might be B$ or Z$.

NUMERIC CONSTANTS AND NUMERIC VARIABLES

Numeric constants are numbers and are specified simply by writing a number in a source statement. Many BASIC systems do provide assistance to the user in that common numeric constants such as π are available by name. The programmer does not have to enter the constant but only specify its name in a source statement.

Numeric variables have simple names, consisting of either one or two characters. The first must be a letter and, if a second character is used, it must be a digit. Examples are: C, D9, M, M9, R, and Z3.

A NOTE ABOUT NAMES

Throughout this chapter we use the naming rules established for early versions of BASIC, calling it "simple BASIC." Many new releases permit longer names—the proposed new BASIC standard allows thirty-one characters, while BASIC for the IBM Personal Computer permits forty. Because BASIC is the first major language covered in this book, it's especially important that the reader concentrate on the principles involved. And, in general, the short names help in this. Statements are thus "bare bones," making it easier to grasp the logic of what they do.

HOW NUMERIC AND STRING VARIABLES ARE USED

The need for a numeric variable is illustrated in the following example, which is given in Figure 3-3. We have a variable named R, which is employee pay rate per hour. Needless to say, a pay rate may vary from one employee to another, so for the calculation in which a paycheck is produced, we always call the pay rate R. As one employee record after another is brought into the computer for processing, the pay rate from that record is moved into numeric variable R. Thus, the pay rate changes as we've shown in the example. For the first employee record, R places $10.50 per hour in the calculation; for the next record, R produces $3.85 per hour;

A Numeric Variable Named R

R – Means Employee Pay Rate Per Hour

| R | 10.50 |

| R | 3.85 |

| R | 4.25 |

A String Variable Named E$

E$ – Means Employee Name

| E$ | R.S. JONES |

| E$ | S.V. SMITH |

| E$ | I.B. TINKLEPAUGH |

Figure 3-3 A Numeric Variable Named
R and a String Variable
Named E$

and, in the third record, R brings $4.25 per hour to the calculation. Therefore, one statement (GROSS PAY = HOURS times RATE) operates for all employees. In BASIC, this would be written $G = H * R$.

The need for a string variable can be shown in the same way. Of course, the string variable is not a number to be used in arithmetic, but it is manipulated within the computer. Let's continue calculating paychecks to illustrate.

In our example of the use of a numeric variable, we had three employee pay rates. Relate them to the three employees JONES, SMITH, and TINKLEPAUGH, which are a string variable named E$. When an employee record that provides pay rate for R is available, it provides employee name for E$. After gross pay is calculated, the paycheck

can be printed by giving the statement PRINT E$, G. This prints the name of the employee now represented by E$, and it follows the name with the gross amount (G) due that employee. (Of course G is a numeric variable.)

ARITHMETIC OPERATORS

Most of the BASIC systems available are capable of at least the five fundamental operations: add, subtract, multiply, divide, and raise to a power. The five signs, called arithmetic operators, that are used in expressions to produce arithmetic are:

+	for addition
−	for subtraction
*	for multiplication
/	for division
↑ (or **)	for exponentiation (raise to a power)

Of course, these operators require two factors (the "a" and the "b" to be added, for example) to perform the arithmetic. If the + and the − signs are placed before only one factor, they are called unary operators and they make the factor positive or negative, respectively.

Parentheses are available and are used in generally the same way as in elementary algebra. One significant difference is that brackets are usually not available. This makes it necessary to use parentheses within parentheses to achieve the effect of brackets. The innermost parentheses perform their normal functions and the outer ones function as brackets.

ORDER OF PRIORITY

Arithmetic operators are executed in a specific order, just as they are in pencil and paper arithmetic. The following is the order of priority, starting with the highest:

a. Operations in parentheses are performed first, starting with the innermost parentheses and working outward.
b. Unary operators (make positive or make negative) are executed.

c. Raise to a power.
d. Multiplication and division.
e. Addition and subtraction.

When operations of equal priority remain, they are executed in order left to right in the expression.

WRITING EXPRESSIONS USING ARITHMETIC OPERATORS

It takes some getting used to to write expressions using arithmetic operators because a source statement must be written all on one line rather than in multiple lines with subscripts and superscripts available. Some typical examples are shown in Figure 3-4.

Normally Written	One-Line in BASIC
$x = ab + c$	X=A*B+C
$x = \dfrac{ab}{c-d}$	X=A*B/(C-D)
$a = 2x + 3y + 8z$	A=2*X+3*Y+8*Z
$x = ab - \dfrac{c}{d}$	X=A*B-C/D
$x = 3a^2 - 5b + 27c$	X=3*A**2-5*B+27*C
$c^2 = a^2 + b^2$ $c = \sqrt{a^2 + b^2}$	C=SQR(A**2+B**2)

Figure 3-4 Examples of One-Line Expressions

RELATIONAL OPERATORS

These are the symbols commonly used to show the relationship between values of quantities, the equal sign (=), the greater than sign (>), etc. They are placed between the quantities to be compared so that the correct decision can be made. Among the relational operators available in most BASIC systems are:

=	equal
<>	not equal
>=	not less than (equal to or greater than)
<=	not greater than (equal to or less than)
>	greater than
<	less than

WRITING EXPRESSIONS USING RELATIONAL OPERATORS

Preparing an expression in which numeric variables are compared is very simple. A>B, X<=Y, and M<>N are examples. However, string variables can also be compared through the use of relational operators.

Possible applications are to determine alphabetical order or to search for a specific set of characters, such as a name. There are usually four relationships that can be tested:

< less than
> greater than
= equal to
<> not equal to

Comparison begins with the first character of each string. For example, if HARRIS was being compared with TINKLEPAUGH, the "H" in Harris is aligned with the "T" in Tinklepaugh and the value of the computer code used for each of those two letters is compared. Assuming that the ASCII code was used, "H" would be less than "T."

Assume that the following expression was used to make the comparison of the two names, HARRIS and TINKLEPAUGH:

IF R$<D$ THEN . . .

The string variable name R$ would bring HARRIS to be compared with TINKLEPAUGH, which was identified by the name D$. In this case, R$ is less than D$ and the decision is affirmative.

A string variable can also be compared with a string constant. Suppose we were searching a file alphabetically. The constant might be the letter "C" and the variable named R$. The following expression compared the two:

IF R$>"C" THEN . . .

If R$ identified HARRIS, the H would be greater than the "C" and the decision affirmative. On the other hand, if R$ brings the name BAKER to the comparison, the decision is negative.

LOGICAL OPERATORS

Although some versions of BASIC offer up to five logical operators, most programmers will use only

AND and OR often. Thus, we'll limit our discussion to those two.

Testing of conditions in order to make decisions is an important part of any programming job. Logical operators make this job easier. They allow relational expressions to be combined and to form a much more complex relationship to be tested.

Two examples are shown below:

IF A>B *AND* A<C THEN . . .
IF A>7 *OR* B=3 THEN . . .

In the first example, the objective is to determine that the value of variable A is within the range of B to C. This could be an age range, with A the age of the person being checked and the values of B and C, being the ages thirty-three and forty-seven.

The second example, which uses the OR operator, checks to see if *either* of two conditions exists before taking action. We've used only simple expressions, but they could be complex.

Although we've shown only numeric relationships being tested in the examples above, the AND and OR operators can also be applied in relational expressions involving strings. They are applied last, after the relationship has been evaluated, and thus work in the same way they do in the examples above.

THE STRING OPERATOR

We'll discuss only one string operator, and it is used to join strings or segments of strings. "Concatenation" is the name given to this joining process and, logically, the operator symbol is one that implies joining. A common and nonambiguous symbol used in simple BASIC is the ampersand (&). It's used in the form M$ = N$ & P$. In this case, string variables N$ and P$ are joined (without a space) to form the string variable M$. However, a string constant could have been used. M$ = N$ & "HARRIS" joins "HARRIS" to N$, forming M$.

ARRAYS

The nature of computers is such that they can perform repetitive tasks very rapidly, and therefore they can operate on large data collections. One of the fundamental ways of organizing data is the array.

Arrays may hold either numeric or string data. An array is named in the same manner as numeric and string variables are named. In simple BASIC, this means a letter is used to name a numeric array and a letter followed by a $ names a string array (F$, for example). Newer versions of BASIC allow much longer names, but the $ always concludes the names of string variables (and arrays) to distinguish them from their numeric counterparts.

BASIC permits either one-dimension arrays, consisting of a series of elements, or two-dimension arrays, which are a group of rows and columns. As we mentioned earlier, each element in the array can be identified individually. This is done by placing the element number in parentheses following the array name. A (17) selects the seventeenth element in a one-dimension array named A, while B$ (3,5) selects the element at the intersection of the third row and fifth column in a two-dimension string array named B$.

What kind of data is placed in an array? Generally, the same kind of data that is tabulated, an example of which appears in Figure 3-5. Here we have an insurance rate multiplication factor array. The notation (1,1) chooses the contents of the first element, a factor of 2.0, while (4,5) selects the element at the intersection of row 4, column 5, and thus brings forth the factor 6.5.

Array elements are used in expressions just like any other variable. A typical expression P = C*M (3,3) takes cost (C) and multiplies it by the contents of element 3,3 in our array M. In this case, a factor of 4.7. The result becomes the value of variable P (premium).

ELEMENT NUMBER →	1,1	1,2	1,3	1,4	1,5
CONTENTS OF ELEMENT →	2.0	3.2	3.3	3.5	3.7
	2,1	2,2	2,3	2,4	2,5
	3.0	3.9	4.0	4.0	4.4
	3,1	3,2	3,3	3,4	3,5
	4.0	4.5	4.7	4.9	5.0
	4,1	4,2	4,3	4,4	4,5
	5.0	5.3	5.7	6.1	6.5
	5,1	5,2	5,3	5,4	5,5
	6.0	7.0	7.6	8.3	9.0

Figure 3-5 The Contents of a Typical BASIC Array

SYSTEM FUNCTIONS

As an aid to simplify programming, certain predefined functions in which all the work is done by the system rather than by the programmer are provided in most versions of BASIC. These are preprogrammed operations, each of which is assigned a name. When the programmer gives this name in an expression, the function is performed and the results automatically included in the evaluation of the expression.

Let's examine some typical system functions, using examples with which the reader may be familiar. SQR(X) is a simple one. When this name is given, it produces the square root of the quantity (X), and this root is used in the expression of which SQR is a part. LOG10(X) is another good example. It produces the common logarithm of the quantity (X), which then becomes part of the expression and is processed in accordance with the operators in the expression.

Listed below are names of some of the system functions that a BASIC system may have. Each is accompanied by a brief description of its function. Some are obviously related to engineering and scientific functions, while others are suited to general use.

Examples of System Functions Frequently Available in BASIC

NAME	FUNCTION
SQR(X)	Take square root of the following expression, which is enclosed in parentheses. Example: A=SQR(N*3/7)
INT(X)	Take largest integer. Example: A=INT(N)
LOG10(X)	Common log of X. Example: A=LOG10(X)
LOG(X)	Natural log of X. Example: B=LOG(X)
SIN(X)	Sine of X (X is an angle measured in radians). Example: S=SIN(X)
COS(X)	Cosine of X.
TAN(X)	Tangent of X.
SGN(X)	Sign of X. Example: A=SGN(X)
ABS(X)	Absolute value of X. Example: A=ABS(R+7*S)
RND	Random number. Example: A=97*RND
LEN(R$)	Determine length of R$. Example: IF A>LEN(R$) THEN 200

SPECIAL SYSTEM FUNCTIONS

Each industry or type of business has some calculations that are done often but which are probably not found among the standard system functions available in BASIC. A pricing calculation, for example, may be used very often and always in the same manner. Many BASIC systems allow the programmer to prepare a customized system function in this case and call it by name just as one does with the standard system functions. The function may be either a numeric function or a string function.

A statement called "define function" (DEF) is used to create a customized system function. Once this function is established, it may be called as many times as necessary by the program in which it is defined. It does not become one of the standard system functions, however, and thus must be provided in each source program in which it's used.

Construction and naming of a function are fairly simple. The first two letters of the function name are always FN. These letters are followed (without a space) by a name conforming to the rules for numeric variables or string variables. For example, FNA is a numeric function and FNR$ is a string function. To summarize: A numeric function is named like a numeric variable and a string function like a string variable.

Thus far we have DEF FN <u>name</u> in our define function statement. Next come the names of the variables to which it will be applied. Up to five variables may be named, the names separated by commas and enclosed in parentheses. DEF FNA (X) or DEF FNB (M, N) are two examples. The first says that function FNA will act on a numeric variable, the X, and the second says the function FNB will act on two numeric variables, M and N.

The names given (X, M, and N in the examples) establish only the form of the variables that the function will act on. They are not the final variable names. B could be substituted for X when the function is actually used, for example.

Last in the define function statement comes the expression that is evaluated when the function is called into action. So our complete function definition statement would take the form: DEF FNA (X) = 9/5 * (X + 2). After this statement is entered in the program, FNA can be used just as any of the standard system functions. Perhaps LET C = FNA (B) would be the form. In this case, the value of the variable named B replaces the X in the expression

9/5 * (X + 2) and the result of the evaluation becomes the value of C.

CONSTRUCTION
OF SOURCE STATEMENTS

Source statements are the instructions that a programmer can issue. They usually consist of an action word (a "verb" if we think of them as a sentence) and a body that provides information necessary to carry out the action.

The best way to study the source statement set available in BASIC is to organize instructions into groups that *work together*—all those associated with displaying information, for example, should be examined at the same time. That is the way the following discussion is organized.

Showing Source Statement Formats

We'll show formats in the same style that a programmer has to write them on a coding form. Let's examine the format. At the left is the line number, which identifies each source statement. All modern systems assign line numbers automatically and provide the capability to reassign line numbers, also automatically, when statements are removed or added.

Some systems still require manual entry, so the programmer must write them out. In addition, some source statements must refer to another line number, and the programmer must provide that line number in the body of the source statement. A GOTO statement, for example, must read: GOTO line number NNNN. In order to provide that line number, the programmer must have kept some kind of record on his coding form.

The COMMENTS section of each source statement, which appears at the right side, is usually of fixed length. Any characters may be typed in there,

so this part of the coding form has no effect on the instruction.

This brings us to the heart of the matter—the positions in which the words and expressions must be entered. We'll call it the "body" of the source statement.

BASIC Source Statement Syntax Diagrams

A problem arises when it becomes necessary to show all arrangements possible within the body of a source statement. In the following section, we've given examples of the most common uses and forms of each statement, but it is impractical to do more than that. Therefore, syntax diagrams like those shown in Figure 3-6 are provided to illustrate the type of information that may appear in each statement, its position with respect to other information, and the punctuation that is necessary to separate the components of the statement.

The keywords are shown in all capitals and appear in the positions they must occupy in the statement. Two sets of symbols are then used to point out the positions of the other components. The enclosures ⟨ ⟩ mean that a component of this type fits in this position. Punctuation needed to separate the component from others is also shown. For example, ⟨component 1⟩, ⟨component 2⟩, means that the comma is the punctuation mark that must be provided if the statement is to be processed properly.

Sometimes, the punctuation chosen depends upon the function to be performed. In this case, the options (, / ; / : /) are shown. This means that a comma, semicolon, colon, or no punctuation at all are the options available.

Components of two different types may occupy a specific position in some statements. A pair of braces { } shows this; they represent an "or" relationship just as if two sets of enclosures ⟨ ⟩ were stacked one on top of the other.

The last situation that may need explanation is

ON ⟨ variable ⟩ GOTO ⟨ line no. 1 ⟩ , ⟨ line no. 2 ⟩ , ⟨ line no. N ⟩

IF ⟨ relation ⟩ THEN { line no. or statement } { ELSE or UNLESS } { line no. or statement }

OPEN ⟨ channel no. ⟩ ⟨ "file name" ⟩ , ⟨ parameter list ⟩ , ⟨ error line no. ⟩

Figure 3-6 Examples of BASIC Syntax Diagrams

the possibility of substituting one keyword for another. This appears in only a few statements, and it is indicated by stacking the two acceptable keywords and separating them by the word "or."

Let's examine three source statements, which are shown in Figure 3-6, to demonstrate how the formats should be read. The first statement is the ON ⟨ ⟩ GOTO. The position of the variable is shown between the keywords. There is no punctuation. At least one line number must be present. If there is more than one, they must be separated by commas.

In the second statement, either a line number or a statement of action may appear after the THEN. If it is desired to specify an alternative action, the ELSE word and an alternative action is provided. If it is desired to add conditions, the UNLESS word followed by a statement of condition is included.

An OPEN statement is the third example. Channel number is followed by file name. A parameter list must be provided. It is separated from other components by commas, and it uses commas for internal punctuation. Finally, a line number may be provided if the program is to go to a specific line number if an error is produced when the OPEN statement is executed.

Statements Discussed

We've chosen a set of "core" statements to explain in detail. They handle the fundamental operations available in BASIC. When a description moves to statements beyond this core, it becomes involved in unique statements available in only one version of BASIC, or at most a few.

First come the statements necessary to enter the data with which the program will operate. They are:

    enter DATA
    READ data
    RESTORE data table pointers

We'll cover statements that operate with the keyboard next. There are two:

    sound BEEP
    accept INPUT

Establishing the size of tables and the fields in which data is held are performed by two source statements. We'll cover these statements next:

    define array DIMensions
    FIELD size

Those statements concerned with handling data in files and buffers appear fourth in order. These are listed below. The reserved word is given in capital letters, and this is supplemented to give it added meaning, as was done above. There are eleven statements in this group:

CLOSE file   PUT in buffer
DELETE current record   READ record
GET buffer contents   RESTORE file pointer
MARK end of file   UPDATE record
OPEN file   WRITE record
PURGE file

Discussed next are the statements that display or print information. They include:

        DISPLAY
        DISPLAY USING
establish IMAGE
        PRINT
        PRINT USING

An extremely useful source statement is the one called LET. Its importance is so great and its use so varied that it is discussed by itself. Essentially, the statement means:

LET the following expression be evaluated.

Statements that make decisions and establish loops have much in common with one another, and they are discussed together. Included are:

FOR and NEXT
IF and THEN
GOTO and ON ⟨ ⟩ GOTO
GOSUB and RETURN

A few of the source statements available have special actions, and we've saved these for last. In this group we have:

PAUSE
enter REMarks
STOP
END
RANDOMIZE

DATA ENTRY STATEMENTS

Data necessary for the execution of a program can be provided in several ways:

a. It may already be present in existing files. In this case, the files are read when the program is being executed.
b. The program may ask the operator to enter the data from the keyboard. In this case, instructions appear on the screen, the operator types in the information, and it is accepted by the INPUT statement.
c. The data may be provided by source statements before the program is compiled. Thus, the data becomes a permanent part of the program.

The three statements that we'll describe in this section perform the data entry outlined in the third case above. They are typed in during entry of the source statements and, therefore, become part of the source program. There are three statements involved, and their formats are shown in Figure 3-7. They have the following meaning:

enter the following DATA
READ data into the specified variable
RESTORE data table pointers

The DATA source statement creates data tables, both numeric and string, and provides the information to be entered in the tables. This operation is used to initially enter information. Although both string and numeric data can be entered, expressions and operators cannot.

```
DATA < entry 1 > , < entry 2 > , < entry N >
READ < variable 1 > , < variable 2 > , < variable N >
RESTORE
```

Figure 3-7 Data Entry Statements Syntax Diagrams

String data is identified by quotation marks and appears in the string data table in the order in which it is given in the DATA statements. The numeric data does not have quotation marks, but it too is entered in a table in the order in which it is provided by the source statement. One DATA statement after another may be used until all the desired data is entered, and numeric and string data may be mixed.

The data tables are only data entry devices. Material in these tables must be associated with the name of a variable so that the program can call it by name.

The READ statement takes an entry from a table and places it in an array element, a string variable,

or a numeric variable. The READ statement is simply a list of names of variables or array elements.

A READ statement starts moving data from the first position of a table, switching back and forth between numeric and string tables as the name of the variable indicates, until all the variables specified in the body of the statement have been handled. The next READ statement continues from the point at which the previous statement left off. (Figure 3-8 illustrates how this works.)

STATEMENTS

```
DATA "HARRIS", "SMITH", "JONES"

DATA 5, 7, 9, 80, 149

DATA 20.73, 15.95, 88.95

DATA "BROWN", 70, "WILSON", 80, "WILLIAMS", 100

READ M$, N$, P$

READ R, S
```

String Data Table	Numeric Data Table	Variables
HARRIS	5	M$ HARRIS
SMITH	7	N$ SMITH
JONES	9	P$ JONES
BROWN	80	R 5
WILSON	149	S 7
WILLIAMS	20.73	
	15.95	
	88.95	
	70	
	80	
	100	

Figure 3-8 Use of DATA and READ Statements

A pointer is automatically maintained to keep track of which position in the table is being read by the READ statement. This applies to the entry of data into the table by the DATA statement as well. Each table (string and numeric) has its own pointer.

The pointers both begin at the first location and step along the locations as each table is used by an enter DATA or READ data statement. A reset action is needed if the same data is to be used a second time by a READ statement, and this is provided by the RESTORE statement. Both pointers are returned to position one when this statement is issued.

The DATA statement is normally provided at the end of the program but may be used anywhere, and the READ statement given as the data is used by the program.

KEYBOARD INPUT STATEMENTS

Two statements, INPUT and BEEP, are described in this section. Both are very simple to construct and use. For readers who wish to look at the syntax diagram before reading this description, it appears in Figure 3-9.

In the preceding section, three ways of entering data for a program to process were mentioned. Each method has specific applications to which it is best suited, and we've discussed the use of the data entry statements. They have one major disadvantage; once entered, they become part of the program and cannot be changed during its execution. Obviously, this is not a good choice of data entry for material that changes often or is otherwise variable.

This brings us to use of the keyboard to enter data while the program is being executed. It is the INPUT statement that allows keystrokes to be accepted. Included in the statement are the names of the variables to be entered and punctuation that controls spacing of the data typed in.

INPUT < variable 1 > , / ; / : / < variable 2 > , / ; / : /
          < variable N > , / ; / : /

BEEP

Figure 3-9 INPUT and BEEP Statement
Syntax Diagrams

Many variables can be defined by one INPUT statement. The number depends upon their type and name. Numeric variables, string variables, and array elements can all be accepted. Use of the INPUT statement to enter information is shown later in examples, but before we get to the examples, let's review the punctuation that is provided with the names of the variables listed in an INPUT statement. There are three symbols:

a. A comma (,) means advance to the beginning of the next zone on the screen to enter the variable. The spacing of zones depends upon the BASIC system in use. A typical arrangement is to divide eighty character positions into five zones of sixteen spaces each. Thus, zone one begins at position one, zone two at position seventeen, etc.
b. A semicolon (;) means do not leave a space between this variable and the next. In this case, the cursor on the screen will move only one position and the data for the two variables will be run together on the screen.

c. A colon (:) means leave one space between variables on the screen.

If no punctuation is provided, the cursor moves to the next line as soon as the variable is entered.

The following example of an INPUT statement accepts the employee name asked for by the DISPLAY statement and moves to the next zone.

DISPLAY "ENTER EMPLOYEE NAME"
INPUT E$,

Shown below are two more examples to illustrate the action of the INPUT statement:

INPUT M, N$
Action: Accepts first typed entry and assigns it to variable M. Moves to start of next zone on the screen to await next entry. Accepts next entry and assigns it to variable N$. Moves to the beginning of the next line on the screen.

INPUT D:T
Action: Accepts the first typed entry and assigns it to variable D. Inserts one space on screen and awaits the next entry. Assigns it to variable T and moves to the beginning of the next line on the screen.

The computer often needs a way to attract operator attention to inform him of a variety of conditions. This is usually done by producing an audible tone through a small speaker in the machine. The BASIC instruction that produces the tone is called a BEEP. Whenever this source statement is given, the tone is produced for a very short time. If the programmer wants to lengthen the tone, he places the BEEP statement in a loop so that it is given over and over again until the operator either takes action or the time established for the loop expires.

ARRAY HANDLING STATEMENTS

One of the first tasks that a programmer must perform is to organize his data. Definition of his arrays is an important part of this work. Most BASIC systems establish a standard size array if the programmer does not otherwise set the limits. That standard size is no greater than ten in either dimension, therefore, a two-dimensional array of ten rows and ten columns is the maximum possible size for an array that is defined only by reference to one of its elements. BASIC calls this "an array defined implicitly."

This brings us to the use of the DIM statement, which is necessary to establish any array other than the standard size, and is always required if an array is to have more than ten columns or rows. When a DIM statement is used, an array is said to have been defined explicitly.

The format of the DIM source statement appears in Figure 3-10. The number of arrays established by each statement depends on the complexity of the definition and the space available in the statement. A one-dimension array needs only the number of rows defined, while a two-dimension array definition must include both the number of rows and number of columns. In simple BASIC, a numeric array is named by a single letter and a string array by a letter and dollar sign.

Use of the DIM statement is very easy, as the following examples illustrate. The first example establishes a string array named Y$, consisting of five rows and ten columns. In the second case, the DIM statement establishes two numeric arrays, A and B. A is a one-dimensional array of ten elements and B is a two-dimensional array of five rows and twenty columns.

```
DIM Y$(5,10)
DIM A(10),B(5,20)
```

Of course, these statements do nothing more than establish dimensions; they do not enter data in the array. Additional statements are required to do that.

There are two basic ways in which data can be entered into arrays or the contents of arrays displayed or printed: (1) one element at a time, and (2) handling the entire array as a unit. If a single element is to be manipulated, it is only necessary to give the name of the array and the location of the element in a statement. For example: READ A$(5,10) will place the next data item it reads from the string data table into the array named A$ at the element located in row five, column ten. To use another example of a statement we've covered: INPUT A$(5,10). This takes data from the keyboard and enters it in the location we just mentioned. DISPLAY A$(5,10) would show the same information on the screen.

Included in some BASIC systems is a keyword that allows a programmer to handle an entire array as a unit; that word is MAT, meaning matrix. When given before the array name in a source statement, it causes that statement to act upon all elements of the array. For example, MAT R refers to all elements in the numeric array named R.

It should be easy for the reader to see how useful this keyword would be when loading data into an array. The source statement DATA can provide the information. When a MAT READ R statement is given, it accepts the data in the order it appears in the DATA statement and assigns it to array R. The array is loaded left-to-right and top-to-bottom.

MAT can also be used in other source statements. MAT PRINT R prints out the contents of array R in the same left-to-right, top-to-bottom form it was loaded, allowing the programmer to deal with an entire array rather than individual elements.

It is also possible to do arithmetic involving an entire array. Suppose, for example, a set of array values had to be updated at the beginning of a new year to reflect the addition of new taxes. In this case, the entire array can be multiplied by a constant to increase every element in the array by an equal percentage. All that is necessary is one statement in the form: MAT S = (C)*R. A new array S is formed after every element in R has been multiplied by C, the constant. All elements maintain their respective positions.

THE FIELD STATEMENT

A field is a group of character positions that holds a specific type of information, although a field may be as small as one position. Student grade, for example, would require only one position if the letter system (A, B, C, etc.) was used but would require more positions in a percentage grade or the point system (4.0, 2.6, etc.). And, of course, the student name field might be as many as twenty positions long.

The purpose of the FIELD statement, which is shown in Figure 3-11, is to establish the length of a numeric or string variable. In the body of the statement, the name of the variable is given and is fol-

DIM < array 1 name (rows, columns)> , < array 2> , < array N>
Figure 3-10 DIMension Statement Syntax Diagram

lowed by the number of positions allocated to that variable and the number of decimal places to be used.

Some examples of a FIELD statement follow:

FIELD M = 5.0
Action: Sets the size of numeric variable M to five digits, with no decimal places.

FIELD N = 8.2
Action: Sets the size of numeric variable N to ten digits, with two decimal places.

FIELD E$ = 20
Action: Sets the size of string variable E$ to twenty character positions.

FILE HANDLING STATEMENTS

Up to now we've discussed two sources of data that a BASIC program may process. The first being the data entered by the DATA statement and the second being information typed in by the operator during program execution. Both sources are important and used often, but files of data are the primary source of information for most BASIC programs.

Files are groups of data external to a BASIC program, and they are held in a permanent storage medium such as tape, disks, diskettes, or cards. Only the simplest BASIC programs operate without using files of data. Therefore, the programmer must learn how to organize and manipulate them. There are several operations involved. First, of course, the file must be established. This requires that a storage medium be selected and the file be given a name. Files are generally named for the type of information they hold and in this respect naming a file is no more complicated than organizing paper files.

After a file is established, there are only a few operations that can be performed on it. Information can be stored in the file and retrieved from the file. In some cases, specific information can be deleted from the file and, naturally, the file itself can be eliminated.

We mentioned earlier that all files are given names but we didn't discuss how one storage medium is chosen from among those available. This depends upon the BASIC system in use, the equipment available, and the operating system. In general, however, each storage medium is given a number or code that the programmer can place in his source statements dealing with files.

In Chapter 1 we discussed how data is organized and how to plan a data file. Some BASIC systems have the capacity to handle two very different types of files. The first is a file in which records are treated as units of information and no less than an entire record is moved to or from a file—this is generally called a "record input-output file." A second type is a file in which individual items are handled by their name. In other words, variables like A$, Z, and Y are stored and retrieved by name. This kind of file is often called a "stream file" and could be thought of as a file in which each record holds only one variable and has a length determined by the size of that variable.

The files, no matter what type, must be opened, named, written, and read, of course. It is much more likely that the reader will be interested in using the record input-output files, however, so we'll limit our discussion to those.

File handling source statements are listed below in alphabetical order. The word entered in the program itself is given in all capitals. Added to this word are others that should help to clarify its meaning.

CLOSE file
DELETE record
MARK end of file
OPEN file
PURGE file
READ record
RESTORE file pointer
UPDATE record
WRITE record

For those readers wishing to see the syntax diagrams of the file handling instructions before reading the explanations that follow, they are shown in Figure 3-12. There is a great deal of similarity among source statements. This is evident in the figure.

OPEN is the first source statement we should consider. It really has two meanings: (1) OPEN—establish or create—a file, and (2) OPEN—gain access to—an existing file. When establishing a file, the programmer must include file parameters

FIELD < name 1 and size > , < name 2 and size > , < name N and size >
Figure 3-11 FIELD Statement Syntax Diagram

OPEN < channel no. >　< file name>　< parameters >　<error line no.>

CLOSE < channel no. >

DELETE < channel no. >

MARK < channel no. >

UPDATE < channel no. >

RESTORE < channel no.>

WRITE < channel no. >　< error line no. >

PURGE < channel no. >　< file name >　<volume no. >

READ < channel no. >　$\left\{\begin{array}{l} \text{REC} < \text{record no.} \\ \text{KEY} < \text{record key} \\ \text{EOF} < \text{line no.} \end{array}\right\}$　< error line no. >

Figure 3-12 Syntax Diagrams for File Handling Statements

such as the access method, the size of records to be used, the size of the file itself, the file name, and the number of the volume on which the file is to be recorded. When wanting to use an existing file, the programmer is able to gain access to the file by simply giving its name.

CLOSE is the next logical statement to examine. It has a very simple function—to end program access to a specific file. Because a file is given a number when opened, the CLOSE statement need only give that number to accomplish its purpose.

This brings us to the PURGE statement, which is used to eliminate a file when it is no longer needed. Positive file identification is required in the PURGE statement, rather than just the file number used in CLOSE. Included must be the file name and number and the number of the volume on which it is stored. The file must have also been closed before the PURGE statement is issued.

READ, WRITE, UPDATE, and DELETE are the source statements that control movement of records between buffers in the computer's memory and files. (A buffer is a set of storage locations established to hold records being transferred.) The actions performed by each are as follows:

a. READ moves a record from a file to a buffer in the computer's memory. The READ statement must provide the file number. There are other specific types of information that can be given.

b. WRITE record moves a record from a buffer to a file. The file number is given in the source statement.

c. UPDATE record is similar to the WRITE statement but deals with a specific record that was read into a buffer and changed. Information needed to identify that record was provided with the READ statement.

d. DELETE record also deals with a record that was previously read into a buffer, and identifying information was provided with the READ statement. When the DELETE statement is issued, that record is removed from the file.

MARK end of file is a simple statement that places an end of file (EOF) indicator in the specified file. The EOF mark follows the current record. If one hundred records are in the file, for example, the EOF mark follows immediately after the one hundredth record. One purpose of this mark is to make it possible for a READ statement to read to the end of file without knowing in advance how many records are in the file.

A RESTORE file pointer statement returns a record counter to the beginning of a file, that is to record one. In the case of tape files, the tape is rewound to the beginning of the file, but for disk and diskette files it is necessary only to reset a record counter because the disk/diskette file is always in motion.

This leads us to a discussion of the statements used to move data into and out of the buffers. Each buffer usually holds all the fields that make up one record. Of course, each field bears a name by which the program can identify it and gain access to only that field without disturbing the rest of the record.

Since field sizes and record sizes are specified in advance, no problems arise in making a field fit.

There are two statements that move information into and out of buffers. Their formats are shown in Figure 3-13. Below, we again have shown the keyword in all capitals and supplemented it with other words to clarify its meaning.

GET data from a buffer
PUT data in a buffer

The GET statement is made up of pairs of field identifiers. The first element of each pair is a numeric expression that defines the starting position in the buffer of the information to be "gotten," and the second element of each pair is the name of the variable into which the "gotten" information is to be placed. These are fields in a record. An employee's name, for example, might start in position six of a record and be placed in a variable called E$. So, the GET statement would specify that the field starting at position six should be moved to the variable named E$. Several pairs of starting points and names of variables can be given in each GET statement, so all the information required for a series of calculations can be obtained simultaneously.

PUT operates so as to move information into a buffer from a variable involved in a calculation. Again, pairs of identifiers appear in the body of the statement. One element specifies the starting location in the buffer where data is to be "put," and the second element defines the data itself.

GET < buffer no. > < numeric expression 1 = variable name 1 > ,
                     < numeric expression 2 = variable name 2 > ,
                     < numeric expression N = variable name N >

PUT   Same Syntax as GET Above

Figure 3-13 GET and PUT Statement Syntax Diagrams

Two examples follow:

GET #4 10=M
Action: Information from buffer #4, starting at position 10, is moved to variable M. Length of M was defined earlier. If it is 5, for example, positions 10 through 14 are moved to numeric variable M.

PUT #4 17=R
Action: Contents of numeric variable R are placed in buffer #4, starting at position 17. The size of R was defined earlier.

Now to some examples of how the file handling statements appear in actual use. Perhaps the best way to illustrate functions is to place several statements in the sequence in which they would be used together, as follows:

OPEN #7 "EMPLOYEES" ERR 2700
READ #7 EOF 1200

UPDATE #7

1200 CLOSE #7

This group of statements and the intervening steps, which are indicated by lines, open the file named "EMPLOYEES" on channel number 7. It then reads one record, revises it, and returns the record with an UPDATE statement. Another statement causes the program to return to read the next record. This process is repeated until the READ statement encounters the end of the file. The EOF 1200 notation means that the program is to go to line 1200 when the end is encountered, and when it does, the CLOSE statement closes the file on channel 7.

In this case, the records were simply read in order, but it is also possible to specify the record to be read by position or by its key. The record identification fits in place of the EOF 1200 we used. For example, the following statements would each read a specific record:

READ #7 REC 13 ERR 2800
READ #7 KEY A$ ERR 2800

The first statement reads the thirteenth record in the file, while the second statement reads a record whose key is the string variable named A$. It should also be noted that the key itself could be provided rather than the name of the variable holding the key.

As we mentioned, a file is established by an OPEN statement. Following are two examples of such statements:

OPEN #5 "ACCOUNTS",6,N,128,I,1000,
4,10,5 ERR 0700
OPEN #3 E$,6,N,128,S,500 ERR 0700

The first statement opens a new (N) file on channel number 5. Its name is "ACCOUNTS", and it is placed on unit 6. Record length is 128 positions, the file is a "keyed" file as indicated by the I, which means indexed. The file is to be established as a

1000-record file. The key is four characters long, and it begins at position 10 in the record. A 5 percent overflow is allowed. If an error is encountered when this statement is establishing this file, the next statement to be executed is in line 0700. Any time after this statement is completed, the program can issue WRITE statements to place records in the file.

The second OPEN statement above opens a file on channel 3. Its name is the contents of string variable E$, which might be something like "EXPENSES-APRIL". This file is to be placed on unit 6. It is new, has records 128 positions in length, and is a sequential file of 500 records.

After the file E$ is established, data can be written into it. Assuming that the file was used for an entire month and it was time to eliminate it, a PURGE statement in the form PURGE #3,E$,6 could remove this file from unit 6.

STATEMENTS THAT DISPLAY AND PRINT

The display screen, or CRT as it is often called, is the primary way in which a small computer communicates with the operator. All screens can show uppercase letters, most can display messages in both upper- and lowercase, and some have the capability to provide complex graphics. The tube, the *T* in Cathode-Ray Tube, is identical to that used in TV sets and, therefore, can provide any picture desired; it is the computer circuits and the programs that determine what is actually shown.

Printers, on the other hand, are limited in their capacity to present information. Most have both upper- and lowercase characters available, and many have the capacity to construct graphics.

We'll cover three major statements in this section and two keywords that appear only in the body of a statement. DISPLAY, PRINT, and IMAGE are the statements, while USING and TAB are the keywords mentioned. (Syntax diagrams for these statements appear in Figure 3-14.)

Some versions of BASIC use the word PRINT for any recording of data, whether that data is placed on the display screen, paper in the printer, or in data files. They choose the destination by placing a channel number after the word PRINT or a letter before it (LPRINT, for example), and this number or letter directs the output to the proper medium.

Some confusion may result from this, particularly for the beginner, so we've used the word DISPLAY to mean "show data on the screen." It should be understood that PRINT can be substituted for this in most adaptations of the language.

The "display" we speak of is the screen on which messages and data appear. Control of it is very simple. There are two instructions available: DISPLAY and DISPLAY USING. When these words are entered in a source statement they have the following meaning:

a. DISPLAY the characters that follow this word or which are named by the symbols following this word.

b. DISPLAY the characters that follow this word or which are named by the symbols following this word, but organize them along the line USING the format (the image) established by the source statement in line NNNNN.

DISPLAY < expression 1 > , / ; / : / < expression 2 > , / ; / : / < expression N >

DISPLAY TAB { < TOF > ; < numeric expression > ; < numeric expression, numeric expression > }

PRINT #1 < expression 1 > , / ; / : / < expression 2 > , / ; / : / < expression N >

PRINT #1 TAB { < TOF > ; < numeric expression > }

DISPLAY USING < line no. > , < expression 1 > , < expression 2 > , < expression N >

PRINT #1 USING < line no. > , < expression 1 > , < expression 2 > , < expression N >

IMAGE < information and edit mask >

Figure 3-14 Syntax Diagrams for Statements That Print and Display

A keyword IMAGE is used to establish the format of a line on both the screen and on the printer. When this keyword is entered in a source statement, it has the following meaning: Establish the IMAGE following this word as the format of characters to be displayed or printed and edit the characters as shown by this format.

Position of the characters within the line is controlled by punctuation, as follows:

None Display, then advance to the beginning of the next line.

Comma Display, then advance to the beginning of the next zone.

Semicolon Display, then advance to the next position after the data provided (this will not leave a space between entries on the line).

Colon Display, then advance two positions after the data provided (this will leave one space between entries on the line).

If no expressions are provided in the DISPLAY source statement, a blank line will appear. This is the way in which vertical spacing is achieved.

The keyword TAB is used somewhat like the tabs on a typewriter are. TAB follows the word DISPLAY, and produces one of three possible actions depending on the expressions that follow it, as shown below:

TAB (n-exp) Move to horizontal position specified by the numeric expression.

TAB (n-exp,n-exp) Move to the horizontal position specified by the first expression and to the vertical position specified by the second expression. This is a way in which starting positions can be established.

TAB(TOF) means move to the top of the form. It moves the completed page up and off the screen, leaving a blank screen (a blank page). The first display position is the first character of the first line.

Shown below are examples of the statements that would be used to construct a simple display of instructions on the display screen.

DISPLAY TAB(TOF) clears the screen.
DISPLAY TAB(20,4) moves the starting point to line 4, the 20th position from the left.
DISPLAY "CHOOSE THE JOB TO BE PERFORMED"

DISPLAY TAB(25,6) moves the starting point to line 6, 25th position from the left.
DISPLAY "1. ACCOUNTS RECEIVABLE"
DISPLAY TAB(25,8) moves the starting point to line 8, 25th position from the left.
DISPLAY "2. ACCOUNTS PAYABLE"
DISPLAY TAB(25,10)
DISPLAY "3. GENERAL LEDGER"
DISPLAY TAB(25,12)
DISPLAY "4. INVENTORY UPDATE"

This produces a list of jobs, and the program pauses with an INPUT statement waiting for the operator to push the proper key number to select the job to be done. We've used only string constants in our example, but it is also easy to use variables, as follows:

DISPLAY "THE COLOR IS:", T$
Action: Displays the information in quotation marks. Moves to the beginning of the next zone and displays the current contents of the string variable T$.

Printing

Printers range in size from the small desktop units to large free-standing machines. They differ in speed and in quality of the printed copy, but most have the same basic characteristics. The paper on which printing is done is usually organized into 80 or 132 columns, with about 60 lines per sheet.

Source statements used for printing are very similar to those used for display, as the reader would expect. (The same basic functions of providing data and locating it on a page are being performed.) The words used in the source statement are PRINT#1 or PRINT#1 USING. They have the following meaning:

a. PRINT the characters following this word or which are named by the symbols following this word.

b. PRINT the characters following this word or which are named by the symbols following this word USING the format (the image) established by the source statement in line NNNNN.

The IMAGE statement is the same as that used with the DISPLAY statements described earlier. It is extremely useful in that a format for specific information, such as columns of numbers in a table can be established in advance and used over and over. If the IMAGE statement were not available, the programmer would have to provide his format each time he printed or displayed data.

There is one printer characteristic that does require it to be handled somewhat differently from a display. This is that printers usually print one entire line at a time and then move down to the next line. Most printers cannot back up. In BASIC, this characteristic limits the use of the TAB keyword to two functions:

TAB (n-exp) Move to the horizontal position specified by (n-exp).

TAB(TOF) Move to the top (first line) of the next page.

Spacing along a line is controlled by the comma, semicolon, and colon punctuation marks described in the DISPLAY statement.

Although the PRINT statement is very similar in action to the DISPLAY statement, it is likely to be of great interest to the reader. Therefore, we'll provide two examples of its use.

PRINT#1 TAB(TOF)

Action: Feeds paper through printer until first line of new sheet is reached. Current position is first position on first line.

PRINT#1 "EMPLOYEE NAME", E$

Action: Prints information in quotation marks, starting at current position on current line, skips to beginning of next zone, prints contents of variable E$, goes to first position of next line.

The IMAGE Statement

Up to this point, we've seen the need for layout planning forms to be used for displayed and printed pages. It should be obvious that organizing the data for display or printing is a fairly complex task and that any tools that would assist a programmer would be welcome. One very important tool is the IMAGE statement.

Of course a programmer must establish the format of each line the first time he uses that format, so the IMAGE statement cannot eliminate this task. Where it is useful is in repetitive use of the same format.

The body of the IMAGE source statement is called the "edit mask." It consists of a series of symbols that determine how the data to be shown is processed before it is printed or displayed. An edit mask is particularly useful in handling numbers, so most of the symbols have to do with editing numeric values.

Symbols available for use in an edit mask and their meaning are shown below. Let's review all the symbols and their effect:

\#   Allow this character to appear.

!   Suppress zeros (Don't display zeros in this position).

,   Insert a comma, unless zeros are suppressed so as to make the comma unnecessary.

.   Insert a decimal point, unless zeros are suppressed so as to make the point unnecessary.

:   Insert a decimal point, stop zero suppression at this point.

;   Insert a comma, stop zero suppression at this point.

−   Add a minus sign if quantity is negative; space otherwise.

+   Add a minus sign if quantity is negative; add a plus sign if quantity is positive; space otherwise.

/   Insert a slash at this point.

A simple example in the following lines shows how useful an edit mask is in establishing the format of a variable when that variable is printed. We start with an unknown number G1, which is gross sales by a salesman. Assuming that it was $10,000.00 for the period, the short program below would print sales commission as follows:

050 LET A = 0.05 (This is the commission of 5 percent.)
060 PRINT#1 USING 070,A*G1
070 IMAGE "SALES COMMISSION $!!!#.##"
Result: SALES COMMISSION $ 500.00

G1 is the gross sales credited to a specific salesman; it was calculated by an earlier routine. Each time that commission is to be printed, the program comes to this routine to print the commission. A is 5 percent. When the PRINT#1 statement is executed, it does the arithmetic (A*G1), although it could have been done earlier and is shown here only to illustrate the power of the PRINT and DISPLAY statements.

The image, which includes part of the message, then edits the product of the arithmetic before the figure is printed. The mask (!!!#.##) suppresses all leading zeros, which are any zeros that appear to the left of the first digit that appears. In the example, one position was unfilled. Then the "5" was encountered and zero suppression stopped. A decimal point was inserted. If the answer had produced a zero in the position immediately to the left of the point, it would have been displayed.

Zones on Both the Screen and Printer

The screen and printer lines are divided into several zones to assist the programmer. When confronted with the task of aligning columns of data, the programmer can simply use the zone spacing provided, rather than work out all the details on a planning sheet and set tab positions for each starting point. A feature that makes use of the zone spacing easy is that a comma placed in a PRINT statement after data to be displayed or printed causes the next printing to start at the beginning of the next zone.

The number of spaces in each zone depends upon the system in use. If 80 spaces were available, each of the five zones would have 16 spaces each, and the 132 spaces on the longest print line could be divided in a similar fashion.

Variations of the Display and Printing Statements

Some BASIC systems allow the edit mask to be provided in the PRINT statement itself, following the word USING. Such a statement would appear in the form:

PRINT#1 USING "####.##",G

In this case, the contents of numeric variable G are printed with four positions to the left of the point and two to the right. No suppression of leading zeros is provided. Whether numbers to the right of the last printed position are truncated or rounded depends upon the system. Assuming that rounding is done, the gross income, the "G" in the above expression, of 3546275 would appear as 3546.28 when the statement is executed.

The word TAB may also be used differently. Earlier examples showed the tab operation to be done first, then the data being printed by another PRINT statement. Some systems allow the TAB word to be placed in the line of information to be printed. An example of such a statement follows. It would print the material shown immediately beneath it.

PRINT TAB(4); "NAME"; TAB(30);
    "ADDRESS"; TAB(60);"DATE"

NAME	ADDRESS	DATE
(start in position 4)	(start in position 30)	(start in position 60)

Ability to Evaluate Expressions

Also overlooked, or at least not stressed up to this point, is the power of the DISPLAY and PRINT statements to cause expressions to be evaluated. Whatever expression is given is resolved first, then the results are printed. Examples are:

PRINT 5*A + 3*Y
PRINT "CIRCLE CIRCUMFERENCE
    IS:":PI*D

In the first case, the expression 5*A + 3*Y is evaluated and the number that results is printed. In the second example, the expression PI*D (π times diameter) is evaluated and the result made part of the printed line in the form CIRCLE CIRCUMFERENCE IS: 25.

THE LET STATEMENT

Because the LET statement is so versatile and powerful, most beginners will find it very easy to use. Its purpose is to cause the expression following the word LET to be evaluated. The result of the evaluation is moved to the numeric variable, string variable, or array element named in the statement. It says: "LET this expression be evaluated and the result assigned to the item named."

Most users would write the expression to be resolved in the same style they would use for pencil and paper arithmetic and elementary algebra. The only significant difference in form is caused by the fact that the expression must all be written on one line; this makes it necessary to show the numeric operator symbols and terms one after another. A good way to illustrate the actions that can be performed by the LET statement is through examples. Several follow:

LET M = 5 Value is assigned to a numeric variable.

LET N$ = "EAGLE" Value is assigned to a string variable.

LET M(3,15) = 29 Value is assigned to a numeric array element.

LET M(X) = 25 Value is assigned to a numeric array element. Element number is the value of X.

M$ = N$ Value is assigned to a string variable from another string variable.

LET S = S + H Simple arithmetic to accumulate a sum total.

LET A = (M + N)/5 More complex arithmetic.

It should be noted that most BASIC systems allow the expressions above to be written without the word LET. In other words, X = 5 is processed just as if it read LET X = 5. Thus, the syntax diagrams shown in Figure 3-15 both apply.

LET < expression >

or

< expression >

Figure 3-15 LET Statement
Syntax Diagrams

DECISIONS, BRANCHES, AND LOOPS

The capacity to make a decision and take action based on an examination of existing conditions is one of the most important features of a computer. BASIC has several statements that make it easy for a programmer to describe the conditions to be examined and the action to be taken.

We've described loops and branches earlier, but a refresher is worthwhile:

a. A loop is a group of statements that are performed over and over.

b. A branch is the act of moving to perform a source statement that is not in sequence. Normally, statements are performed in 1,2,3,4,5 . . . order. If statement 2 caused statement 5 to be performed next, that would be a "branch."

BASIC source statements in this class are:

FOR and NEXT
GOSUB and RETURN
GOTO and ON . . . GOTO . . .
IF . . . THEN . . .

Syntax diagrams are shown in Figure 3-16. The reader should examine them before reading the following descriptions.

FOR < variable > = { expression or variable } TO { expression or variable } STEP { expression or variable } { WHILE or UNTIL } < condition >

NEXT < variable >

GOSUB < line no. >
ON < variable > GOSUB < line no. 1 > , < line no. 2 > , < line no. N >

GOTO < line no. >
ON < variable > GOTO < line no. 1 > , < line no. 2 > , < line no. N >

IF < relation > THEN { line no. or statement } ELSE { line no. or statement }

IF < relation > THEN { line no. or statement } UNLESS < condition >

Figure 3-16 Syntax Diagrams for FOR/NEXT, GOSUB, GOTO, and IF/THEN/ELSE Statements

The FOR/NEXT Loop

The FOR statement and the NEXT statement are, respectively, the beginning and end of a loop. Usually, the same operations are repeated but the data being operated on is different.

Calculating the retail markup on a series of toys might be a good example to illustrate. The markup is always the same percentage, perhaps 40 percent, but the toy to which it is applied changes and so does the final price of the toy. So a series of wholesale prices are processed by the loop and a series of retail prices are calculated. The number of times the loop is performed depends upon the number of toys to be priced.

The FOR statement includes the name of a control variable and the limits of that variable. As long as the variable is within those limits, the loop continues. Steps following the FOR statement are performed until a NEXT statement including the name of the same control variable is reached. Then the program returns to the related FOR statement and the value of the control variable is checked again. When a limit is reached, the program leaves the loop and continues at the statement following the NEXT statement.

Each time the loop is performed, the value of the control variable is incremented by one (stepped by +1), but this can be changed by the addition of the keyword STEP to the FOR statement. STEP is followed by the amount the variable is to be changed. For example, a +2 produces a step of two each time the loop is performed, and a −5 would reduce the control variable by five.

Up to this point we've thought of the limits of the control variable and the steps as constants. The limits might be 1 TO 10 and the STEP +2, for example. Both the limits and the step value may be expressions to be evaluated, however. For example, the lower limit could be stated as A-B, the upper limit as X+2 and the step as 2*Y/Z.

Some BASIC systems add even more decision-making power to the FOR statement. They allow the keyword WHILE or UNTIL at the end of the statement and follow the keyword with a condition. In this case, the control variable must not only be within the limits stated, but the condition must also be met if the loop is to be performed. If the condition is not met, the program moves on to the line following the NEXT statement just as it would if the control variable was not within limits.

An example of the loops created by the FOR and NEXT statements appears in Figure 3-17. The upper section shows a single loop, beginning at line 050 and ending with line 130. At line 050, the FOR statement establishes A as the control variable and 1 to 25 as the limits of the variable. If A is within the limits, it is increased by one and the program beginning at line 060 is performed. The value used to step the variable can be changed, however, by the addition of the word STEP followed by the value of the step. A STEP 2 is shown in the figure.

All the statements on lines 060 through 120 are performed before the end of the loop is reached. The statement NEXT A then causes the program to go back to line 050 and test the limits of the variable again. If the test shows that the limits have been exceeded, the program goes to line 140 for the next instruction.

An example of two loops used together is shown in the lower position of the figure. Operation is basically the same. The main loop is started in the normal manner, and the subloop (or inner loop) is entered as the value of control variable B dictates.

When loops appear within other loops, the term used to describe them is "nested." The number of nested loops possible depends upon the BASIC system being used. Loops may not cross one another, however.

GOSUB and RETURN Statements

The GOSUB and RETURN source statements allow the program to leave its sequential order, go to the source statement in a specific line number and then return to the source statement that follows the GOSUB statement. These statements are unconditional; that is, no conditions are tested to determine whether or not they are executed. Part of the body of a GOSUB statement is the line number of the source statement to be executed next. On the other hand, the RETURN statement has no body at all; the first RETURN statement encountered causes the program to come back to the line immediately following the GOSUB statement that caused the branch to take place.

An example follows:

```
040 GOSUB 350
050 Statement
```
Action: The program goes to line 350 for the next statement to be executed. If this is

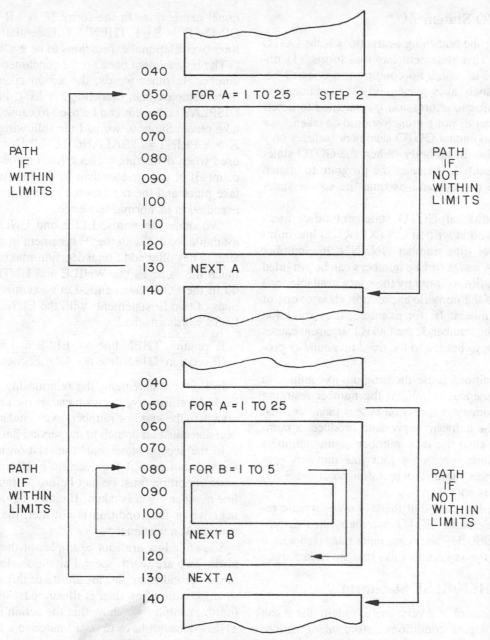

Figure 3-17 Examples of FOR/NEXT Loops in BASIC

the only GOSUB statement active, the first RETURN statement encountered brings the program back to the line following this GOSUB statement, which is 050.

Although GOSUB by itself is an unconditional statement, some BASIC systems make possible the addition of the word ON accompanied by a condition. This changes the statement from an unconditional branch into one that evaluates a numeric expression before branching. The form is a simple one: ON variable GOSUB. It operates in the same manner as an ON . . . GOTO statement, which is described below.

The GOTO Statement

Next among the branching instructions is the GOTO statement. This statement has two forms: (1) unconditional, in which no conditions are tested before the branch takes place, and (2) conditional, in which a numeric expression is evaluated to determine whether or not a branch should be taken.

The unconditional GOTO statement includes only a line number in its body. When the GOTO statement is executed, it causes the program to branch to that line number and execute the source statement there.

The conditional GOTO statement offers more flexibility, and is written ON (X) GOTO line number NNNNN, line number NNNNN, line number NNNNN. A series of line numbers can be provided in the body, limited only by the space available, and the value of the numeric expression chooses one of the line numbers. If, for example, the expression (X) yields the number 3, the GOTO statement causes the program to branch to the third line number provided.

Two conditions cause the program to continue in normal sequence: (1) When the number resulting from the numeric expression is less than one, and (2) when the numeric expression produces a number greater than the total number of line numbers listed. If there were only four line numbers provided and the numeric expression produced 8.23, the branch is not taken.

It should be noted that there is no automatic return possible in the GOTO statement like that provided in GOSUB. The programmer must plan source statements for any return links that are necessary.

The IF/THEN/ELSE Statement

The IF statement is a very useful one in that it can evaluate complex conditions before taking action. In the simplest form, the word IF is followed by two numeric expressions separated by a relational operator. (IF $A - B > C - D$, for example.) The last expression is followed by the keyword THEN and a line number (IF $A - B > C - D$ THEN 00700). In this case, the program goes to line 00700 if the expression yields an affirmative decision but continues on in normal sequence if a negative decision is reached.

As the next step to add power to the IF statement, the logical operators AND or OR (only one, not both or two of each) can be used to join two rela-tional expressions in the form: IF $A - B > C - D$ OR $C - D > E - F$ THEN . . . Essentially this allows two relational expressions to be evaluated.

The IF statement need not be concluded by a line number. In other words, the action taken can be more complex than branching. A LET, PRINT, or DISPLAY statement can be used to cause action to take place. Suppose we had the following case: IF $X > Y$ PRINT#1 "BALANCE OK." This might be used when deducting a check from a checking account. If X was greater than Y, the printing would take place and the next source statement would be executed in its normal sequence.

Two other keywords, ELSE and UNLESS, are available for use with the IF statement in some systems. They offer additional decision-making power, much the same as the WHILE and UNTIL words do in the FOR statements. Let's examine the formats of two IF statements with the ELSE and UNLESS words attached:

IF relation THEN line no. ELSE line no.
IF relation THEN line no. UNLESS condition

In the first statement, the relationship is examined. An affirmative decision causes the program to branch to the first line number given, and a negative decision causes a branch to the second line number.

In the second statement, the relationship is examined, but even if the decision is affirmative another condition must be met before a branch to the line number given is taken. If either the decision is negative or the condition is not met, the program continues in sequence.

Shown below are four examples of the IF statement. Two are worth special attention. In the case of the second example, the ability of this statement to work with string data is illustrated. And, in the fourth example, we show that the action following THEN does not have to be a branch to a line number, but may be an imperative statement such as the DISPLAY statement we've provided.

IF N = 5 THEN 040
Action: A numeric variable (N) is checked to see if it is a 5. If it is, the program goes to line 040 for the next statement to be executed.

IF M$ = "SEAM" THEN 040
Action: A string variable is checked to see if it is "SEAM." If it is, the program goes to line 040 for the next statement.

IF M(3,7) = (A − B)/C THEN 040

Action: An element of array M is compared with the results of the expression A minus B divided by C. If they are equal in value, the program goes to line 040 for the next statement.

IF N>10 THEN DISPLAY "NO. IS GREATER THAN 10."

Action: The IF/THEN statement may also be used to produce actions other than branching. In this case, numeric variable N is checked. If its value is greater than 10, the message to that effect is shown on the display screen.

SPECIAL SOURCE STATEMENTS

There are several statements that are difficult to categorize, so we'll cover them in a group called special source statements. Included in this group are:

insert REMarks
STOP
END
PAUSE
RANDOMIZE

The insert REMarks statement is a very simple one: Whatever follows the abbreviation REM (or its substitute *) is entered in the source listing. It has no effect on execution of the program. Remarks statements are used to give titles to groups of statements that perform a specific function. A remark using the * symbol but with no information in the body is often used to create spaces between titles and the steps, thus making it easier to read the titles and to separate the routines from one another.

The STOP and END statements are nearly identical in function. Both terminate the program, but END serves to mark the physical end of the source program as well as to terminate it while STOP serves only the latter purpose.

These statements end processing so that no problems are encountered by the next program. For example, the STOP or END statement closes all open files.

PAUSE is one statement that may not be available in some versions of BASIC. When it is encountered, the program stops, awaiting some operator action. Most often this is the pressing of a key on the keyboard. PAUSE can be used if the program encounters some simple problem that the operator can correct.

Instructions to correct the problem would be displayed, then the program would pause. If a key must be depressed, that fact would be given in the instructions and, after correcting the problem, the operator would press the key and the program would resume.

One feature provided in some BASIC programming systems is a random number generator. There are scientific uses for such a feature, but a more popular application may be with computer games where the results are to be based on chance. A RANDOMIZE statement resets the generator to an unpredictable starting point, and the RND function acquires the name of the number produced by the generator. When RND appears in an expression, it places the random number in the expression, to be evaluated as the expression states.

A SAMPLE PROGRAM

Included in this section is a sample program. If the reader is able to understand the action taken by each step, the reason the step is necessary, and the results produced, he is well prepared to take the self-test.

Before anyone tries to analyze how a program operates, one must have a clear understanding of what that program is intended to do. So that's where we'll begin with this sample.

The purpose of this program is to check the sales orders turned in by novelties salesmen. Each salesman has a standard order sheet on which the items available for sale are listed. Next to each item on the list, he enters the total number of that item he has sold, does the arithmetic necessary, and turns over his order to the computer operator.

As a first step in processing the orders, the operator checks the sales by running this simple program. The results state the number of items sold by each salesman and the total value of the sale.

Simple BASIC requires that the names of variables be very short. So, before any program is written the programmer should make a list of his variables and assign them names that make it easy to remember what the name stands for. If we do that for the sample program, we come up with the following list:

Variable
Name   *Meaning*

N   Number of items on the standard order sheet. (The number of different items offered for sale.)

P   Price of each item.

M   Number of salesmen.

S   Total dollar value of the sales made by each salesman.

S1   Total number of items sold by each salesman.

C   Number of each item sold, as read from the order sheet (Item 1, Item 2, etc., a substitute for the name of the item).

Next, let's look at the program itself and locate the sections that perform the primary functions. A source list follows. In it, we've used PRINT to operate the display screen and PRINT#1 to operate the printer.

```
010  READ N
020  FOR I = 1 TO N
030  READ P (I)
040  NEXT I
050  READ M
060  FOR J = 1 TO M
070  PRINT
080  PRINT "*** SALESMAN ":J
090  LET S = 0
100  LET S1 = 0
110  FOR I = 1 TO N
120  PRINT "ITEM NUMBER"; I:
130  INPUT C
140  LET S = S + C*P(I)
150  LET S1 = S1 + C
160  NEXT I
170  PRINT#1 "SALESMAN" ,J
180  PRINT#1 "NUMBER OF ITEMS":S1
190  PRINT#1 "TOTAL ORDER = $":S
200  PRINT#1
210  NEXT J
220  DATA 5
230  DATA 2.25, 3.15, 1.85, 5.40, 3.20
240  DATA 3
250  END
```

Data to be used by this program is entered in lines 220, 230, and 240. The reader should recall, however, that the DATA statements may appear anywhere in the program. They put information into data tables, while READ statements take it out and assign it to variables.

Figure 3-18 illustrates the interaction between DATA and READ statements for this program. Line 220 puts a 5 in the data table; line 010 reads the 5 and assigns it to variable N, the number of items on the standard order sheet. Line 230 enters the prices of the five items available into the data table; line 030 reads them from the table and assigns them to elements 1 through 5 of a one-dimension array named P. Last, line 240 enters a 3 into the data table; line 050 reads it and assigns it to variable M, the number of salesmen involved.

There are three loops. The first reads the prices into the array P and is composed of lines 020, 030, and 040. It is performed five times.

The next two loops are "nested." An outer loop, from lines 060 through 210, uses control variable J and has an upper limit of M. Since M is the number of salesmen, this outer loop will be performed three times. An inner loop consisting of lines 110 through 160 has an upper limit of N, which is the number of items offered for sale on the order sheet. In our case, this is five items, so this loop will be performed five times for each time the outer loop is executed. Thus, the inner loop will be performed fifteen times.

Lines 080 and 120 do not print; they display. If no channel number is specified in this case, the display screen is selected. A channel #1 must be included in order to use the printer. Therefore, line 080 shows a title SALESMAN 1 (or 2, or 3) on the screen. This is followed by the notation ITEM NUMBER 1 (or 2, 3, 4, 5). The computer operator is thus instructed to read a specific salesman's order sheet and type in the quantity sold for item 1 (2, 3, 4, or 5). This number, which appears on the screen, is accepted by the INPUT statement in line 130 and assigned to variable C. Thus, the computer knows the value of C for the following calculations.

Now the calculations are performed. Line 140 does the arithmetic for dollar value and line 150 adds up the number of items sold. In each case, the total accumulates until the five items for one salesman are processed. Then lines 170 to 200 print out the totals for one salesman.

When line 210 is reached, it causes the outer loop to be repeated for salesmen 2 and 3. Only when all three salesmen's orders have been processed is the outer loop ended. This causes the program to drop to lines 220, 230, and 240, the nonexecutable DATA statements, and finally to reach line 250, the END statement.

When the program is thus concluded, the opera-

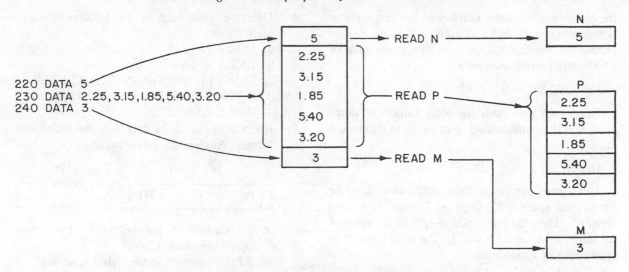

Figure 3-18 Data Used in the Sample Program

tor has the printed output. Of course, this can then be compared with the sales orders and the orders checked for accuracy.

The next step is the analysis of this sample program in a line-by-line examination. This is provided below:

010 READ N

Accepts the first item from the numeric data table and assigns it to variable N. This is a 5 and is the number of items in the price list.

020 FOR I = 1 TO N
030 READ P (I)
040 NEXT I

Based upon N being 5, this loop reads five items from the data table. These are the prices of five products, and they are placed in a one-dimension array named P (prices). Element number is I, which goes from 1 to 5.

050 READ M

Reads another item from the data table. A 3 in this case, representing the number of salesmen involved. The variable M is now assigned 3.

060 FOR J = 1 TO M

Establishes the main (outer loop). M is the number of salesmen, so this loop will be performed once for each salesman. In this case, that is three times.

070 PRINT

Creates one blank line on the screen.

080 PRINT "*** SALESMAN":J

Shows the word "SALESMAN" on the screen, followed by the value of control variable J, which starts at 1. Therefore, the first time this loop is performed, the screen shows: "SALESMAN 1."

090 LET S = 0
100 LET S1 = 0

Sums S and S1 are initially set to zero.

110 FOR I = 1 TO N

Establishes the inner loop. N is the number of different items. So this loop is performed once for each different item. In this case, that is five times.

120 PRINT "ITEM NUMBER":I:

Shows the words "ITEM NUMBER" on the screen, followed by the value of control variable I, which starts at 1. Therefore, the first time this loop is performed, the screen shows: "ITEM NUMBER 1."

130 INPUT C

The operator enters the quantity of item number 1 that salesman 1 sold.

140 LET S = S + C*P(I)

This multiplies the number sold of this item (C) by the price (P) from array element P(I) meaning the element is the same number as the item number being processed, and this runs 1 through 5. The product is then added to S, which is the sum of goods sold by this salesman.

150 LET S1 = S1 + C

This expression adds the total number of items sold. C is the number sold. It is added to the current sum, S1.

160 NEXT I

This closes the inner loop, and causes it to be performed again. "I" steps to 2, then 3, 4, and finally 5. Then the loop ends. S will be the value of all items sold, and S1 will be the total number of items sold by a salesman.

170 PRINT#1 "SALESMAN",J

This prints out SALESMAN 1 the first time, because control variable J is 1 on the first performance of the main loop. It is 2 on the second pass, and 3 on the third.

180 PRINT#1 "NUMBER OF ITEMS":S1

This prints out the number of items sold (S1) by this salesman.

190 PRINT#1 "TOTAL ORDER = $":S

This prints out the total dollar value of items sold (S) by this salesman.

200 PRINT#1

This spaces one line at the end of each salesman's printout.

210 NEXT J

This closes the main (outer) loop and causes it to be performed again. J steps to 2, then to 3. Then the loop ends.

SELF-TEST FOR CHAPTER 3

1. Which of the following *string variables* is named incorrectly?
   a. S$ b. B$ c. A3 d. Z$
2. What are the rules for naming numeric variables in the simple BASIC we've covered?
3. What distinguishes string constants from numeric constants?

4. Describe what each of the following statements do:
   a. DIM A (10,25)
   b. LET S = (A+B)/2
   c. PRINT#1 "PROGRAM COMPLETE"
   d. DATA "HARRIS",70,"GILMAN",90, "WILLIAMS",75
5. Records in our file of data have the following format. Answer the related questions.

1	7	30	36	45
E1	E2	H1	G	D

   a. E1 is employee number field. How many characters does it have?
   b. E2 is employee name. What is wrong?
   c. H1 is hourly pay rate. Write the statement to get it, assuming that the record for this employee is in the buffer associated with file 2.
   d. Assuming that we have calculated gross pay, put it in the employee record in the field labeled G.
6. What does the acronym BASIC mean?
7. What are arithmetic operators? Show the five commonly used in BASIC.
8. What are relational operators?
9. Which of the following are string constants?
   a. "PRICE EACH"
   b. "147A4"
   c. "JONES"
   d. "YOUR GRADE IS 75."
10. Why is an IMAGE statement and its edit mask useful?
11. Expressions must be written on one line in BASIC source statements. This requires some study in order to get correct results. Write the statements for the following calculations:
    Pencil and Paper Form
    a. $A = \dfrac{bh}{2}$
    b. $P = X3 + 78X + A$
    c. $C = \sqrt{3X+N}$
    d. Amount of payment (A) equals the total loan (T) plus interest charges (I) divided by months to pay (M).
12. The OPEN statement has two functions and forms. What are the functions?

In questions 13 through 23 write a one-line statement to meet the requirements given.

13. Provide in a DATA statement the names, prices, and quantity on hand (in that order) of the following:
3 chairs at $99.95 ea.
14 clipboards at $2.50 ea.
40 pads of paper at $0.90 ea.

14. Enter the first set of the above information into variables.
T$ Type of product
P Price each
Q Quantity on hand

15. Place headings on display screen (spaced at zones) for entry of the same information.

16. Enter one line of the same data from the keyboard.

17. Place headings on the printer (spaced at zones) for printout of the same information.

18. Print one line of the data.

19. Subtract your current check (C) from current balance (B), and form new balance (B1).

20. Find the number of cubic feet (T) of insulation needed in your attic floor if the dimensions are L (length), W (width), and D (depth).

21. Perform the same task (any task) ten times.

22. Make a decision based upon age (A) of the job applicant. If 40 or over, go to line 500. If not, continue in sequence.

23. Perform the subroutine beginning at line 700 and then return to the next instruction.

24. If we have the following statements as part of a program, what is the value of X when the statement in line 20 is finished?
10 READ A, B, C
20 X = A**2 + 3*B − C
30 DATA 10, 20, 30

25. What is wrong with the following simple programs?

a. *FIRST PROGRAM*
10 READ X,Y,Z
20 LET C = X*Y/Z
30 DISPLAY C
40 DATA 5, 10
50 END

b. *SECOND PROGRAM*
10 FOR I = 1 TO 5
20 INPUT A
30 IF A > 3 THEN 60
40 PRINT "NUMBER IS GREATER THAN 3"
50 LET C = A + B
60 PRINT "NUMBER IS LESS THAN 3"
70 NEXT I

c. *THIRD PROGRAM*
10 READ X,Y,Z
20 LET A = X*Y + 2Z
30 PRINT#1 "YOUR GRADE IS": A
40 DATA 90,100,35
50 END

d. *FOURTH PROGRAM*
10 FOR A = 1 TO 3
20 FOR B = 1 TO 5
30 LET X = Y + N
40 LET C = X**2/P
50 NEXT A
60 NEXT B
70 PRINT X
80 PRINT C

4

Pascal

INTRODUCTION

Most names given to programming languages are abbreviations. FORTRAN, for example, is short for *for*mula *tran*slator, and RPG means report program generator. On the other hand, Pascal was the name of a French mathematician and philosopher who lived in the seventeenth century. In 1642, Blaise Pascal invented a mechanical adding machine that used teeth on gears to represent numbers. In some respects, this was the first digital calculator.

Of course, Pascal didn't develop the programming language bearing his name. That was done by a Swiss computer scientist, Niklaus Wirth, and the language was introduced about 1970. As of this writing, there is no accepted ANSI standard for Pascal, but there is general agreement as to the structure and functions of Pascal statements and of the program structure.

A short section of a Pascal program is shown in Figure 4-1. Most of the words can be understood immediately, but the action produced and the relationship of one statement to another will obviously require some study.

BEGIN and END are simple enough. They say "begin to perform the following statements," and "this is the end of a group of related statements." This is an extremely important feature of Pascal—each logical block of statements is bounded by a BEGIN statement and an END statement.

The body of the program is organized into blocks, if more than one block is needed to perform the functions of the program. A system of indentation is often used to show which blocks are parts of others. It is also possible to give a block a name and to then simply write the name of that block in the place in the program where the block is to be executed.

Pascal also requires that specific information be provided at the beginning of the program. This material, which is called a "declaration," includes data descriptions such as the name and types of variables used in the program.

RESERVED WORDS AND NAMES

No matter what they are called, every programming language has a limited set of words that the programmer may use; Pascal's are shown in Figure 4-2. A general term used to describe these words is the "instruction set." Other terms the reader may encounter are keywords, reserved words, standard identifiers, and predeclared names. Although there is some similarity between the terms used in all the high-level languages, there are also differences that may be confusing. In this chapter on Pascal, we'll use three terms:

a. Reserved words, which are most of the words that cause action to take place. BEGIN, END, GOTO, FOR, UNTIL, DO, and THEN are examples.
b. Standard identifiers, which are names already assigned to functions, procedures, data types, constants, and files.
c. Identifiers, which are the names the programmer may originate.

```
PROGRAM EXPENSES(INPUT,OUTPUT);
CONST ELEMENTS=5;
TYPE DEPARTMENT=(ADM,PROD,ENG,MKTG,QC,ERR);
VAR EXPENSES: ARRAY[DEPARTMENT] OF REAL;
    DEPT: DEPARTMENT;
    INVOICE,TOTAL: REAL;
    DEPTNR,I: INTEGER;
BEGIN
DEPT:=ADM;
FOR I:=1 TO 6 DO
BEGIN
  EXPENSES[DEPT]:=0;
  IF ELEMENTS > ORD(DEPT) THEN DEPT:=SUCC(DEPT)
END;
WHILE NOT EOF DO
BEGIN
  READLN(DEPTNR,INVOICE);
  IF DEPTNR > 7 THEN DEPTNR:=3;
  CASE DEPTNR OF
    0       :EXPENSES[ADM]:=EXPENSES[ADM]+INVOICE;
    1       :EXPENSES[PROD]:=EXPENSES[PROD]+INVOICE;
    2       :EXPENSES[ENG]:=EXPENSES[ENG]+INVOICE;
    3,4,5   :EXPENSES[ERR]:=EXPENSES[ERR]+INVOICE;
    6       :EXPENSES[MKTG]:=EXPENSES[MKTG]+INVOICE;
    7       :EXPENSES[QC]:=EXPENSES[QC]+INVOICE
  END; (*CASE*)
END; (*WHILE NOT EOF*)
TOTAL:=0;
DEPT:=ADM;
FOR I:=1 TO 6 DO
BEGIN
  TOTAL:=TOTAL+EXPENSES[DEPT];
  IF ELEMENTS > ORD(DEPT) THEN DEPT:=SUCC(DEPT)
END; (*FOR I*)
WRITELN('EXPENSES' :16);
WRITELN('ADMINISTRATION: $' ,EXPENSES[ADM]:16:2);
WRITELN('PRODUCTION:      ' ,EXPENSES[PROD]:16:2);
WRITELN('ENGINEERING:     ' ,EXPENSES[ENG]:16:2);
WRITELN('MARKETING:       ' ,EXPENSES[MKTG]:16:2);
                           ' ,EXPENSES[QC]:16:2);
                           ' ,EXPENSES[ERR]:16:2
```

Figure 4-1 A Section of a Pascal Program

Reserved Words		Standard Identifiers	
AND	MOD	**Data Types**	**Functions (cont'd.)**
ARRAY		BOOLEAN	LN
	NIL	CHAR	ODD
BEGIN	NOT	INTEGER	ORD
		REAL	PRED
CASE	OF		ROUND
CONST	OR	**Constants**	SIN
		FALSE	SQR
DIV	PACKED	TRUE	SQRT
DO	PROCEDURE	MAXINT	SUCC
DOWNTO	PROGRAM		TRUNC
		Files	
ELSE	RECORD	INPUT	**Procedures**
END	REPEAT	OUTPUT	GET
			NEW
FILE	SET	**Functions**	PACK
FOR		ABS	PAGE
FUNCTION	THEN	ARCTAN	PUT
	TO	CHR	READ
GOTO	TYPE	COS	READLN
		EOF	RESET
IF	UNTIL	EOLN	REWRITE
IN		EXP	UNPACK
	VAR		WRITE
LABEL			WRITELN
	WHILE		
	WITH		

Figure 4-2 Keywords Available in Pascal

Reserved Words

As a first step toward understanding the language, let's examine the reserved words. They are listed in alphabetical order in Figure 4-2, but the best way to study their actions is to place them in groups, and that is the method used in the following paragraphs.

Taking from the list the words used to make declarations, we have:

CONST (constant)   PROGRAM
FUNCTION   TYPE
LABEL   VAR (variable)
PROCEDURE

In general, each of these is followed by an identifier (name) that the programmer constructs. The reserved word shows that the identifier is a certain kind of program component.

Next come the words used as operators, either arithmetic, relational, or special. We have six in this group, including:

AND   MOD (modulus)
DIV (divide)   NOT
IN   OR

Of course there are operator symbols (+ , − , etc.) as well. The action produced by each of these

words and symbols is described in the section dealing with operators.

Four reserved words define the way in which data is organized. They are:

ARRAY   RECORD
FILE   SET

These are four types of "structured" data that Pascal uses. The reader should recognize records, files, and arrays immediately. "Set" is a data organization unique to Pascal; it is described later in this chapter. Each of these words is accompanied by an identifier that names a specific array, a specific file, etc.

Now, we're getting down to the words that produce action in the statements. Included in this group are:

BEGIN   ELSE   IF   UNTIL
CASE   END   REPEAT   WHILE
DO   FOR   THEN   WITH
DOWNTO   GOTO

Some, such as BEGIN, DO, and GOTO, produce action, while others, such as IF, UNTIL, and WHILE, establish or test conditions. These are many of the action words the programmer may use. Some versions of Pascal have words added to the instruction group, but most readers should be able to understand the additions once they are familiar with those we cover.

There are four words left on the list: NIL, OF, PACKED, and TO. These are rather specialized, so we'll describe them later along with statements of which they are a part.

Standard Identifiers

Also shown in Figure 4-2 is a list of the standard identifiers provided in Pascal. Again, the best way to study the action they perform is to discuss them in groups.

First, the names of data types:

BOOLEAN   INTEGER
CHAR (character)   REAL

Integers are whole numbers, while "real" in Pascal means numbers with decimal places. CHAR means a single character from the machine's character set. And last, BOOLEAN means information that produces a "true" or "false" result.

Next, the constants. There are only three: FALSE,

TRUE, and MAXINT (which means the maximum size of the integer that can be handled by the system). Remember, these are only names; they have values established by the system.

Two standard file names, INPUT and OUTPUT, are provided. In general, INPUT is used to mean an input from a keyboard while OUTPUT is display or printing.

The last two groups of standard identifiers may cause some confusion at first glance because they seem to include action words that should have been placed in the list of reserved words. In fact, they are used in statements just as the reserved words are.

Functions are the easiest to explain so let's begin with them. When the standard identifier for a function appears in an expression, it acts upon its argument (the quantity in parentheses), performs the calculation specified, and returns a value to the expression. TRUNC (X), for example, truncates the value of X, returning an integer to the expression if the function is applied to a number with decimal places.

Standard functions available in Pascal include:

ABS (X)	Absolute value of X.
ARCTAN (X)	Arctangent of X.
CHR (X)	Return the character in position of X in set. X is a number.
COS (X)	Cosine of X.
EOF	End of file.
EOLN	End of line.
EXP (X)	Exponential of X. The value of the base of natural logarithms (e = 2.71828) raised to the power X.
LN (X)	Natural log of X.
ODD (X)	True if X is odd number; otherwise, false.
ORD (X)	Ordinal number (position) in the set of values of which the argument (X) is a member.
PRED (X)	Predecessor of X.
ROUND (X)	Round X.
SIN (X)	Sine of X.
SQR (X)	Square of X.
SQRT (X)	Square root of X.
SUCC (X)	Successor of X.
TRUNC (X)	Truncate the fractional part of X. TRUNC (5.5) = 5.

Standard identifiers for procedures are next to be discussed. These names can be used in a statement just as a reserved word is. Most deal with inputs and outputs, however, and their overall purpose is to provide data for the program to operate on and to display, print, or store results. We have twelve words in this group. Each is described later in the chapter when we construct statements and provide examples of how statements are used.

Identifiers Originated by the Programmer

Every programming language has rules that govern naming. Among the items that may be named in Pascal are:

a. variables f. functions
b. programs g. procedures
c. constants h. arrays
d. data types i. files
e. sets   j. records and fields

If the reader is familiar with the severe limitations imposed on the naming of variables in simple BASIC—a maximum of two characters may be used—he should appreciate the freedom allowed by Pascal. The rules are as follows:

1. Names may be of *any length*.
2. They must *begin with a letter*.
3. They must *not include blanks or punctuation marks*.
4. They must *contain only letters or numbers*.
5. They must *not use a reserved word*.

In practice, of course, it's not common to use lengthy names if for no other reason than they take up too much space.

Pascal does limit the size of names in one way though; the compiler recognizes only the first eight characters. Thus, the programmer is free to use as many characters as he sees fit, but the first eight characters must not duplicate the first eight characters of any other name.

To illustrate: The word "EMPLOYEE" has eight characters. If it was used to name variables EMPLOYEENAME, EMPLOYEEPAYRATE, and EMPLOYEEAGE, the compiler could not distinguish one variable from another. This problem could be solved by abbreviating: EMPNAME, EMPPAYRATE, and EMPAGE.

Reserved Symbols

We've already talked about the reserved words and standard identifiers; they each have a specific meaning and are limited in the way they can be used. The same holds true for many of the symbols. Some are used for operators, others for constructing statements, and still others for enclosing expressions or providing comments. Because some of the symbols have several uses, a good approach is to point out their use as the various statements and operations are described. That's what we'll do.

PROGRAM STRUCTURE

Some languages require that information for the program be provided in a specific form and order. Pascal is an example of this. It has very rigid rules concerning how a program must be organized.

Readers who are moving through this book in sequence will be able to compare Pascal to BASIC. BASIC is a "free form" language in many respects, so the contrasts are likely to be great.

We can begin the examination of a Pascal program structure, which is shown in Figure 4-3, by establishing three divisions: (1) header, (2) declarations, and (3) body. The program is named in the header section, and any files it uses are listed. This information follows the word PROGRAM and takes the form: PROGRAM program name (file name, file name . . . file name);.

Next, the declarations are given and, even within the declaration section, a specific order must be followed. Of course, some declarations may not be necessary simply because the program does not use the kind of information they provide. The order in which the information must be given is: labels, constants, data types, variables, procedures, and functions.

A label is a line number. If there are any statements in the program that refer to other line numbers, as is often the case in branches, those line numbers must be given in a label declaration. This is done in the form: LABEL 500;. (If there are no labels, then the label declaration is not included.)

Constants used by the program are declared next, although the standard constants are not. A constant is an actual value. If the user wishes to establish constants for his program so that he may use their names they are declared in the form: CONST K = 2.751; or CONST MINSIZE = 12;. Another example: CONST TAX = 4.5;.

Next comes a declaration of data types used by

PROGRAM   name   (file names);

LABEL   declaration

CONST   declaration

TYPE   declaration

VAR   declaration

PROCEDURE   declaration

> Procedure

FUNCTION   declaration

> Function

BEGIN

     Main Body

END

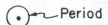 Period

Figure 4-3 The Structure of a Pascal Program

the program. The standard data types (real, integer, character, and Boolean) need not be defined but all others must be. This subject is complex; it is sufficient to say at this point that it is often desirable to prepare names for new data types. There are several forms the data type declaration may take. Examples are:

TYPE DAY = (MON, TUES, WED, THURS, FRI, SAT, SUN);
TYPE WEEKDAY = MON..FRI;

In the next part of the declaration section, the variables used by the program are named and declared to be a specific data type, either one of the standard types or one of the types given in the type declaration described above. A variable declaration statement takes the form:

VAR X, Y, SUM: INTEGER;
VAR GRADE: CHAR;

Now the procedures and functions to be used are declared. A procedure is a short program itself. When that program is to be performed, its name is given in a statement.

A function on the other hand is the name of an operation, such as square root (SQRT). It is used in an expression and could take the form: A: = SQRT (N). In this case, the square root of N is found and assigned to the variable A.

Now to the program itself. Very simple programs may not be subdivided, but most programs will be. The overall program, often called the main body, is bounded by a BEGIN statement and an END statement. Subdivisions may be bounded by the same words, but the END statement is followed by a semicolon (END;) rather than by a period (END.) as it is for the overall program.

FORMS OF STATEMENTS

There are two basic forms that statements may take: (1) isolated, and (2) compound. The isolated statement is the typical one-line statement. It starts with one of the valid reserved words or standard identifiers and concludes with a semicolon.

A compound statement is actually a group of statements. They are bounded by the words BEGIN and END, in the form:

BEGIN
    Statement 1;
    Statement 2;
    Statement 3;
    Statement 4
END;

Note that the word BEGIN does not require a semicolon nor does the last statement appearing before the word END.

Compound statements are frequently used where the action to be taken as a result of certain conditions is more complex than can be accomplished

with a single statement. The BEGIN/END "limiters" show that the entire compound statement is executed as if it were a single statement.

DATA TYPES

Over the next few paragraphs we'll devote our attention to data types. Most are no different than those used in BASIC; however, Pascal has very strict rules about how data types are declared and organized, and the reader must understand the terms involved before the rules make sense.

Among the very first points to be made is that there are two classes of data: (1) the simple, or "scalar" and (2) the compound, or "structured." The structured types are made up of the scalar types.

Included in the scalar types are integers, real numbers, characters, and Boolean. Also among the scalar types are items the programmer may list. The order in which each item appears indicates its place on the scale with respect to the other items.

"Structured" data includes the arrays, strings, records, and files we know about and two new types, sets and lists. These structured types are composed of combinations of the scalar types as the programmer chooses.

Figure 4-4 illustrates the data types available. We've provided examples of those that should be familiar, but examples of others are reserved for the sections in which the specific data type is described. The only exception to this is "string." An example of string data is given in the figure to emphasize that string data is not CHARacter data, although characters do make up strings. CHARacter data is a single character.

After having read the rules regarding naming, the reader may wonder how Pascal determines which variables are numbers and which are characters. There is certainly nothing in the name (identifier) itself that makes it possible. Therefore, a declaration of data type is required, and the programmer must prepare such statements for inclusion in the declaration section.

Among the subjects discussed in this chapter, the reader is likely to find the subject of user-defined data types the most difficult to understand. It has two basic applications. The first is to define the organization of the compound data structures: the arrays, records, and sets.

The second application of the user-defined data

TYPE	EXAMPLE

A. SCALAR
  1. Standard
        Integer . . . . 74500,1982, − 72, 5, + 781
        Real . . . . 2.52, − 34.0, + 0.5427
        Character . . . . "B", "(", "7"
        Boolean . . . . TRUE, FALSE

  2. User-Defined
        Enumerated . . . . DEPARTMENT = (MFG,ADM,SALES,ENG,SERV);
        Subrange . . . . PASSGRADE = 60 . . 100;

B. STRUCTURED
        Set
        Array
        String . . . . THIS IS A STRING, ADAMS,J.R.,SYCAMORE ST.
        Record
        File
        List (Pointer)

Figure 4-4 Data Types and Examples

type deals with simple variables. Here it is of limited value. A name, the *data type*, is given and it is followed by all the values that comprise that type of data.

MONTH, for example, can be declared to be a data type. Of course, the twelve months that make up the year would be the elements of that type.

A type declaration of the enumeration style takes the form shown below:

TYPE MONTH = (JAN, FEB, MAR, APR,
              MAY, JUNE, JULY, AUG,
              SEPT, OCT, NOV, DEC);

This establishes a data type called MONTH and limits the elements to the material within the parentheses. So any variable that is declared to be of the type MONTH must be one of the months listed.

The second form that a type declaration may take is a subrange declaration. An example can be applied to the type MONTH. Of course, a section of the year is SUMMER. It could be declared a subrange in the form: TYPE SUMMER = JUNE . . AUG;. Notice that only the beginning element (JUNE) and the ending element (AUG) need be given. The two periods showing the range are always provided.

The question of course is: What is the value of user-defined data types in the case of simple variables? First, let's examine what the TYPE declaration does: It gives a name to a sequence of known elements and places them on a scale. (The lowest value is the first entered and the highest value is the last entered.)

This establishes a scale for comparison. All the relational operators and three functions can be applied to user-defined data types. We'll see later how these functions and operators take advantage of the scale established by user-defined data type declarations.

OPERATORS AND FUNCTIONS USED IN PASCAL

Operators are the signs or words that make the computer perform arithmetic, comparisons, or special operations with the data items. There are two basic kinds of operators: (1) arithmetic and (2) relational and logical.

The arithmetic operators are the add, subtract, multiply, and divide signs with which we're all familiar. Relational operators include the "equal to," "greater than," and "less than" signs, while logical operators include AND, OR, and NOT. In Pascal, each data type (integer, real, etc.) can be processed by some operators but not others.

Most of the operators used in Pascal are very

similar to those in other languages. Relational and logical operators include:

= equal to   < > not equal to
> greater than   > = greater than or equal to
< less than   < = less than or equal to
AND
OR
NOT

And four of the arithmetic operators, plus (+), minus (−), multiply (*), and divide (/), are those commonly used in all languages. In Pascal, however, the divide symbol (/) applies only to real numbers; the abbreviation DIV is used with integers.

Another operator, "MOD" for "modulus," is also available only for use in integer arithmetic. Written in the form "7 MOD 2," this operator produces the remainder of division. For example, the expression 7 MOD 2 divides 7 by 2 and yields the remainder of 1; the quotient is not used.

Next we have the special functions that can be performed. "Take absolute value" or "square this data item" are examples. These functions are made to happen or "called" by entering a short word in an expression, just as an arithmetic sign is used.

Most of the functions in Pascal's repertoire are also familiar.

We mentioned above that some operators applied only to specific data types. A good way to summarize this relationship is to tabulate it. We've done just that in Figure 4-5. The upper section lists operators, while the bottom section is devoted to functions. Notice that the result data type is listed as well and that it is not always the same as that of the operand data type.

As in all languages, operators in Pascal also have a specific order in which they must be applied if they are to produce the results intended. Ranging from the highest precedence (those operations done first) to the lowest (those operations done last) Pascal operators are executed as follows:

Highest   NOT, − (make negative)
          *, /, DIV, MOD, AND
          +, −, OR
Lowest   = , <>, < =, > =, <, >, IN

We haven't yet mentioned parentheses, which may be inserted to set off terms and operators that must be treated as a single quantity. Parentheses within

OPERATOR	OPERAND DATA TYPES	RESULT DATA TYPES
+, −, *	Integer, Real	Integer, Real
/	Integer, Real	Real
DIV, MOD	Integer	Integer
=, <>, <, >, <=, >=	All Scalar Types	Boolean
AND, OR, NOT	Boolean	Boolean

FUNCTIONS	OPERAND DATA TYPES	RESULT DATA TYPES
ABS, SQR	Integer, Real	Same as Operand
ARCTAN, COS, EXP LN, SIN, SQRT	Integer, Real	Real
CHR	Integer	Character
ODD	Integer	Boolean
ORD	All Scalar Types, except real	Integer
PRED, SUCC	All Scalar Types, except real	Same as Operand
ROUND, TRUNC	Real	Integer

Figure 4-5 Operators, Functions, and Data Types

parentheses may also be used. As in BASIC, the first action is to remove the parentheses, starting with the innermost set. After parentheses have been removed, the remaining operators are applied. When operators of equal precedence remain, they are executed in left-to-right order.

THE PROGRAM SYNTAX DIAGRAM

Perhaps the best method to illustrate how a program is organized is to show the overall program syntax diagram and relate it to a program listing. The syntax diagram is shown in Figure 4-6 and the related program listing in Figure 4-7.

Across the top of the syntax diagram we have the program header. It includes the program name and the names of files that will be used. Item 1 in the listing shows how this is actually written.

Now the line in the syntax diagram leads to a block showing seven possible kinds of entries: label, const, type, var, procedure, function, and begin. This indicates the order in which these entries must appear. Of course, the word BEGIN is where the program starts. All the others are part of the declaration section.

A semicolon ends the LABEL declaration. After leaving the semicolon, which is shown in a circle in the syntax diagram, the flow line returns to the trunk and proceeds to the CONST declaration; it does not turn back upward to the PROGRAM header statement. This illustrates how to read the flow of the diagram.

Next to be entered are the constants. They follow the reserved word CONST one after another. Each consists of a name and a value, and each is terminated by a semicolon. The loop following CONST in the syntax diagram shows this, while item 2 in the program listing points out how the constants would be written. When all constants have been identified, the flow line leads back to the trunk and to the next declaration, which is data type.

Beginning with the reserved word TYPE, this declaration statement provides identifiers (names) and types one after another. Each type is terminated by a semicolon, and the loop shown in the syntax diagram may be repeated as many times as necessary to define all data types. There are two in our program listing; they are pointed out by item 3.

Variables are the next component to be declared. The flow line leaving the type declaration enters the trunk and leads to the VAR section. Here, one identifier (name) after another is written with commas separating them. These entries are then declared to be a certain type. After a semicolon terminates that declaration, another variable or series of variables may be declared to be a specific type. Shown in the program listing are several entries, which are identified by item 4.

After the last variable declaration, the flow line returns to the trunk and moves on to the PROCEDURE declaration. The procedure name is given, followed by the parameter list. The word "block" in the syntax diagram indicates that the procedure itself is then given and that its organization is very similar to a program. An example of a procedure declaration is pointed out by item 5 in the listing. Notice that it includes declarations of variables and BEGIN and END statements. It could also include statements using the name of a previous procedure.

One procedure after another may be declared, but each must bear the reserved word PROCEDURE. This is shown by the way the flow line in the syntax diagram reenters the PROCEDURE section.

Function declarations follow the last procedure to be given. These consist of the word FUNCTION, followed by the function name, the parameter list, and the data type that the function produces. As the syntax flow line shows, the declaration then proceeds to the "block" rectangle. This indicates that the program steps that perform that function must be provided.

Now the declaration section is complete and the body of the program is encountered. Keep in mind that the programmer has not given a single instruction to make the computer perform the task he wishes. None of the procedures or functions declared will be performed until the body of the program is reached and the name of that procedure or function is used in a statement.

The first BEGIN statement in the body (item 6 in Figure 4-7) starts the program. Statements are separated by a semicolon. Thus, the system knows it has one statement to be performed when it encounters this punctuation mark. Our sample program listing shows that the program itself may be very simple, consisting in this case of only three statements. All of the statements are the names of procedures declared above, however, so the program is much more complex than it appears to be.

The END statement will be encountered several times during execution of this program, but in all cases except one, it is punctuated by a semicolon

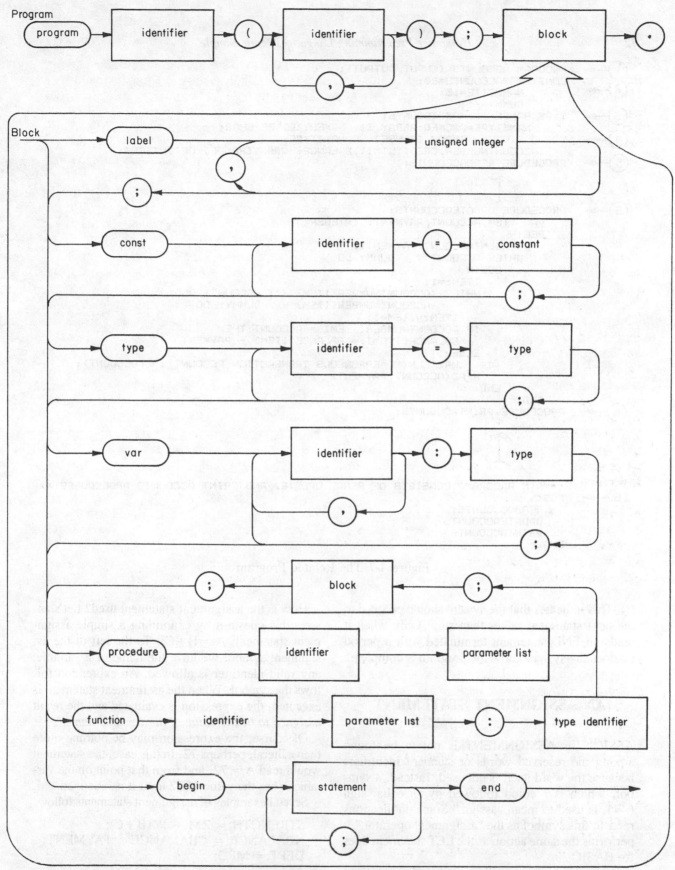

Figure 4-6 The Program Syntax Diagram

71

```
①→  PROGRAM ACCOUNTS (INPUT, OUTPUT);
②→  CONST MAXACCOUNTS=20;
          NAMESIZE=15;
          DUMMY=-1;
③→  TYPE RANGE=1..MAXACCOUNTS;
          NAMETYPE=PACKED ARRAY [1..NAMESIZE] OF CHAR;
④→  VAR CUSTOMER: ARRAY [RANGE] OF NAMETYPE;
         ACCOUNTNUMBER,CREDITLIMIT,BALANCE: ARRAY[RANGE] OF INTEGER;
⑤→  PROCEDURE READACCOUNTS;


⑤→  PROCEDURE UPDATEACCOUNTS;
         VAR ITEM,ACCOUNT,PAYMENT: INTEGER;
         BEGIN
             READLN(ACCOUNT,PAYMENT);
             WHILE ACCOUNT < > DUMMY DO
                 BEGIN
                     ITEM:=1;
                     WHILE (ACCOUNTNUMBER[ITEM] < > ACCOUNT) AND
                           (ACCOUNTNUMBER[ITEM] < > DUMMY) DO
                         ITEM:=ITEM+1;
                     IF ACCOUNTNUMBER[ITEM] = ACCOUNT THEN
                         BALANCE[ITEM]:= BALANCE[ITEM] - PAYMENT
                     ELSE
                         WRITELN('  ERRONEOUS TRANSACTION ACCOUNT : ',ACCOUNT);
                     READ(ACCOUNT,PAYMENT)
                 END
         END;
⑤→  PROCEDURE PRINTACCOUNTS;



    (*MAIN PROGRAM, CONSISTS OF READ, UPDATE, AND PRINT ACCOUNTS PROCEDURES *)
⑥→  BEGIN
         READACCOUNTS;
         UPDATEACCOUNTS;
         PRINTACCOUNTS
    END.
```

Figure 4-7 The Related Program

(;). This indicates that the system should proceed to the next statement rather than stop. Only when it reads an END statement terminated with a period (.) does the system know the program is complete.

AN ASSIGNMENT STATEMENT

ASSIGN or ASSIGNMENT is not to be found among the reserved words or standard identifiers because the word itself is not used. Instead, a symbol, which is a colon followed by an equal sign (:=), is used to mean "assign." Some publications refer to this symbol as the "assignment operator." It performs the same action as the LET statement does for BASIC.

How is the assignment statement used? Let's answer this question by examining a simple assignment statement: $A:=B+C;$. To the left of the assignment symbol we have the name of a variable; any valid identifier is allowed. An expression follows the symbol. When the assignment statement is executed, the expression is evaluated and the result *assigned to be the value of the variable named*.

Of course, the expression may be nothing more than a literal, perhaps 72. In this case, the statement would read $A:=72$, and from that point on the variable A has the value of 72 until it is redefined.

Several examples of assignment statements follow:

$$STRENGTH:= ZM + P/(B+C);$$
$$NBALANCE:= CBALANCE - PAYMENT;$$
$$DEPT:= MFG;$$

STATEMENTS THAT DISPLAY, PRINT, AND ACCEPT KEYBOARD INPUTS

This section deals first with the use of the READ and READLN statements to accept data typed in at the computer keyboard. It then describes how the WRITE and WRITELN statements are used to produce displays on the screen and to print on the forms in a printer.

Pascal handles the keyboard data as a character stream INPUT file and the display screen or printer as a character stream OUTPUT file. Since nearly all programs would have typed inputs and displayed or printed outputs, the two standard file names INPUT and OUTPUT would be provided along with the program name in most Pascal programs.

READ and READLN Statements

Accepting an input from the keyboard is very simple. Of course, the operator must have received some instructions as to what is to be typed in, and the program should have displayed those instructions. After having given the instructions in the manner we describe soon, the program issues a statement to accept the inputs. It takes the form:

READ (M, N, O);

Here, the M, N, and O are the names of variables. The READ statement is thus expecting three separate inputs from the keyboard. The first becomes the value of variable M, the second the value of variable N, etc.

To relate this to an everyday task, assume that the instructions appear on the screen to enter the date, an employee's name, and hours worked. This would be spread out on the screen so as to allow space for entries in the form:

ENTER THE FOLLOWING FOR EACH EMPLOYEE:

DATE: NAME: HOURS WORKED:

A READ statement like the following would be issued to take the typed inputs:

READ (DATE, NAME, HRSWKD);

This time, the date typed in becomes the value of the variable named DATE, the employee's name becomes the value of the variable NAME, and, finally, the hours worked becomes the value of the variable called HRSWKD.

A READ statement accepts only the variables it has listed and remains on the same line. In order to move to the next line, a READLN statement must be used. This statement accepts all of the variables named from the current line and moves to the beginning of the next line.

In many cases, it is necessary to accept inputs whose length is unknown. Therefore, some way must be provided to allow the program to sense when an input is complete. There are two such indicators available EOLN (end of line) and EOF (end of file). The indicators, which are special characters in most systems, can be produced by the depression of certain keys for the keyboard input applications. A carriage return, for example, may produce the EOLN character, and a JOB COMPLETE key the EOF.

Pascal has two standard functions, named EOF and EOLN, to sense these indicators. When these function names are given in a statement, they determine whether an EOF or EOLN condition exists and return a yes or no answer. The READ and READLN instructions can thus be made part of a loop that continues to read until EOF or EOLN occurs. At that point, the loop ends and the program moves on to the next statement.

WRITE and WRITELN Statements

These statements are very similar to the READ statements, taking the form:

WRITE (A,B);
WRITELN (GROSSPAY, DEDUCTIONS, NETPAY);

In both of the cases above, the actual value of the variables named within the parentheses is displayed on the screen or printed. A WRITE statement remains on the same line after being executed, while the WRITELN version moves to the beginning of the next line after displaying or printing the material specified. If a statement is given in the form WRITELN;, a blank line is created.

A WRITE/WRITELN statement may also provide the actual information to be printed either by itself or with variables. For example:

WRITE ('YOUR GRADE IS', G);

This will display the characters in single quotation marks followed by the current value of the variable G, as in:

YOUR GRADE IS 80

Both the WRITE and WRITELN statements have the ability to evaluate expressions before the printing is done. In other words, only the result is printed. Suppose we had the following case:

WRITE ('THE SUM IS', A + B);

In this situation, A and B are added to form the result to be printed, and the line produced would appear:

THE SUM IS 199

Although the statements appear easy to use, setting up the proper format of the display is not. Since the methods available vary from one system to another we can only give some representative examples.

First, the standard procedure named "PAGE" can be called in by a PAGE statement to provide a top-of-form command. This clears the screen and moves a pointer to the first position of the first line. If issued to the printer, this statement moves the form up to a new sheet. Of course, the WRITELN; statement (a blank WRITELN) skips a line, and this can be used as many times as necessary.

Both of the above deal with controlling the vertical format of the screen or printed page. Next we'll discuss how the format of a line is established.

Spacing of information along a line is controlled by information provided in the WRITE/WRITELN statement itself. First, the minimum field width for an item to be displayed or printed can be defined by a number following that item in the WRITE/WRITELN statement. This overrides the system conventions and takes the form:

WRITE (EMPNAME: 20);

It establishes the minimum width allowed for the variable EMPNAME (employee name) as twenty positions. The name is then blocked to the right in

the twenty positions, and if the name has fewer than twenty letters, blanks appear on the left. If more than twenty letters are present in the name, they are printed, so the programmer should set the field width to the size of the longest name expected. (Although we've used an actual value, twenty, for field width, Pascal allows an expression to be used as well. Of course, the expression must be capable of being evaluated to a positive integer.)

A series of information to be printed can be given and the format established in a single statement. For example, the following WRITELN statement places a student's name on the screen and shows his grades for a series of subjects:

WRITELN (SNAME: 20,E:6,M:6,PE:6,T:6,C:6);

This produces the display shown in Figure 4-8.

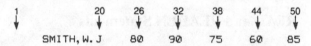

Figure 4-8 Student Grades Produced by the WRITELN Statement

Let's examine next a line in which there is both a string constant and a variable of the real data type to be printed. A statement to print such a line could take the form:

WRITELN ('ENGINEERING: $', EXPENSES [ENG]:16:2);

It produces the following line:

ENGINEERING: $ 789.41

The constant, which consists of the word ENGINEERING: followed by several spaces and a dollar sign, begins at the current print position and extends over the number of character positions within the quote marks.

On the other hand, the variable, which is named EXPENSES [ENG], has its size and spacing specified in the statement. Minimum width is sixteen positions. Since this is a real number, we can also specify the number of decimal places; this is done by the entry :2, which sets two decimal places. Thus, the variable EXPENSES [ENG] is blocked to the right in a sixteen-position field and has two decimal positions printed.

STATEMENTS CONCERNED WITH DECISIONS, BRANCHES, AND LOOPS

There are six statements in this group:

    IF . . . THEN . . . ELSE . . .
    CASE . . . OF . . .
    WHILE . . . DO . . .
    REPEAT . . . UNTIL . . .
    FOR . . . TO or DOWNTO . . . DO . . .
    GOTO . . .

The statements in this group are discussed together because they have one thing in common: The ability to change the order in which the program statements are executed. Syntax diagrams for all appear in Figure 4-9.

Let's examine the overall action of each statement first, then go into the details. We'll begin with the simplest, the GOTO statement.

The GOTO Statement

The purpose of the GOTO statement is to give the line number of the next statement to be performed. Its format is uncomplicated, consisting of only the reserved word and the line number in the form: GOTO 500;.

When executed, this statement causes the statement at line 500 to be performed and the program to continue from that point. Of course, the line number must be given a LABEL declaration.

The block structure of Pascal places some severe limitations on the use of the GOTO statement that we did not see in BASIC. A GOTO statement may branch only within a block or upward into a higher block. In the latter case, the block in which the GOTO statement appears is part of the higher block.

The CASE Statement

Next to be examined is the CASE statement. If we were to convert this statement to English, it would read something like: "Examine the item specified, and in the CASE . . . OF . . . perform a specific action." For all practical purposes, there is no limit on the number of alternative actions.

Suppose, for example, the computer operator had been given a list of jobs displayed on the screen and was asked to depress a key corresponding to the job he wanted the computer to perform. A READ in-struction would accept that keystroke and it would be assigned to a variable, perhaps KEYNUM. Now the programmer wants to determine what the key number is and select the appropriate job. A CASE statement can be used to do this, as follows:

    CASE KEYNUM OF
        1: statement;
        2: statement;
        3: statement;
        4: statement
    END;

The syntax diagram in Figure 4-9 shows the flexibility of the CASE statement. Immediately following the word CASE, the programmer may place an expression to be evaluated. In our example above we used a single variable so that the evaluation was simple. The expression must evaluate to one of the constants given in the list of alternatives, however. (We used 1, 2, 3, and 4 in the example.) These are called the "CASE labels," and they *must be a nonreal data type* such as integer, character, or Boolean.

The loop around the word "constant" (the case label) shows that more than one case label may appear in a line. If this is done, they are separated by commas. In our example, it might have been desirable to take the same action if either key 1 or key 2 was depressed. So, the CASE statement could have been constructed:

    CASE KEYNUM OF
        1, 2: statement;
        3: statement;
        4: statement
    END;

The outer loop simply shows that the case labels (the constants) and alternative actions follow one another after being punctuated by a semicolon. This continues until the last action, which does bear the semicolon.

Notice that the CASE statement must be terminated by an END; statement aligned with CASE. A BEGIN statement is not used, however.

The IF Statement

So far we've discussed an unconditional branch, the GOTO statement, and a conditional branch with multiple paths, the CASE statement. We have an-

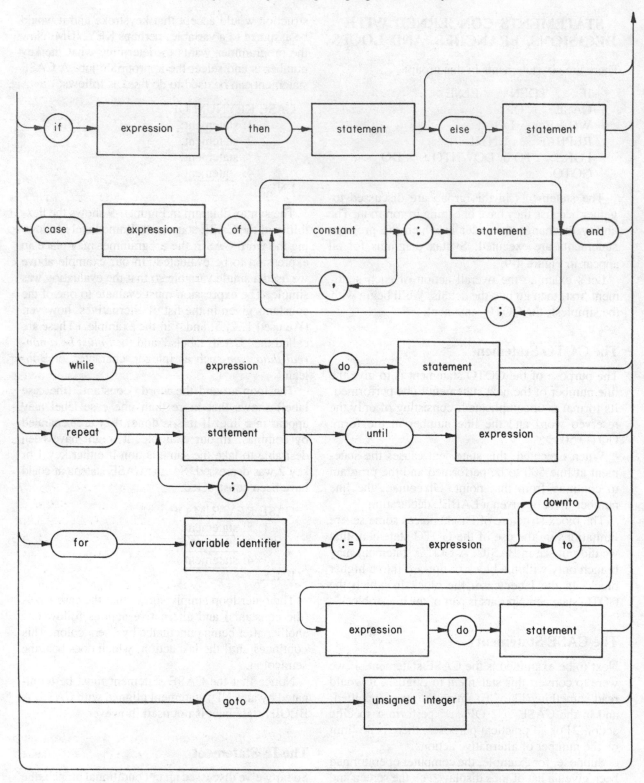

Figure 4-9 Syntax Diagrams for Statements Concerned with Decisions, Branches, and Loops

other statement in this group that is used for conditional branches; it is the IF statement.

Writing this statement in English is fairly simple: IF this condition exists, THEN take a certain action; otherwise (ELSE) take a different action. Notice that the English version of the statement is easily fitted onto the syntax diagram in Figure 4-9. What the syntax diagram shows though is the fact that ELSE and the second action, which follows the word ELSE, need not be provided. If it is not, the program simply goes to the following statement when the tested condition is not found. Implied by the syntax, the expression following the word IF must evaluate to a yes or no, true or false, condition. IF A>B, IF MONTH = 7, and IF M<>N are examples of such expressions.

The operators AND and OR can be used in the expressions to make them very powerful and yet evaluate to a yes or no answer. We'll use one example here to illustrate:

```
IF A>B AND A< = C THEN SIZE: = MEDIUM
   ELSE SIZE: = OTHER;
```

When the IF statement is constructed without the ELSE alternative, it has a form like that below:

```
IF (AGE < 65) AND (AGE > 18) THEN
   WRITELN ('MEETS AGE LIMITS');
```

This statement is complete. If the conditions are not met, the next statement in sequence is executed.

Statements That Perform Loops

Pascal offers an excellent selection of statements that can cause an operation to be done over and over, a loop in other words. There are three sets of statements available:

```
FOR . . . TO . . . DO . . .
WHILE . . . DO . . .
REPEAT . . . UNTIL . . .
```

Each set has features that make it a better choice than the others under specific conditions. What they do have in common is the ability to examine a condition and perform an action only as long as that condition exists.

Since the FOR statement is very similar to the FOR statement used in BASIC, we'll discuss that one first.

The FOR Statement

The FOR statement establishes the name of a control variable and sets the limits of that variable. As long as the variable remains within those limits, the action specified by the DO is performed. Each time the action is performed, the control variable is stepped up by one and tested. When the variable exceeds the limit, the action is no longer taken. The program then proceeds to the next statement in sequence.

The syntax diagram shown in Figure 4-9 adds to this explanation. The control variable, which is sometimes called a "counter variable," is named immediately after the word FOR. Any name that is a valid identifier may be used. An assignment symbol (: =) then leads to two expressions. These are evaluated to provide the limits that the control variable must remain within if the loop is to continue.

A simple example is shown below:

FOR NUM: = 1 TO 10 DO <u>Statement</u>

Here a variable named NUM is checked to see if it is from one to ten. If it is, the statement following DO is performed and the variable is stepped up by one and tested again. If it is still with limits, the statement is performed again. When the variable reaches eleven, the statement is *not performed* and the program moves on.

An alternate form uses the word DOWNTO, replacing TO. This simply reduces the control variable by one each time the loop is performed so the lower limit will be passed rather than the high limit.

Thus far we've considered the possibility of only one statement being performed repetitively as a result of the FOR loop. Most often, however, a compound statement is executed. It takes the form:

```
FOR NUM: = 1 TO 10 DO
   BEGIN
      Statements
   END;
```

The WHILE Statement

Let's begin this description by looking at the syntax diagram. It's much simpler than the FOR statement and should be read in English as: While this condition exists, do the following. As in the case of the FOR statement, the condition is tested before the action is taken. Thus, the action may not be taken at all.

Two major differences between the FOR and the WHILE statements show up quickly: (1) only one expression can be evaluated by the WHILE statement, and it must evaluate to a yes/no, true/false condition, and (2) there is no automatic counting mechanism in the WHILE statement. Any changes in the condition being examined must be produced by other statements. The loop initiated by the WHILE statement continues as long as the condition being tested for in the expression exists.

Again, the word "statement" in the syntax diagram may mean either one statement (an isolated statement) or several (a compound statement). As we know, the compound statement starts with the word BEGIN and is terminated by the word END.

Two examples of the WHILE statement are shown below. One uses an isolated statement and the other a compound statement.

WHILE KEY = 0 DO READ (KEY);

This example is reading the keyboard for a key to be depressed. It performs the operation over and over until a key is depressed and the variable named KEY changes from zero to some other number.

WHILE A>B DO
BEGIN
        Statements
END;

As long as the variable A is greater than the variable B, the statements bounded by the BEGIN and END statements are performed over and over.

The REPEAT Statement

The third in our series of loop statements available is the pair REPEAT . . . UNTIL, meaning repeat this action until this condition exists. It is similar in operation to the WHILE statement. However, the WHILE statement has the tested condition existing before it starts and it continues as long as the condition remains. On the other hand, the REPEAT statement does not have the tested condition existing when it starts. It continues until the tested condition occurs. This may seem to be a subtle difference to most readers, but it is an important one.

The syntax diagrams for the REPEAT and WHILE statements differ enough to merit a close examination. In the REPEAT statement, the statement(s) that comprise the loop follow immediately after the word REPEAT. These statements will be performed once before the condition is tested for the first time. A compound statement need not be bounded by the words BEGIN and END, although they may be used if the programmer chooses. After the last statement is executed, the condition is tested. If it still does not exist, the loop is repeated; if the condition does exist, the program continues with the next statement in sequence.

In contrast, the WHILE statement tests the condition before performing the action. If the condition exists, the action is taken; if it does not, the program continues with the next statement in sequence. Since the action comes after the test is made, compound statements must be bounded by the conventional BEGIN and END.

Examples of the REPEAT statement can also be shown simply. Although the expression being evaluated may be complex, it must be capable of being evaluated to a yes/no, true/false condition, so we can use a simple expression to illustrate how the statement works.

REPEAT
    TOTAL: = T + NEW;
    READ (NEW);
UNTIL TOTAL > = MAXTAX;

In the example, two statements add numbers entered from the keyboard until the variable named TOTAL is equal to or greater than the variable named MAXTAX. At that point the program proceeds to the statement following UNTIL.

FILES AND THE STATEMENTS THAT HANDLE THEM

A good step to take first in this section is to review the description of files given in Chapter 1. There we said that a file held a group of related information and that the information consisted of a number of records. Each record was identical in format to all other records in the file, and records were often, in turn, made up of fields of data.

When we reached Chapter 3 and discussed the

files that BASIC could handle, the "stream" file was introduced. In this case, there were no records in the file, simply a stream of data. The same idea was applied to the inputs from the keyboard and the outputs to the display or printer in this chapter. The keyboard was considered the INPUT file and the display or printer the OUTPUT file.

File Names and Declarations

There are several important rules concerning how the program is told about files:

a. The names of files used by the program, if they already exist, must be given in the program header just as the INPUT and OUTPUT files are given. This would take the form:
PROGRAM TAXCALCULATOR (INPUT, OUTPUT, SALES, PREYEAR, NEWTAX);
b. The files must again be identified in the TYPE declarations, in the form:
TYPE file name = FILE OF data type;
c. Finally, the file must be declared as a variable in the VAR declaration, in the form:
VAR file name: FILE OF data type;

Note that neither the file element size nor the total file size is declared. Element size is established when the first element is entered into the file, and overall size changes as data is added.

Establishing a File

One statement is used to either establish a new file or remove an existing file; that statement is RE-WRITE, which appears in the form: REWRITE (file name);. If the file name is that of an existing file, that file is declared to be empty. If the name is a new one, a new, empty file named as specified is created. The next step, then, is to place data in the file.

Ordinarily, a list of parameters with which the file must operate is provided when a file is established and later used. Such things as access method are normally given in the REWRITE statement and some of the other file handling statements. These depend on the specific implementation of Pascal, however, and are not defined in the basic language requirements.

There are also other statements available in some implementations of the language. SEEK (file name, record number) and SEEKKEY (file name, key value) are used in one of the most popular implementations. They allow direct access and indexed access that we consider in the following paragraphs.

We've discussed ways in which programs gain access to data in files. Sequential access is the simplest method. File elements are simply recorded one after another, and new elements are added at the end. In this case, a pointer keeps track of which element is to be handled next. Imagine the pointer as the stylus on the arm of a phonograph. It is reset to the beginning of the file when the phonograph is turned on and moves from one musical selection to another as the record is played. If power is turned off, the stylus stops at the point at which the music will resume when power is reapplied. Think of the file reading or writing instructions as applying power to the phonograph when they are using the file and removing it when they are not.

The second way in which programs can gain access is called the direct access method. A more complex method of counting the elements is established and an element can be chosen by number.

The most sophisticated access method is called "indexed" or "keyed." Each element is given a unique key by which it can be identified and written, read, or revised.

Most Pascal systems will provide more than one form of access. However, standard Pascal provides only the sequential access method, so we'll limit our description to that method.

The Pointer and Reading and Writing

Pascal uses a special symbol to represent the position of the pointer in the file, a small arrow pointing upward (↑). This symbol is written immediately after the file name, in the form file name ↑, or SALES ↑.

This identifier can be used like a variable in an assignment statement to show what information is to be placed in the file. For example, the following statement says that data is to be placed in the current position of the file named SALES.

SALES ↑: = name of data to be entered

However, this statement does not actually do the recording. The PUT procedure must be used for that, in the form:

PUT (SALES);

Instead of this two-step method, the programmer is more likely to choose the statement available in most implementations that combines both. That statement is WRITE, and it appears in the form:

WRITE (file name, data to be entered);

This statement places the data to be entered in the current position and moves the pointer to the next position. Of course, the PUT statement also moves the pointer after the data is entered in the file.

Naturally, a file is recorded so that its contents can be used later, and this requires that the file be read. Position of the pointer is one of the first things that must be considered. Since it is at the end of the file after the last WRITE statement (or PUT statement) is executed, it must be returned to the first position in the file before reading can begin. This action is performed by a statement called RESET. All that need be given is the file name, so the RESET is written in the form:

RESET (file name); or RESET (SALES);

When this statement is executed, the pointer is returned to the first position in the file.

Either a one-step or two-step method may be used to read. The two-step method consists of an assignment statement and a GET statement.

The first statement assigns the contents of the current file position (↑) to the variable named, and the GET statement actually acquires the data from the file. If we used actual variable and file names, these statements could be written:

SALESREC: = SALES ↑;
GET (SALES);

The first record is taken from the file named SALES and given the name SALESREC in the computer. After the GET statement is executed, the pointer is moved to the next position in the file. Thus, the next time this pair of statements is executed, the second record is read (and the pointer is moved to the third position).

A READ statement is the one-step method used to acquire data from a file in some implementations of Pascal. It combines the functions of GET and assign and is written in the form:

READ (file name, name of variable); or
READ (SALES, SALESREC);

This statement takes the record selected by the pointer, brings it into the computer, and assigns it to the variable named SALESREC. After the statement is executed, the pointer is moved to the next position.

Sensing the EOF Mark

Up to now, the EOF (end of file) mark has not been used by any of the statements. This mark, which is a special character or combination of characters, is very important to the handling of sequential access files. The system automatically places it after the last element in a file, so the programmer can rely on it being there.

There is a standard function that examines a file and determines if the pointer has reached the EOF mark. Appropriately enough, this function is named EOF. It must be used in an expression and related to a specific file. When this is done, the EOF function returns a true or false result on which a conditional decision can be based. A simple example used to sense the end of our SALES file would be written:

EOF (SALES)

Of course, this is not a statement so it has to be made part of a statement to be useful. Perhaps: WHILE NOT EOF (SALES) DO . . . In this case, the statements following DO are performed until the EOF mark is reached. An arrangement like this permits a file to be read when the programmer does not know many of the elements it holds.

STATEMENTS THAT
ESTABLISH AND USE ARRAYS

An array in Pascal is a table of information, consisting of one element after another or of rows and columns of data.

Pascal arrays are organized in the common way, but some of the terms used are unique, and Pascal requires that, like other data types, arrays be declared in the declaration section.

Let's begin with a simple array, a one-dimensional array of integers. This array is shown in Figure 4-10 and is identical in organization to the arrays described earlier. It has a name, which conforms to

STEP I - THE TYPE DECLARATION
TYPE RATE = ARRAY [1..10] OF INTEGER

RATE

```
[ 1]  _____
[ 2]  _____
[ 3]  _____
[ 4]  _____
[ 5]  _____
[ 6]  _____
[ 7]  _____
[ 8]  _____
[ 9]  _____
[10]  _____
```

STEP 2 - THE VARIABLE DECLARATION
VAR INTERESTRATE : RATE

INTERESTRATE

```
[ 1]  _____
[ 2]  _____
[ 3]  _____
[ 4]  _____
[ 5]  _____
[ 6]  _____
[ 7]  _____
[ 8]  _____
[ 9]  _____
[10]  _____
```

Figure 4-10 A One-Dimension Array Named
INTERESTRATE

the rules for identifiers, and each element has a number that allows that element to be selected for use. In Pascal, that element identifier is called the "index."

When an array element is to be chosen for use, both the array name and index must be provided, in the form: INTERESTRATE [9]. This designation selects the ninth element of the array named INTERESTRATE. The element is used just like any other variable.

A two-dimensional array consists of rows and columns. Both a row and column index must be given to select an element in a two-dimensional array, and this is done in the form INTERESTRATE [7,3]. This identifier would choose the element at the intersection of the seventh row and third column. Of course, elements in two-dimensional arrays may also be used just like any other variable.

So far the description of arrays in Pascal could apply to the arrays in BASIC. Now, however, we will begin to see some differences in their handling.

First, as with all Pascal data, characteristics of the data must be declared before it can be used. This brings us to the subject of how arrays are declared.

Declaration of Arrays

Arrays must be covered by a TYPE statement and a VAR statement, as is the case with files, which we just discussed. Let's begin with the TYPE declaration for a list (one-dimensional array) of ten numbers to illustrate the format of the declaration. Such an array would be declared:

TYPE data type = ARRAY[1..10] OF INTEGER;

Assuming that the array was a table of interest rates, the data type might be declared as to RATE, and therefore, the declaration would appear:

TYPE RATE = ARRAY[1..10] OF INTEGER;

Now the array must also be declared as a variable. If the above statement were used for the TYPE declaration, then the VAR declaration could be:

VAR INTERESTRATE:RATE;

A shortcut in these declarations is possible; the VAR declaration can define data type directly. But this has the disadvantage that no other variable can be assigned to be that data type. If we use the shortcut to declare our array in this case, no TYPE declaration is required, and we can change our VAR declaration to read:

VAR INTERESTRATE:ARRAY[1..10] OF INTEGER;

Notice that there is no data type named RATE when the variable is declared directly.

Regardless of whether the two-step declaration or the shortcut is used, the result is that an array consisting of ten elements, each capable of holding integers, is established. The array is empty, of course, and data must be placed in each element before the array will have any value. We'll discuss how that is done after the declaration of multidimensional arrays is described.

The declaration statement for a two-dimensional array is the same as that shown for the one-dimensional array except the second dimension is added within the square brackets. If we use exactly the same names that we used earlier, the declarations for a two-dimensional array would appear:

TYPE RATE = ARRAY[1..10,1..10] OF INTEGER;
VAR INTERESTRATE:RATE;
   or
VAR INTERESTRATE:ARRAY[1..10,1..10] OF INTEGER;

These statements establish an array having ten rows, ten columns, and one hundred elements.

Selection of an Array Element

The contents of an array element may be used in a variety of ways, but before we discuss that subject, a brief recap of how an element is selected would be useful. First, the array name is a variable and may be used in a statement just as any other variable is. Next, the element number is always given in square brackets immediately after the array name (no space between array name and element number). Two examples are:

INTERESTRATE[7] A one-dimensional array
INTERESTRATE[3,8] A two-dimensional array

However, the element number may also be the result of an expression being evaluated. Suppose, for example, the interest rate to be chosen was based on the loan applicant's income, current debts, and credit rating. Each of these factors would first be rounded off so that the expressions would evaluate to an integer between one and ten and then they would choose an element in a two-dimensional array. Selection of the element could be stated:

INTERESTRATE[I-D,CR]

In this case we have three variables, I for income, D for debts, and CR for credit rating. Income minus debts evaluates to an integer to select a row, and credit rating selects the column. At the intersection of the selected row and column is the rate of interest this applicant will be charged.

Using the Content of an Array

The content of each array element is a variable and may be used as such in expressions. Each may be printed or displayed, for instance. A display of the interest rate selected for the loan applicant is displayed if it is given in the statement:

WRITE (INTERESTRATE[I-D,CR]);

We have created arrays so far, but have not filled them with data. This is done with the assignment statement (:=). In order to enter the interest rates in our one-dimensional, ten-element array named INTERESTRATE, we would use the assignment statement as follows:

INTERESTRATE[1]: = 7;
INTERESTRATE[2]: = 8;
INTERESTRATE[3]: = 10;
INTERESTRATE[4]: = 11;
INTERESTRATE[5]: = 12;
INTERESTRATE[6]: = 14;
INTERESTRATE[7]: = 16;
INTERESTRATE[8]: = 18;
INTERESTRATE[9]: = 19;
INTERESTRATE[10]: = 20;

STRINGS AND THEIR USE

A "string" is a collection of characters from the character set, such as a name, address, an instruction, or a catalog number. WILLIAMS, 9035295 = 17N, and THIS IS A STRING are examples.

We've used string constants in our description of the WRITE and WRITELN statements. WRITELN ('YOUR GRADE IS', G) is an example. The 'YOUR GRADE IS' is a string constant, and the programmer is free to use these in statements that display and print. They are always enclosed in single quotation marks.

What we haven't discussed up to now are string variables. The data type CHAR was covered among the simple, standard data types REAL, INTEGER, and BOOLEAN, but *a variable of the data type CHAR is only one character, not a string*. In Pascal, a string variable is thought of as a structured data type, and naturally it is composed of characters.

String variables are held in arrays, which are declared to be of the simple data type CHAR. Let's look into the declarations involved. They are slightly different than declarations for numeric arrays because the length of string variables is not known in advance. In other words, size of numbers is set by the system and thus the programmer doesn't need to specify their length when a numeric array is organized but he must specify string size.

If we assume that we wish to prepare an array of

the names of students in a class we could do it in the following manner.

TYPE NAME = PACKED ARRAY[1..15] OF CHAR;
VAR STUDENTNM: ARRAY[1..20] OF NAME;

The TYPE declaration establishes that each element of the array holds up to fifteen characters, the size of the student name. In the VAR declaration, the array is named STUDENTNM and it is set to twenty elements each of the type NAME. (PACKED is a term indicating that the character codes are stored so that they occupy the minimum space.)

Now the string variable STUDENTNM can be used and indexed in the same manner as references to elements in numeric arrays. The name of the variable is given and it is followed by the index in the form: STUDENTNM[5]. This reference can be used in a variety of statements as any variable may. For example, when the array is to be loaded with names, the following statement could read the name entered from the keyboard: READLN (STUDENTNM[5]);.

Whatever name was typed in would be placed in the fifth element of our student name array. And to print an output reporting the grade: WRITELN (STUDENTNM[5], GRADE[5]);. This statement gets the name from one array and the corresponding grade from another.

STATEMENTS THAT ESTABLISH AND USE RECORDS

Since recordkeeping is one of the most useful functions computers perform, all the modern high-level languages include statements that establish records and manipulate their contents. Pascal's statements are very easy to use.

Before we examine the statements, however, let's review what a record is and what its components are. A record is a collection of data related to one entry in a file. The registration form for an automobile is a good example of a record. A typical state has files holding millions of such records, each identified by a registration number and the vehicle owner's name.

Related to each automobile is a variety of information. This includes owner's name and address, which is all characters; vehicle weight, which is an integer; fee paid, which is a real number; and finally the answers to some questions given in yes/no, or Boolean form. Thus, a typical record may hold data of all four standard Pascal data types as well as special types defined by the programmer.

Each section of the record is a field. Fee paid, for example, may be a five-position field for the typical car. Organizing a record in Pascal requires that the record be named, the fields be named, and the data type to be provided in each field be stated.

Record Declaration

As the reader would expect after having gotten this far into Pascal, records and their fields must be declared in the declaration section of the program. This is done in the TYPE declaration because a record is a structured data type.

It may be a good idea to examine the syntax diagram of the record declaration statement in Figure 4-11 before we construct a declaration. This begins with the word TYPE, which is followed by a name chosen by the programmer and the word RECORD.

Now we'll examine a typical declaration of a record and discuss some of its components. The declaration is shown below. It prepares the format for a student record in a file of such records, perhaps called the student file. Logically, the type is declared to be STUDENTREC.

TYPE STUDENTREC = RECORD
NAME: PACKED ARRAY[1..25] OF CHAR;
NUMBER: INTEGER;
CREDITS: INTEGER;
GRADEAVG: REAL;
YEARSTARTED: INTEGER;
END;

The fields making up the record use most of the standard data types. The name is a string variable. As discussed in the previous section, fields are held in arrays, so the field declaration states this and shows that the NAME field is twenty-five characters long.

Next comes student NUMBER, obviously an integer data type, as is the CREDITS field. GRADEAVG is the point system (3.6, 2.0, etc.) so its data type is REAL. Finally, YEARSTARTED is the INTEGER data type.

In a record such as this there could be several yes or no entries as well. Financial aid eligibility, for

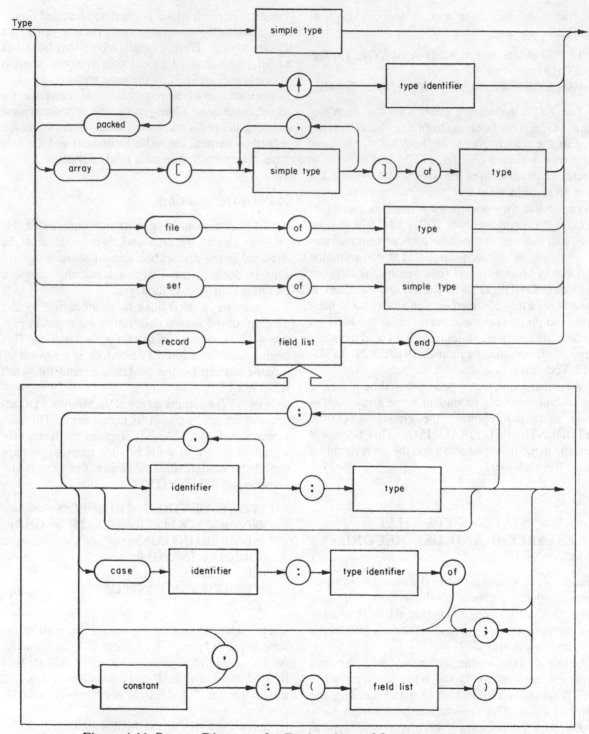

Figure 4-11 Syntax Diagrams for Declarations of Structured Data Types

example, might require a simple BOOLEAN answer of TRUE or FALSE. Such entries would be declared to be of the type BOOLEAN.

At this point, a record format has been established but no records have actually been created. All that has been accomplished is to state that a type of record named STUDENTREC is made up of fields named in the list and those fields will each hold data of a certain type.

The next step, obviously, is to enter the information in the record format and then place that record in a file in a permanent storage medium such as a diskette. We'll describe how data is gathered for a record in the following paragraphs.

To begin, a variable must be declared. A variable named SR should be a good choice. Of course, the data type must be included in the variable declaration, and that data type is STUDENTREC as we stated in our TYPE declaration. Thus, our variable declaration would take the form:

    VAR SR:STUDENTREC;

Gaining Access to Record Contents

A question now arises: What is the source of the information that is to be placed in the records? Most likely, it would be the keyboard when an operator read information from an application and typed it in. Thus, statements would be required to place instructions on the display screen and read the typed inputs. We've covered the READ/READLN and WRITE/WRITELN statements already, so the reader should understand how data is entered from the keyboard. Our purpose here is to show how the data is entered into specific fields of a record.

In order to select a field for the entry of data we give the variable name and the name of the field. (Keep in mind that the variable, SR in our case, has already been declared to be of the type STUDENTREC.) In our student record, field selection takes the form:

    SRNAME
    SRNUMBER
    SRCREDITS
    SRGRADEAVG
    SRYEARSTARTED

Thus, a read or write statement can use the fields as individual variables, in the form: READLN (SRCREDITS); to obtain data for the record, and WRITELN (SRGRADEAVG); to print or display an output.

The WITH Statement

The reader must have noticed that repeating the variable name before every field name requires extra time. This brings us to the use of the WITH statement, which makes it possible to deal directly with each field in a record and to eliminate the separate variable name. The WITH statement takes the form:

    WITH SR DO
        BEGIN
            WRITELN (NAME);
            WRITELN (YEARSTARTED);
            WRITELN (CREDITS);
            WRITELN (GRADEAVG)
        END;

Although we've shown only a display or printing of record contents, any of the statements normally used to process data of this type can be applied. Previous credits could be added to new credits or a new grade average calculated, for example.

SETS AND THEIR USE

Here's a data type that is not available in some of the major languages but which can be very useful. It's called a set, which means a group of items of the same basic kind. A list of civic clubs, for example, would be a set, as follows:

    [ROTARY, KIWANIS, LIONS, ELKS, MOOSE,
    OPTIMISTS]

The kind of items in the set is called the "base type," and items are scalar in nature; that is, the system places the entries on a scale. We've seen this arrangement earlier when we discussed enumeration of data types.

Before we describe the ways in which sets are declared and constructed, let's examine some simple uses to show the kind of thing that can be done with sets. One of the operations available is called intersection. It compares two sets and lists common members.

Another useful operation is difference. When it

is performed, the items that are in the first set but not in the second set are identified.

A third operation that can be performed on sets is called union. As this implies, the sets are merged to form a composite. Of course, the duplicated items appear only once in the resulting set.

Union, intersection, and difference are all caused to take place by arithmetic operator symbols we identified earlier: ($+$) causes the union operation, ($-$) causes the difference operation, and (*) causes the intersection operation. They are used in the form:

[set 1] + [set 2], [set 1] $-$ [set 2], and [set 1] * [set 2].

Four of the relational operators ($=$, $<>$, $<=$, and $>=$) are also available for use with sets. They all yield a true or false indication when acted upon. The equal ($=$) and not equal ($<>$) are easy to understand, but the other two are more complex.

First is the $<=$ sign, which in this case is used to test whether one set is within another. For example:

[set 1] $<=$ [set 2] tests to see if set 1 is part of set 2.

Second, we have the sign $>=$, which tests the same relationship but in the reverse order. For example:

[set 1] $>=$ [set 2] tests to see if set 1 contains set 2.
(In other words, if set 2 is part of set 1.)

Perhaps the most useful operator of all and the most frequently used is one unique to sets; it is called IN. The purpose of this operator is to determine if a specific expression—let's just say item—is within a specific set. It is used in the form:

Expression IN [Set]

Suppose we wanted to test a word just typed in from the keyboard to determine if it is a valid response. All valid responses would be in the set. Then the operator IN would determine if the response was in the set.

Now to the construction of sets. Sets are constructed within square brackets, and may be either fully enumerated (all members listed) or the limits given in the same manner as the subrange declaration.

First, we have a set that outlines student grade limits. We establish a set called passing grades in the form:

PASSGRDS: = [60..100]

This produces a set of integers ranging from sixty through one hundred. If a variable such as a student grade was examined for passing or failing, this set could be used in the form:

IF STDGRD IN PASSGRDS THEN . . .

Sets are one of the structured data types available in Pascal. If a set is to be used in a program, it must be declared as a data type and then, of course, a variable must be declared to be of that data type. Beginning with the type declaration we could have:

TYPE ANIMALS = (CAT, DOG, RAT, . . .);

This declaration enumerates (lists) the name of every animal that can be of the data type ANIMAL. Next we have another type declaration:

TYPE ZOOPOP = SET OF ANIMALS;

This declaration establishes the data type ZOOPOP as being a set, and the members of any set of the type ZOOPOP must be selected from those enumerated in the type ANIMALS.

Now we're ready to declare our variables, which are the animals held in the Detroit Zoo (DETZOO) and the Houston Zoo (HOUZOO). The names in parentheses are the names of the variables. Thus, the variable declaration would appear:

VAR DETZOO, HOUZOO: ZOOPOP;

When this declaration is completed, the system knows that variables DETZOO and HOUZOO are: (1) of the data type ZOOPOP; (2) are sets, since ZOOPOP has been declared to be a set; and (3) must include only the animals listed in the ANIMALS declaration, since ZOOPOP is a SET OF ANIMALS.

At this point, however, neither of the variables have any animals listed in their sets. They've simply been established as being sets. So the next step is to fill in the contents of the variables DETZOO and HOUZOO. This is done with the assignment statement, which may list the full contents of the set or use a subrange form of enumeration. For example:

DETZOO: = [CAT, DOG, 3, 4, 5, 6];
HOUZOO: = [CAT..RAT];

Variable DETZOO is fully enumerated while the HOUZOO uses the subrange form. The two periods (..) indicate that the HOUZOO spans the range CAT to RAT in the list of animals originally given. Remember that the original list is entered in order, so if all the items between two points in the list are to be included in a set, only the starting and ending point need to be given.

The variables DETZOO and HOUZOO can now be applied to useful work. For example, the zoo populations can be checked by any of our three basic operations. The animals that the Houston Zoo has but the Detroit Zoo does not have can be found by:

ZOODIF: = HOUZOO – DETZOO;

Of course, the variable ZOODIF would have had to be declared to be the type ZOOPOP. It would also have had to be assigned to be an empty set, in the form ZOODIF: = [ ];. When the two sets are compared by the difference operation, the variable ZOODIF becomes a set of animal names.

Of course, the IN operator we spoke of earlier could also be used. It could be used to determine if a certain zoo held a certain animal. For instance, it is easy to find out if any of the zoos have a parrot:

IF PARROT IN HOUZOO THEN . . . ;

In summarizing sets, we can conclude that their preparation requires a good deal of work. Once this is done, however, the use of sets is relatively simple.

THE LIST TYPE DATA STRUCTURE

So far we've introduced five types of structured data: arrays, strings, records, sets, and files. Once established, the first four types are basically fixed throughout the program. Files, on the other hand, may be changed, but standard Pascal limits those changes to adding to the file or elimination of the file. Thus, there is a need for a structured data type that allows changes to be made more easily; that data type is the *list*, which is also called the pointer type.

As in the housewife's grocery list, items can be added to or removed from Pascal lists. Items can be inserted at any point or removed from anywhere in the list and yet the list will always remain intact.

While this may seem impossible, it is actually accomplished easily. Stored along with each element placed in the list is a pointer that gives the location of the next list element. Some systems may store two pointers, one the location of the previous element and the other showing the location of the succeeding element, and even more complex linking is possible.

To summarize: A list is a collection of elements each of which points to the next. Thus, the elements do not have to be contiguous in storage in order to maintain a definite order.

The pointer type data structure is not often used in simple programs, so we'll limit our discussion to some of the basic ideas involved and the use of the standard procedure NEW and the reserved word NIL.

The first step is, of course, to declare the type, just as we did for arrays, records, etc. The syntax diagram for the declaration of the structured data types was shown in Figure 4-11 on page 84. Across the second line, we have the pointer type; it is the arrow in the circle.

What isn't shown, however, is the fact that elements in this type of data structure are records and that they must be included in the TYPE declaration. As we know, the record declaration requires that the fields in the record be listed. Therefore, a type declaration for a pointer structure is needed.

At least one of the fields in each record will hold the address of the next record. So if we had a very simple list of part numbers, the two fields in the record might be named PARTNUM and LINK. The actual part number goes into the first field and the address into the LINK field.

A type declaration would set the stage for the establishment of a list like that shown in Figure 4-12 but not actually create it. The declaration and use of variables are necessary to do that.

To prepare the structure for use, a standard procedure NEW must be issued in a statement. It assigns a beginning address, and now the list can be started.

The link must also be established. However, we are still at the first record in the list, and there was no previous record. NIL is placed in the LINK field of the first record entered, showing the end of the list.

Variables are then stored in the list, with the actual data going into one field of each record and linking addresses into another. Now the second record and subsequent records will lead to the first no matter what their actual physical locations are. Of course, this process continues until all the information is stored.

If the information in the list was to be printed, a pointer in our example would start at its current

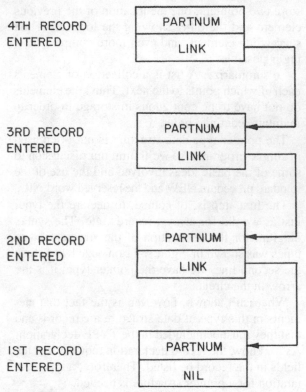

4TH RECORD ENTERED

PARTNUM

LINK

3RD RECORD ENTERED

PARTNUM

LINK

2ND RECORD ENTERED

PARTNUM

LINK

1ST RECORD ENTERED

PARTNUM

NIL

Figure 4-12 Organization of the List Type Structured Data

position. So the last record entered would be the first to be retrieved and printed. Records are then linked by the addresses stored, and retrieval would continue until the first record was reached. At that point, NIL indicates the end of the list.

PROCEDURES

In Pascal, a procedure is a group of statements that, collectively, bear a name and are treated as a unit. The procedure name may be used as a statement itself to cause the group of statements to be executed.

The next step is to separate procedures that are standard, that is, automatically provided by the system, from those that the programmer may create. We'll call the latter type user-defined procedures.

User-Defined Procedures

A point that should be reviewed before we go further is that user-defined procedures appear in the procedure declaration section, not in the body of the program. Only the procedure name is given in the body.

An example of a user-defined procedure name is shown in Figure 4-13. Here we have a procedure whose purpose is to calculate and list student grades. Several times during execution of the program, it is necessary to perform this operation. Each time, the procedure's name appears in the program body, and this acquires and executes the statements comprising the procedure.

Although the statements involved in the procedure remain the same each time it is used, the data that it processes may not. This may make it necessary for the procedure and the main program to exchange certain information. This information is specified in a part of the procedure declaration called a parameter list.

Before we delve into the contents and construction of a parameter list, let's examine the structure of a procedure that doesn't require such a list; such a procedure declaration is shown in Figure 4-14. It begins with the reserved word PROCEDURE, which is immediately followed by the procedure's name, and is terminated by a semicolon. If a parameter list is required, it is placed between the name and the semicolon.

Appearing below the procedure name are any *declarations that apply to only this procedure;* these are called "local references." They may include the same kind of declarations allowed in the overall program declarations: LABEL, CONST, TYPE, VAR, PROCEDURE, and FUNCTION.

Parameter Lists

We'll examine the need for a parameter list by first showing the two basic ways in which a procedure is applied. The simplest case is one in which the procedure is called in to use several times but always operates on the same items, although the values differ. If these items are declared at the beginning of the program, in the "global references" following the program header, the procedure can use their names freely in its body, and no parameter list is needed. An example of such a procedure call appears in the main body of the program in the form of a statement:

PRINTACCOUNTS;

The second basic way in which a procedure is

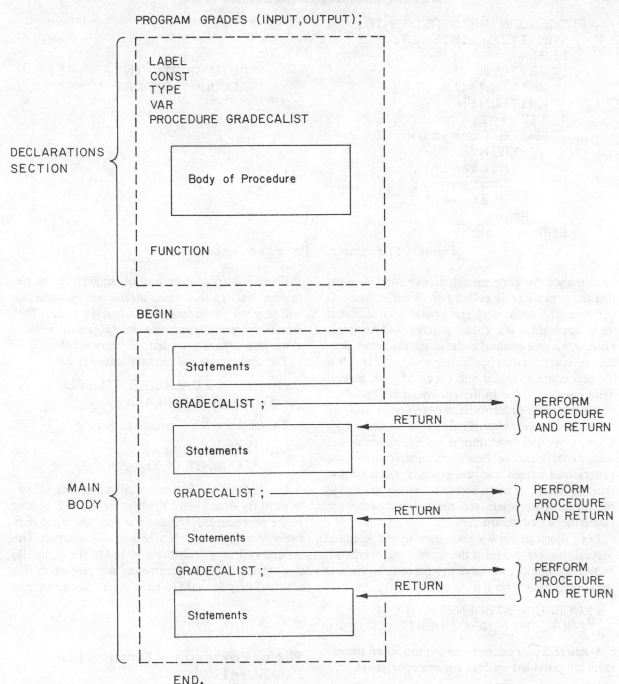

PROGRAM GRADES (INPUT,OUTPUT);

DECLARATIONS SECTION

LABEL
CONST
TYPE
VAR
PROCEDURE GRADECALIST

Body of Procedure

FUNCTION

BEGIN

MAIN BODY

Statements

GRADECALIST ;

RETURN

PERFORM PROCEDURE AND RETURN

Statements

GRADECALIST ;

RETURN

PERFORM PROCEDURE AND RETURN

Statements

GRADECALIST ;

RETURN

PERFORM PROCEDURE AND RETURN

Statements

END.

Figure 4-13 Example of Procedure Use

```
PROCEDURE PRINTACCOUNTS;
  VAR ITEM: INTEGER;
  BEGIN
    WRITELN ('                    AUTO PARTS INC.     ');
    WRITELN ('                    ACCOUNT REPORT ');
    WRITELN;
    ITEM:=1;
    WHILE Condition DO
      BEGIN
        Statement;
        Statement;
        Statement
      END
  END;
```

Figure 4-14 Example of Procedure Declaration

used makes the parameter list necessary. Assume that the procedure is called two or more times. It performs the same way but operates on different items each time it's called. Somehow, the items must be given a general name in the procedure declaration and then the specific names substituted when the procedure is called and executed. The general names are provided in the parameter list and used within the procedure itself. *These names indicate the kinds of items that the procedure will handle.* Then, when the procedure is called, names of the same basic kinds of items are substituted for the generalized names and the procedure acts on the specific names. The generalized names are called the formal parameters and the specific names are called the actual parameters.

Let's illustrate how a procedure might be called several times to perform the same basic operation. In the declaration we have the procedure title and the formal parameter list:

PROCEDURE STUDENTAVG (COURSE: COURSEFILE; NOSTUDENTS: INTEGER);

When this procedure is called, the actual parameters are provided. A call, for example, could be:

STUDENTAVG (ENGLISH,24);

The procedure would then gain access to the course file for ENGLISH and perform the calculations for twenty-four students. Naturally, the next call would provide an actual parameter list with a different course title and number of students. When parameters are passed to a procedure in this manner (the actual value given), they are said to have been "passed by value."

There is also another way of organizing the parameter list. In this case, the names of variables will be given to the procedure when it's called. This requires that the parameters be shown to be variables in the parameter list. as shown below.

The declaration and formal parameter list:

PROCEDURE CALACCOUNTS (VAR A: INTEGER; VAR B: REAL);

The calls and actual parameter lists:

CALACCOUNTS (M,N);
CALACCOUNTS (X,Y);

In this case, the first call of the procedure substitutes M for A and N for B wherever A and B appear in the procedure. Naturally, the procedure acquires the value of M and N when it is executed. The second call says "substitute X and Y for A and B, respectively." When parameters are passed in this manner, they are said to have been "passed by reference."

Placing Procedures or Functions in a Parameter List

Not mentioned up to now is the fact that the parameter list may also include the names of procedures and functions that are to be passed to a procedure. This is a complex subject, but the principles are the same as those we just described.

A general name (the formal parameter) for the procedure or function can be used in the body of the procedure to show the position that the function or procedure call is to occupy. Then, when the procedure is called, the actual names to be used would be given. This is shown below.

The declaration and the formal parameter list:

PROCEDURE CALCULATE (PROCEDURE PROC2; FUNCTION FUNC1: INTEGER; VAR A,B:REAL);

The call and the actual parameter list:

CALCULATE (MOBAL,RATES17,X,Y);

Whenever the procedure call is issued, MOBAL is substituted for PROC2, RATES17 for FUNC1, X for A, and Y for B. Another call could then provide another list of actual parameters to be substituted for the formal ones. In this manner, a procedure can be used several times in a program or be transported to another program without being changed internally.

FUNCTIONS

By now, readers should understand what a standard function does and how it's used. Now we'll cover the declaration and creation of nonstandard functions—those that the programmer creates. Let's call them special functions for the purpose of this discussion.

The function declaration is the last entry in the declaration section. Like procedures, the function is not only named in the declaration, but all the statements comprising the function are actually written out.

Function declarations in Pascal are similar to the creation of customized functions in BASIC, although there are differences. A typical function declaration is shown in Figure 4-15. In the heading we have the word FUNCTION followed by the name assigned by the programmer. In general, the names are kept short. After the name we have the parameter list and the data type of each parameter. These are enclosed in parentheses and define the types of variables that the function will operate on when it is called.

We know that the names provided in the parameter list are called formal parameters and may not be the actual names given when the function is used. While an X might appear in the parameter list, the actual name of the variable could be GROSSPAY when the function is applied. Naturally, the actual parameter must be of the same nature as the formal parameter. If, for example, the formal parameter is an integer, so must the actual parameter be. Following the parameter list is a definition of the data type the function provides when it is executed.

Thus the heading is simple enough; it gives the name, the type of parameters the function will op-

SYNTAX OF HEADING

FUNCTION name (parameters and type) data type:

Example of Function

```
FUNCTION POWER (X: REAL; Y: INTEGER): REAL;
   VAR W,Z: REAL;
       I: INTEGER;
   BEGIN
      W:=X;
      Z:=1;
      I:=Y;
      WHILE I > 0 DO
         BEGIN
            IF ODD(I) THEN Z:=Z*W;
            I:=I DIV 2;
            W:=SQR(W)
         END;
      POWER:=Z
   END;
```

Figure 4-15 A Typical Function Declaration

erate on, and, finally, the type of data the function will return to the expression in which it is used.

Next we have the body of the function. It may consist of several statements, including declarations. Any such declarations are "local," meaning that they apply only to this function.

Within the body of the function, one of the statements prepares the value to be returned to the expression that called the function. We've shown it (POWER:=Z) last in our example, but it need not be last; it may appear in any position following the statements that produce the value.

SAMPLE PROGRAM—
ACCUMULATING EXPENSES

Earlier in this chapter we showed a section of a program to illustrate the appearance of a program written in Pascal (Figure 4-1). Now we'll examine how this program (Figure 4-16) operates. Its purpose is to accumulate expenses by the department to which they are charged and provide a total of the expenses charged to all departments. Several important features of Pascal are illustrated: loops, the CASE statement, indexing of an array, use of the SUCC function, entering information from the keyboard, and printing the program results. It also shows very clearly the advantages of user-defined data types.

Let's examine the overall organization before moving to a line-by-line analysis. After the program header, the declaration section occupies the next six lines. The main body starts with the BEGIN statement in the eighth line and concludes with the END statement in the last line.

Input data is shown in the left column near the bottom of Figure 4-17 and the printed results appear on the right side of the same figure.

Several parts of the declarations section in Figure 4-16 deserve special attention. First, the second line declares the value of a constant named ELEMENTS to be five. This value is used twice in the program. A TYPE declaration in the third line sets out a type named DEPARTMENT and then establishes that the departments are ADM, PROD, ENG, MKTG, QC, and ERR.

Three lines of variable declarations then appear. The fourth line is interesting. It sets up a one-dimensional array named EXPENSES, indexed by DEPARTMENT. This produces the array shown in

Figure 4-17, which is the area in which expenses will be accumulated.

Now let's analyze the main body. The ninth line sets the variable DEPT to a value of ADM and thus sets a starting point. Work will begin with the Administration Department.

Next we have a FOR loop. Its purpose is to clear the array EXPENSES to zeros. The index is a department, and the first index is ADM because line nine set DEPT to ADM. The ADM element is cleared first.

In this loop, we make use of ELEMENTS (which is a five), the ORD function, and the SUCC function. If five is greater than the ordinal of the current department (which is ADM and thus the ORD is 0), then the value of the DEPT is set to the successor of the current DEPT. Since ADM is current, PROD (Production) is its successor. After line thirteen is completed the first time, DEPT:=PROD.

The array is thus indexed by one department at a time and each element cleared. After being performed six times, the loop ends.

Another major section of the program, the data entry phase, now begins. It is dependent upon the WHILE statement, which waits for the EOF condition. This will not be present until the operator presses a certain key to indicate the entries are complete, so the entry phase continues as long as the operator sees fit. In our case, we have only eight entries, those in the input data list (Figure 4-17).

The READLN statement (Figure 4-16) acquires the department number and invoice amount, assigning them to variables DEPTNR and INVOICE, respectively. Certain department numbers are invalid, so if the number is greater than seven, it is changed to three and all invalid data is collected in one place.

Next, the CASE statement examines the department number (DEPTNR) and accumulates the amount of the invoice in the proper array element. Department 0 charges are added to ADM, 1 to PROD, 2 to ENG, etc. Invoices for departments above number 7 and for departments 3, 4, and 5 are all accumulated in the element that holds charges made to an invalid department number.

After the operator depresses the key that indicates entries are complete, EOF becomes true and the input loop is ended.

An assignment statement then clears the variable TOTAL by setting it to zero. Now the charges accumulated for all departments must be added. This is done by another FOR/DO loop.

```
PROGRAM EXPENSES(INPUT,OUTPUT);
CONST ELEMENTS=5;
TYPE DEPARTMENT=(ADM,PROD,ENG,MKTG,QC,ERR);
VAR EXPENSES: ARRAY[DEPARTMENT] OF REAL;
    DEPT: DEPARTMENT;
    INVOICE,TOTAL:  REAL;
    DEPTNR,I:  INTEGER;
BEGIN
DEPT:=ADM;
FOR I:=1 TO 6 DO
BEGIN
  EXPENSES[DEPT]:=0;
  IF ELEMENTS > ORD(DEPT) THEN DEPT:=SUCC(DEPT)
END;
WHILE NOT EOF DO
BEGIN
  READLN(DEPTNR,INVOICE);
  IF DEPTNR > 7 THEN DEPTNR:=3;
  CASE DEPTNR OF
     0         :EXPENSES[ADM]:=EXPENSES[ADM]+INVOICE;
     1         :EXPENSES[PROD]:=EXPENSES[PROD]+INVOICE;
     2         :EXPENSES[ENG]:=EXPENSES[ENG]+INVOICE;
     3,4,5     :EXPENSES[ERR]:=EXPENSES[ERR]+INVOICE;
     6         :EXPENSES[MKTG]:=EXPENSES[MKTG]+INVOICE;
     7         :EXPENSES[QC]:=EXPENSES[QC]+INVOICE
  END; (*CASE*)
END; (*WHILE NOT EOF*)
TOTAL:=0;
DEPT:=ADM;
FOR I:=1 TO 6 DO
BEGIN
  TOTAL:=TOTAL+EXPENSES[DEPT];
  IF ELEMENTS > ORD(DEPT) THEN DEPT:=SUCC(DEPT)
END; (*FOR I*)
WRITELN('EXPENSES' :16);
WRITELN('ADMINISTRATION: $' ,EXPENSES[ADM]:16:2);
WRITELN('PRODUCTION:      ' ,EXPENSES[PROD]:16:2);
WRITELN('ENGINEERING:     ' ,EXPENSES[ENG]:16:2);
WRITELN('MARKETING:       ' ,EXPENSES[MKTG]:16:2);
WRITELN('QUALITY CONTROL: ' ,EXPENSES[QC]:16:2);
WRITELN('DEPTNR ERROR:    ' ,EXPENSES[ERR]:16:2);
WRITELN('TOTALS:        $' ,TOTAL:16:2)
END.
```

Figure 4-16 The Expenses Program

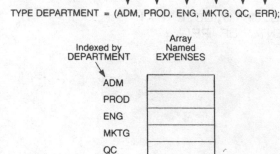

ORD 0 , 1 , 2 , 3 , 4 , 5

TYPE DEPARTMENT = (ADM, PROD, ENG, MKTG, QC, ERR);

Indexed by
DEPARTMENT

Array
Named
EXPENSES

ADM

PROD

ENG

MKTG

QC

ERR

INPUT DATA		THE REPORT	
DEPT NO.	INVOICE AMT.	EXPENSES:	
0	117.45	ADMINISTRATION: $	117.45
7	2100.98	PRODUCTION:	111.80
9	323.77	ENGINEERING:	554.65
1	56.80	MARKETING:	17185.50
1	55.00	QUALITY CONTROL:	2100.98
2	554.65	DEPTNR ERROR:	323.77
6	7300.00	TOTALS:	$ 20394.15
6	9885.50		

Figure 4-17 Data Associated with the Expenses
Program

First, however, the array index is restored to the first element, ADM. The FOR/DO loop then steps the index from one department to another. This is similar to the way in which the array was cleared earlier. This time, however, the contents of each array element are added to TOTAL, and after the program goes through all six elements, TOTAL is complete. The loop ends and the program moves on to the printing phase.

The WRITELN statements produce the report shown in Figure 4-17. Let's examine some of the instructions. First, a line titles the report 'EX-PENSES'; the 16 following 'EXPENSES' is minimum field size. Next, the word 'ADMINISTRA-TION' followed by a colon, spaces, and a dollar sign is enclosed in single quotation marks, so this line is printed exactly as it appears. Notice that the other departments and the TOTALS line are all the same size as ADMINISTRATION; the ending quote mark establishes this.

Following each department title, this program prints the amount accumulated. It does so by referencing the array EXPENSES and using the department (ADM, PROD, etc.) as an index to select a specific element. The contents of that element are acquired and printed by the WRITELN statements.

Minimum field size is specified as sixteen, and the number of decimal places as two. This aligns the amounts in the report.

The main body of the program concludes with the END statement. Note that it is the only END statement terminated by a period.

SELF-TEST FOR CHAPTER 4

1. Pascal programs have three major sections. The first is the program header. What are the other two?
2. What items may be declared in the declaration section?
3. In the left column below are the names of four declarations. Enter a number in the right column to show the order in which they must appear:

    Order

    CONST   _____

    VAR   _____

    LABEL   _____

    TYPE   _____

4. Which of the following are invalid identifiers, and why?
    a. 2-SECT
    b. JAM5
    c. EMPLOYEE
    d. LABEL 1
    e. **TOTAL
5. How are comments shown in Pascal?
6. What are the four standard simple data types?
7. List four of the structured data types described in this chapter.
8. One of the standard functions allowed for use with the integer data type is SQR (Square). What is the result of SQR(X) if X is 7?
9. Which of the following functions are arithmetic and which are character?
    ARCTAN, SUCC, PRED, ABS.
10. If A: = TRUNC(X); is evaluated and X is 2.975, what is the value of A?
11. Which of the following are not legal integers, and why?
    a. 17
    b. −579
    c. 3,475
    d. 5.75
12. Which of the following are not legal real numbers, and why?

a. 0.521

b. .5

c. +11.5

13. Operator precedence is extremely important. If an expression included the following operators, what is the order in which they would be applied?

$-$, ( ), +, and >

14. Evaluate A: = 4 + 2*3/5 using the proper precedence of Pascal operators.

15. Why couldn't the operator DIV be used in the above expression?

16. What does this statement do? WRITELN ('GOOD MORNING');

17. If you wanted to be able to add more words on the same line as GOOD MORNING, what changes would have to be made to this statement?

18. Write an assignment statement to average ENGLISH and MATH grades and name the result AVGRADE.

19. Write a declaration for the variables INTERESTRATE, PERCNTPAID, and BALDUE stating that they are real numbers.

20. Statements in Pascal may be either single or compound. What two reserved words must bound a compound statement?

21. Describe the basic difference between the WHILE/DO and the REPEAT/UNTIL repetitive loops.

22. Assume that the following TYPE declaration is used:

TYPE COLOR = (RED, BLUE, YELLOW);

Describe what each of the following functions will produce:

a. PRED (BLUE)

b. PRED (RED)

c. SUCC (BLUE)

d. ORD (RED)

e. ORD (BLUE)

23. Explain what each of the following statements do:

a. VAR J: INTEGER;

b. REWRITE (NEWFILE);

c. RESET (OLDFILE);

d. END.

e. (*PRINT CUSTOMER ACCOUNTS*)

f. WRITELN;

g. ITEM: = 5;

h. BEGIN

INITIALIZEACCOUNTS;

REVISEACCOUNTS

END.

i. COSTS[DEPT]: = lCOSTS[DEPT] + CHARGES;

24. Write statements to accomplish the following:

a. Create three blank lines on the display screen.

b. Display your name on the display screen and remain on the same line.

c. Declare DEDUCTIONS to be real, EMPNO to be integer, and JOBCODE to be character.

d. Select the first element in a one-dimensional array named EMPNO, read from the keyboard the employee number typed in, and place it in the array.

e. Add DEPOSIT to BALANCE.

f. Find the MONTHPAY (monthly payment) if AMTOWED is to be repaid over thirty-six months.

g. Create a fifty-element, one-dimensional array of integers. Name the array EXPENSES.

h. Determine whether applicant age APPAGE is above MINAGE (minimum age for job) and if so, display the message AGE OK.

5

COBOL
Common Business Oriented Language

INTRODUCTION

We've defined COBOL several times so far, but we'll do it again here for readers beginning at this chapter. *COmmon Business Oriented Language* are the words from which the acronym is derived. COBOL is one of the oldest major programming languages, so a review of its history is a good place to start our description.

As one would gather from its name, the primary use of COBOL is in business data processing. All major computer manufacturers offer it with their machines, and it is widely used. In general, BASIC is most popular with the very small machines and COBOL with medium and large business installations.

A committee called CODASYL, for *Conference on Data Systems Languages*, initiated the development of COBOL in 1959, and the first version, called COBOL-60, was published as a result of this committee's work. An ANSI version of COBOL appeared first in 1968, with a newer version in 1974. These are often referred to as ANS-68 COBOL and ANS-74 COBOL, respectively. The description in this chapter is based on the 1974 standard.

As one moves further into this chapter, one is certain to recognize that COBOL statements are very easy to read and understand. This is due to the fact that they are near English in their composition. It does, however, make for long statements when compared to those in BASIC and some of the other languages. This is a virtue of the language in two respects. First, it makes the transition from an English statement of the action to be performed to a COBOL statement fairly easy. Secondly, it makes the program easy to understand and thus reduces the need for a great deal of explanation.

The Four Divisions

Many reference books on the subject of COBOL begin by showing the four major divisions of a COBOL program, which are the identification, environment, data, and procedure divisions. We'll do the same but approach them in reverse order however, beginning with the procedure division.

Figure 5-1 shows the divisions and the sections that make them up. Although the procedure division appears last, it is, for all practical purposes, the program itself. It includes all the statements of what is to be done. Here is where the executable instructions are given by the programmer.

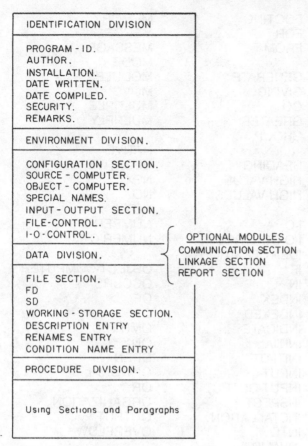

```
IDENTIFICATION  DIVISION

PROGRAM - ID.
AUTHOR.
INSTALLATION.
DATE WRITTEN.
DATE COMPILED.
SECURITY.
REMARKS.

ENVIRONMENT  DIVISION.

CONFIGURATION   SECTION.
SOURCE - COMPUTER.
OBJECT - COMPUTER.
SPECIAL  NAMES.
INPUT - OUTPUT  SECTION.
FILE - CONTROL.
I - O - CONTROL.

DATA   DIVISION.

FILE  SECTION.
FD
SD
WORKING - STORAGE  SECTION.
DESCRIPTION  ENTRY
RENAMES  ENTRY
CONDITION  NAME  ENTRY

PROCEDURE   DIVISION.


Using  Sections  and  Paragraphs
```

OPTIONAL MODULES
COMMUNICATION SECTION
LINKAGE SECTION
REPORT SECTION

Figure 5-1 The Four Divisions of a COBOL
Program

Coming just before the procedure division is the data division. It describes the data to be handled. Name, length, and value of fields, records, variables, and constants are given here. This is an extremely useful feature. COBOL was one of the first languages to provide such a separate data definition. This allows a programmer to find his data descriptions easily and simplifies changes.

Still working our way backward, we reach the environment division. This is the division intended to make a COBOL program transportable from one machine to another. It defines the characteristics of the surroundings in which the program must operate and, if all standards were rigidly enforced, would be the only division that needed to be changed when a COBOL program was moved from one data processing installation to another.

The environment division defines the types of computers involved in handling the program. What type accepted the source? What type will execute the object, and which files are assigned to the vari-

ous physical devices available? are questions answered in this division. The environment division has to be prepared each time a COBOL program is moved to a new "environment"; it is unique to every application.

At the top of each program but discussed last here is the identification division. We can assume that this part was included to help make a COBOL program self-documenting, for it includes nothing more than what a programmer often provides in remarks or comments with other languages. Program name, author, installation, date written, date compiled, security, and remarks make up the identification division. The remarks portion is unrestricted as to length, so the programmer may provide his program description here. The compiler treats the identification division entries as other languages treat comments; it stores them and prints them but otherwise ignores them. Only the program name is a required entry.

Reserved Words

The 1974 ANSI standard lists over 300 reserved words, which are shown in Figure 5-2. As we move through this chapter, we'll use many of them in our explanations, examples, and syntax diagrams. These words have a certain meaning to the COBOL compiler and must not be used in any other way. Some computer manufacturers have added to the list of reserved words used by their compilers, but we certainly have enough words to deal with in the ANSI list.

ORGANIZATION OF A PROGRAM

Before we examine each of the divisions of a COBOL program and the appearance of statements in them, it is necessary to understand the organization of the entries provided in each division. Overall, the scheme is:

DIVISION
SECTION
PARAGRAPH
SENTENCE

Sections, if they are necessary, are blocks within divisions. Paragraphs are blocks within sections, and sentences make up paragraphs. This is the basic hierarchy. We'll refine it division by division after discussing the coding form.

ACCEPT	DATA	FOOTING	MEMORY
ACCESS	DATE	FOR	MERGE
ADD	DATE-COMPILED	FROM	MESSAGE
ADVANCING	DATE-WRITTEN		MODE
AFTER	DAY	GENERATE	MODULES
ALL	DE	GIVING	MOVE
ALPHABETIC	DEBUG-CONTENTS	GO	MULTIPLE
ALSO	DEBUG-ITEM	GREATER	MULTIPLY
ALTER	DEBUG-LINE	GROUP	
ALTERNATE	DEBUG-NAME		NATIVE
AND	DEBUG-SUB-1	HEADING	NEGATIVE
ARE	DEBUG-SUB-2	HIGH-VALUE	NEXT
AREA	DEBUG-SUB-3	HIGH-VALUES	NO
AREAS	DEBUGGING		NOT
ASCENDING	DECIMAL-POINT	I-O	NUMBER
ASSIGN	DECLARATIVES	I-O-CONTROL	NUMERIC
AT	DELETE	IDENTIFICATION	
AUTHOR	DELIMITED	IF	OBJECT-COMPUTER
	DELIMITER	IN	OCCURS
BEFORE	DEPENDING	INDEX	OF
BLANK	DESCENDING	INDEXED	OFF
BLOCK	DESTINATION	INDICATE	OMITTED
BOTTOM	DETAIL	INITIAL	ON
BY	DISABLE	INITIATE	OPEN
	DISPLAY	INPUT	OPTIONAL
CALL	DIVIDE	INPUT-OUTPUT	OR
CANCEL	DIVISION	INSPECT	ORGANIZATION
CD	DOWN	INSTALLATION	OUTPUT
CF	DUPLICATES	INTO	OVERFLOW
CH	DYNAMIC	INVALID	
CHARACTER		IS	PAGE
CHARACTERS			PAGE-COUNTER
CLOCK-UNITS	EGI		PERFORM
CLOSE	ELSE	JUST	PF
COBOL	EMI	JUSTIFIED	PH
CODE	ENABLE		PIC
CODE-SET	END	KEY	PICTURE
COLLATING	END-OF-PAGE		PLUS
COLUMN	ENTER	LABEL	POINTER
COMMA	ENVIRONMENT	LAST	POSITION
COMMUNICATION	EOP	LEADING	POSITIVE
COMP	EQUAL	LEFT	PRINTING
COMPUTATIONAL	ERROR	LENGTH	PROCEDURE
COMPUTE	ESI	LESS	PROCEDURES
CONFIGURATION	EVERY	LIMIT	PROCEED
CONTAINS	EXCEPTION	LIMITS	PROGRAM
CONTROL	EXIT	LINAGE	PROGRAM-ID
CONTROLS	EXTEND	LINAGE-COUNTER	
		LINE	
COPY	FD	LINE-COUNTER	QUEUE
CORR	FILE	LINES	QUOTE
CORRESPONDING	FILE-CONTROL	LINKAGE	QUOTES
COUNT	FILLER	LOCK	
CURRENCY	FINAL	LOW-VALUE	
	FIRST	LOW-VALUES	

(Continued)

RANDOM	ROUNDED	START	UNIT
RD	RUN	STATUS	UNSTRING
READ		STOP	UNTIL
RECEIVE	SAME	STRING	UP
RECORD	SD	SUB-QUEUE-1	UPON
RECORDS	SEARCH	SUB-QUEUE-2	USAGE
REDEFINES	SECTION	SUB-QUEUE-3	USE
REEL	SECURITY	SUBTRACT	USING
REFERENCES	SEGMENT	SUM	
RELATIVE	SEGMENT-LIMIT	SUPPRESS	VALUE
RELEASE	SELECT	SYMBOLIC	VALUES
REMAINDER	SEND	SYNC	VARYING
REMOVAL	SENTENCE	SYNCHRONIZED	
RENAMES	SEPARATE		WHEN
REPLACING	SEQUENCE	TABLE	WITH
REPORT	SEQUENTIAL	TALLYING	WORDS
REPORTING	SET	TAPE	WORKING-STORAGE
REPORTS	SIGN	TERMINAL	WRITE
RERUN	SIZE	TERMINATE	
RESERVE	SORT	TEXT	ZERO
RESET	SORT-MERGE	THAN	ZEROES
RETURN	SOURCE	THROUGH	ZEROS
REVERSED	SOURCE-COMPUTER	THRU	
REWIND	SPACE	TIME	
REWRITE	SPACES	TIMES	
RF	SPECIAL-NAMES	TO	
RH	STANDARD	TOP	
RIGHT	STANDARD-1	TRAILING	
		TYPE	

Figure 5-2 COBOL Reserved Words

Coding Form

A sample coding form is shown in Figure 5-3. The heading material is similar to that for most systems and is eighty columns wide, also a common arrangement. Note that the contents of columns 1 through 3 remain the same for the entire page and are shown only in the upper left corner. The same is true for columns 73 through 80. They hold program identification and appear in the upper right.

Once we reach the body, however, the unique COBOL features appear. There are six positions provided for numbering the lines. The first three often provide the page number of the coding form and the second three (columns 4, 5, and 6) give the line number within a page. We have only twenty-five lines per page in our sample which, of course, need only two columns to number. The last position of each line number is normally left at zero, in the style: 030. This allows as many as nine elements to be inserted between line 030 and line 040 without having to renumber, a great convenience because insertion and removal of statements is normal during program development.

Column 7 provides some important information about the material on each line. Ordinarily, this column is blank, but if the line is only a comment, column 7 includes an asterisk (*). If the line begins with a continuation of a word from the previous line, column 7 contains a hyphen (-). This causes the word to continue without a space.

Next, in columns 8 through 72, we have the area that holds the COBOL statements. Area A occupies columns 8–11 and area B columns 12–72. Some types of entries must begin in area A and others in area B. When the divisions are discussed in detail, the use of the two areas will be explained.

The rest of the form is divided by vertical lines every four positions. (We've shown those up through column 24.) These lines provide guides for indentation schemes. Columns 73–80 provide space for additional information the programmer wishes to insert concerning program identification.

COBOL CODING FORM

PAGE 1 NO 0,0,3	PROGRAM						PAGE	OF	
	PROGRAMMER				DATE		IDENT.	73	80

LINE NO 4 6	7 8	12	16		40	72
01	0		ADD N-HOURS TO EMP-HOURS.			
02	0		ADD N-WAGE TO EMP-WAGE.			
03	0		MOVE EMP-NO- IN TO PREV-EMP.			
04	0		READ TIME-FILE, AT END MOVE 'EOF' TO EOF-FLAG.			
05						
06						
07						
08						
09						
10						
11						
12						
13						
14						
15						
16						
17						
18						
19						
20						
21						
22						
23						
24						
25						

Figure 5-3 The COBOL Coding Form

Relationship of Divisions to One Another

Now let's discuss the way in which the environment, data, and procedure divisions work together. One good way to show how the divisions are related is to use specific examples of files and data items. Two such examples are given in the following paragraphs.

Suppose a file of employee records, which is held on a disk, is to be updated by the program. Beginning in the FILE-CONTROL paragraph of the INPUT-OUTPUT SECTION in the environment division, the file name, EMPLOYEE-FILE, is assigned to the equipment holding the disk on which the file is stored. (Figure 5-4 shows the entry.) This establishes a connection between the COBOL program and specific equipment. Next, the basic organization of the file is stated, and the key is given. Now the compiler knows both the kind of equipment and the file characteristics involved.

In the data division, the file description (FD) paragraph of the FILE SECTION defines the contents of the file as to names and sizes of fields. The data record in the file is called EMP-RECORD, and it is made up of a series of fields. The compiler now knows the name, size, and type of elements the procedure division will be dealing with. Last in the data division is the WORKING-STORAGE SECTION; it also gives names of data items that the procedure division will be using.

Now we reach the procedure division itself, where actions to be taken appear. When we reach the EMP-UPDATE SECTION, the instructions to open and read the EMPLOYEE-FILE can be given. All links to the equipment and operating system have been defined. And, of course, the record size, field size, and data names have been established.

The second example, which is shown in Figure 5-5, is a simpler one. A data item named PAY-

```
ENVIRONMENT DIVISION.
        .
        .
        .
INPUT-OUTPUT SECTION.
FILE-CONTROL.
    SELECT EMPLOYEE-FILE
    ASSIGN TO System Name              Defines the file and
    ORGANIZATION IS INDEXED            its organization.
    ACCESS MODE IS RANDOM
    RECORD KEY IS EMP-NMBR.
        .
        .
        .

DATA DIVISION.
FILE SECTION.
FD EMPLOYEE-FILE
    LABEL RECORDS ARE OMITTED
    DATA RECORD IS EMP-RECORD.
01  EMP-RECORD.
    05  EMP-NMBR              PIC X(5).    Defines the organization
        .                                 of a record in the file.
        .
        .
    05  EMP-NAME              PIC X(20).
WORKING-STORAGE SECTION.
        .
        .
        .
PROCEDURE DIVISION.
        .
        .
        .
B000-EMP-UPDATE SECTION.
    OPEN INPUT EMPLOYEE-FILE.               Reads a record
    READ EMPLOYEE-FILE KEY IS EMP-NMBR.     from the file.
```

Figure 5-4 First Example of the Relationship Between Divisions

```
DATA DIVISION.
FILE SECTION.
        .
        .
        .
WORKING-STORAGE SECTION.
77   PAY-RATE                        PIC 99V99.  } Defines an
                                                  } — Independent
                                                  }   Data Item.
        .
        .
        .
PROCEDURE DIVISION.
        .
        .
        .
   READ EMPLOYEE-FILE KEY IS EMP-NMBR.
        .
        .
        .
   MULTIPLY HRS-WKD BY PAY-RATE GIVING GRS-PAY.  } Uses the
                                                  } — Independent
        .                                         }   Data Item.
        .
        .
```

Figure 5-5 Second Example of the Relationship Between Divisions

RATE will be used in the program. It is named and its size given in the WORKING-STORAGE SECTION of the data division. (A value could also be established here.) The procedure division can now use this data item, but will have to provide a value for PAY-RATE.

THE IDENTIFICATION DIVISION

The purpose of this division is to name the program, describe its origin, and, if the programmer chooses, give a statement of its purpose. Only the PROGRAM-ID paragraph is mandatory; the others are optional.

All paragraph titles begin at margin A, are hyphenated as shown in Figure 5-1, and are followed by a period. The program name must begin with a letter and conform to the naming rules; some systems allow only eight characters in the name. A period follows the program name.

The optional paragraphs and their contents may appear in any order. Since the compiler does not check the contents of the entries, the programmer is free to use them as comments.

THE ENVIRONMENT DIVISION

This is the division that adapts the data and procedure divisions to a specific computer and, theoretically, is the only division that would change when a COBOL program is moved from one type of computer to another. It consists of two sections: (1) the CONFIGURATION SECTION and (2) the INPUT-OUTPUT SECTION.

The CONFIGURATION SECTION includes only two standard paragraphs, one naming the computer on which the program is compiled, the source computer, and the second naming the computer on which the program will be run, the object computer. Although these are normally the same, it is possible for them to be different.

The second section is far more important. Called the INPUT-OUTPUT SECTION, it relates the data files used by the program to the equipment available at a specific installation, and it defines the characteristics of those files to the system. It also provides certain instructions regarding the use of the input-output equipment.

There are two paragraphs in the INPUT-OUTPUT SECTION. The first is the FILE-CONTROL paragraph. Through a series of entries that take the form: SELECT file-name ASSIGN TO device-name, the FILE-CONTROL paragraph links a file to equipment. Following each assignment are entries concerning the organization of the file, its access mode, and the name of the file key (if one is used). This information is required by the computer's operating system in order to manage the files properly.

The second paragraph in the INPUT-OUTPUT SECTION is called the I-O-CONTROL paragraph, and it is optional. Certain features and operations unique to the application can be specified in this paragraph.

THE DATA DIVISION

Provided in the data division are the names and descriptions of the files, records, fields, data groups, and data items the program will be using. Two sections are required. A FILE SECTION identifies files and records and gives the name and description of items within the records. The second section is called the WORKING-STORAGE SECTION; it names and describes data groups and individual data items that are used with the program but which are not described in the file section.

Three other sections are available in the data division: a COMMUNICATION SECTION, a LINKAGE SECTION, and a REPORT SECTION. Each has a special use. The COMMUNICATION SECTION is concerned with telecommunication messages, the LINKAGE SECTION is used to pass information between programs, and the REPORT SECTION is used with the report writer module of COBOL. We'll confine our discussion to the two sections that are likely to be of most interest to the reader, the FILE and the WORKING-STORAGE sections.

Naming Data

Early in the process of learning a new programming language, a programmer must become familiar with the rules governing the way in which data is identified and described to the system. In COBOL, data is defined and described in the data division. The naming rules are simple and easy to apply:

a. Each name must be unique.
b. Reserved words must not be used.
c. Names may be up to thirty characters long.
d. The first character must be a letter or a number.
e. Other characters must be letters or numbers, with one exception: a hyphen may be used.
f. Blanks must not be used, and the last character in the name must not be a hyphen.

Describing Data

COBOL uses an interesting way to describe a data item. A reserved word PICTURE, or PIC, follows the name of the item to describe its size and contents. PIC X(80), for example, says that this item is eighty positions in length and that it holds alphanumeric data, which is indicated by the X.

There are two other code characters for data types, A and 9. Thus, we have the following codes for the type of data that may appear in a data item:

A Alphabetic. Only letters A–Z and blanks may appear.
X Alphanumeric. Any valid character may appear. This includes letters, numbers, and punctuation.
9 Numeric. Only numbers may appear in this data item.

The A and X codes are followed by a number in parentheses, like the PIC X(80) we showed above. On the other hand, the code 9 for numeric may be shown in either of two ways: A 9 followed by the same parentheses-style definition of size, or a series of 9s written out one after another. Each 9 in the series represents one position that the number may have.

The number in parentheses is called the repetition factor. It tells the compiler how many spaces to provide for a specific data item.

Relationship of Data Items

Now that the rules concerning names and descriptions have been discussed, the next step is to examine how the relationship of one data item to another is shown. COBOL uses level numbers to indicate these relationships. There are five possibilities:

Level No.	Meaning
01	A data group, most often a record, including fields or other subdivisions
02–49	Fields within a record or subdivisions within a data group
77	An independent data item
66	Used with RENAMES
88	Condition names

Since 66 and 88 are related to rather specialized uses, we'll skip them and concentrate on the frequently used codes. Let's begin this discussion with the level number 77, an independent data item.

An independent data item is one of the items that the program uses but: (1) is not part of a data group or (2) is not known by the same name if it is part of a group or record. Two independent data items are shown in Figure 5-6. The level code for the independent data item appears in area A and the name and description in area B.

```
Col. 8    12


   77  PREV-ORD-NUM        PIC 9(5).
   77  VALUE-SOLD          PIC S99V99.
```

Figure 5-6 Examples of Independent Data Items

Next we'll look at the description of fields and records and show how level numbers are used to indicate what fields make up a record. A simple record is shown in Figure 5-7. It holds all the information related to a specific part held in stock by an auto dealer and is called a part record. It begins with part number, and includes part description, cost, and number in stock. (This same style is used to show the organization of other data groups as well.) Where the word FILLER is shown, that section of the record is usually set to blanks by the programmer.

Notice that the level number 01 begins in column

```
Col. 8    12

   01  PART-RECORD.
       03  PART-NUMBER         PIC X(7).
       03  FILLER              PIC X(2).
       03  DESCRIPTION         PIC X(24).
       03  FILLER              PIC X(6).
       03  COST                PIC 99V99.
       03  FILLER              PIC X(2).
       03  NUM-IN-STOCK        PIC 999.
```

Figure 5-7 Example of a Record Description

8, while the level number 03, identifying a field, begins in column 12. If further subdivision of the fields was necessary, continued indentation and level numbers would be used.

Setting the Beginning Value

In some cases, it is necessary to establish the initial value of a data item defined in the data division so that the program will begin with a known quantity. Constants must, of course, be set to a value, and other items may be as well. This is done by the VALUE clause, VALUE being one of the reserved words.

Immediately following the PIC definition of the data item, a VALUE clause is inserted in the form PIC X(80) VALUE . . . The reserved word SPACES can be used. VALUE SPACES, for example, produces a field of blanks. Another form VALUE'—' also produces a blank field. Whatever information appears within the quotation marks following VALUE becomes the initial value of the related data item. The quotation marks are used only with alphabetic data (A) and alphanumeric data (X). Pure numbers, data type 9, do not use quotation marks. A data item TOTAL-AMT PIC 999V99, for example, would be given an initial value in the form: TOTAL-AMT PIC 999V99 VALUE 43.75. (Note that the VALUE clause is used in the WORKING-STORAGE SECTION, not the FILE SECTION.)

Organizing Numeric Data

We mentioned earlier that the code 9 following PICTURE or PIC indicates that the data item is a number. EMP-NUM PIC 9999, for example, says that the data item EMP-NUM is a four-position number.

Now we must consider decimal point position, signs, and punctuation as well. First, the decimal point position is shown by a V, in the form: TOTAL-AMT PIC 999V99. This statement says that there are three positions to the left of the decimal point and two to the right. If the number is a large one, the repetition factor style can be used. TOTAL-AMT PIC 9(5)V9(3) says there are five positions to the left and three to the right of the decimal point.

Next, the sign (+ or −) of the number is important in many cases. Unless there is an indicator placed with the PICTURE clause, no sign can be used. The indicator is an S, and it precedes the first 9, in the form: TOTAL-AMT PIC S999V99.

Editing Data for Display or Printing

Whenever numbers held within the computer are displayed or printed, they must appear in the form that humans are accustomed to reading. For example, 003445655 should be read $34,456.55 when it appears in a report. This requires that a dollar sign be added, the zeros on the left be eliminated, a comma inserted, and a decimal point inserted. Of course, the computer must be told what to do, and this is also done by a PICTURE clause.

Assume that there is a data item named PRICE which has a PICTURE 99V99, meaning a number with two positions on each side of the decimal point. The actual value of PRICE is 3550. Thus, the number must be converted to a readable form before it is printed. This is done by a PICTURE clause, $99.99, provided for this field in the printed line. Thus, when 3550 is moved to the print line field, it becomes $35.50, and this is what is actually printed in the report.

COBOL has a wide variety of editing possibilities. Let's examine one more before moving on.

Assume that a very large number may exist within the computer. To print it we could provide a PICTURE clause: PIC $$$$,$$9.99. The currency sign is floating, suppressing zeros down to the last integer position, and a comma is inserted for thousands. Of course, the comma is not inserted if the zero suppression makes it unnecessary. If 57695401 was moved into this field, it would appear $576,954.01. On the other hand, 00000059 would appear $0.59.

COBOL SYNTAX DIAGRAMS

Nearly all programming languages use some type of diagram to explain the construction of their source statements. If a reader has gone through earlier chapters, he knows why syntax diagrams are necessary. For those beginning here in Chapter 5, we'll provide a brief introduction to the subject.

Source statements in most languages may take a variety of forms, depending on their specific use.

It's very difficult to provide examples of every possibility because the more complex statements may have a great many combinations. In addition, the meaning of specific examples might be misunderstood. Therefore, a "possibilities diagram" using generic rather than specific names is prepared, and the diagram uses certain symbols to illustrate all valid arrangements of the words and names that form a statement.

Syntax diagrams are available for all four divisions, but we're concerned with those for the statements in the procedure division. A typical diagram is the one used for the ADD statement, which is shown in Figure 5-8. Let's begin our explanation by examining words. Those capitalized and underlined in the form ADD, TO, ROUNDED, and SIZE ERROR are mandatory if the feature they represent is to be used. The ROUNDED phrase is an option, as is the SIZE ERROR phrase. Other capitalized words also appear in the syntax diagrams but are not underlined. These words may be added to make a sentence more readable if the programmer wishes, but they are not mandatory. ON is an example of such a word.

Now to the lowercase words. These are the generic terms describing what the programmer may place in the positions the words occupy in the syntax diagram. In our ADD statement, the term "literal" means a number may be placed there, 187 perhaps. On the other hand, the term "identifier" means that the name of a data item, perhaps FICA-DED, may occupy this position. Of course, the number that this data item holds is used when the arithmetic is done.

Next to be examined are the symbols involved in the diagram. The square brackets indicate that the feature is optional. The ROUNDED phrase, for example, can be left out and yet the statement will be executed. When brackets appear within other brackets, it means that the feature shown by the outer brackets is optional but, if it is used, the feature within the inner brackets is again optional.

Braces on the other hand indicate that a choice must be made among the items offered. In our ADD statement, the first number following the word ADD must be provided, but the braces show that the number may be provided in literal form *or* a data item named.

The three periods (. . .) are called the ellipsis points. They show that the previous option may be repeated as many times as the programmer sees fit.

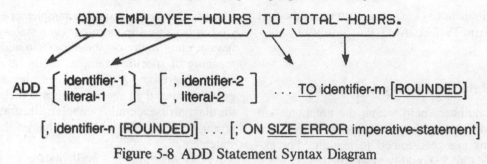

Figure 5-8 ADD Statement Syntax Diagram

In the ADD example, we have shown that one number must follow ADD and that a second may. The ellipsis points show that a third, fourth, fifth, etc. number may also be included.

Except for the period shown at the end of the ADD sentence, the punctuation marks are optional. They are included only to make the sentence more readable.

THE PROCEDURE DIVISION

This is the division in which the programmer provides the executable statements that carry out the functions the program is to perform. It has no preassigned section or paragraph names, requiring only that the division name be given at the beginning of the coding, in the form: PROCEDURE DIVISION.

The programmer is therefore free to organize the body of the procedure division as he sees fit. Let's examine first the basic component available, the COBOL sentence. The sentence consists of one or more statements and is terminated with a period. A simple sentence would consist of a single statement, but a complex sentence may include several statements. As we'll see when we examine the functions performed by each statement, nearly all statements begin with a verb. ACCEPT, CALL, DIVIDE, MOVE, SEARCH, and WRITE are examples.

In very simple programs, the sentences may follow immediately after the PROCEDURE DIVISION heading, and no further organization is necessary. Of course, most programs are not simple, consisting of hundreds of statements. This makes it desirable to group sentences into paragraphs or sections and identify them by the function they collectively perform.

Paragraphs are given names that conform to the general naming rules. They may be up to thirty characters long, and they begin in area A of the coding form.

If necessary, sections named by the programmer can be introduced in the procedure division. Section names, too, conform to the naming rules, can be a maximum of thirty characters, and must begin in area A. The word SECTION is appended to the name constructed by the programmer.

When a paragraph heading is provided for a group of sentences, it allows the program to handle that group as a unit, a procedure. The PERFORM statement can then select paragraphs or sections to be executed in their entirety. PERFORM *paragraph or section name,* for example, causes all the statements in the group named to be executed; then the program resumes with the sentence following the PERFORM statement.

To summarize the organization of the procedure division: Only the name PROCEDURE DIVISION is mandatory. If further organization is necessary, the hierarchy is:

> SECTION
> > Paragraph
> > > Sentence
> > > > Statement

STATEMENTS THAT PERFORM ARITHMETIC

There are five COBOL statements that perform arithmetic: ADD, SUBTRACT, MULTIPLY, DIVIDE, and COMPUTE. The first four are the equivalent of the arithmetic operator symbols (+ ,

−, *, and /) that we discussed in BASIC and Pascal. In COBOL, however, the operation can be written out, in the form: ADD A TO B or SUBTRACT A FROM B.

On the other hand, the COMPUTE statement uses the operator symbols just as BASIC and Pascal do, and the symbols available are very similar. If the reader is familiar with the way in which BASIC and Pascal do arithmetic, he should find the COMPUTE statement very easy to use.

Although the ADD, SUBTRACT, MULTIPLY, and DIVIDE statements are themselves simple, there are several variations available. (Typical syntax diagrams appear in Figure 5-9.) One good way to illustrate how they perform is to provide some examples of statements and show the results that they produce. In order to make the examples realistic, we'll use identifiers (names) for our data items that the reader may encounter in everyday use.

The ADD Statement

There are two basic forms of the ADD statement. Both allow use of the ROUNDED phrase and ON SIZE ERROR phrase. The ROUNDED phrase causes the result (the sum in the case of addition) to be rounded off. If, for example, the result had three positions to the right of the decimal point but the field into which the result was placed had only two, the result is rounded to two positions.

The ON SIZE ERROR phrase is followed by a statement of what to do if a size error results from the ADD statement. While the ROUNDED phrase applies to only decimal places (positions to the right of the point), the ON SIZE ERROR phrase applies to the integer part. Suppose the receiving field had four positions—perhaps a maximum number of 9999.99—but the result of an addition produced a value of 23597.23. This amount cannot be moved into the receiving field with meaningful results, thus a size error has occurred. The statement following the ON SIZE ERROR phrase would, in this case, cause a branch to some type of error recovery routine in which the operator is warned about the invalid operation.

Now we can examine the GIVING phrase. It states where the result is to be placed. Without the GIVING phrase, the result is placed in one of the fields involved in the addition operation. With the GIVING phrase, the result is placed in the field (or fields) specified by the GIVING phrase.

Below are some examples of the ADD statement. Note that additional punctuation could have been included in the positions shown by the syntax diagrams.

ADD DEPOSIT TO BAL.
  The amount of DEPOSIT is added to BAL and the result appears in BAL.
ADD DEP-1, DEP-2, DEP-3, to BAL.
  Three deposits are added to BAL and the result appears in BAL.
ADD TAX TO COST ROUNDED.
  TAX is added to COST. Result is rounded, then placed in COST.
ADD TAX TO COST GIVING TOTAL.
  TAX is added to COST and the result is placed in TOTAL.
ADD OTIME TO BASERT GIVING GROSSPAY ON SIZE ERROR GO TO . . .
  Overtime is added to the base rate. If the resulting gross pay is greater than the maximum number that the GROSSPAY field can hold, go to an error routine.

The SUBTRACT Statement

The SUBTRACT statement is also easy to use, and it has the two basic forms—one without the GIVING phrase and one with it. Both the ROUNDED and ON SIZE ERROR phrases may be used. Examples follow:

SUBTRACT CHECK-1 FROM BAL.
  The amount of CHECK-1 is subtracted from BAL and the difference appears in BAL.
SUBTRACT CHECK-1, CHECK-2, CHECK-3, FROM BAL.
  All three checks are subtracted from BAL and the final result appears in BAL.
SUBTRACT COST FROM PRICE GIVING PROFIT.
  COST is subtracted from PRICE and the difference placed in PROFIT.

The MULTIPLY Statement

Again we have a simple statement that may or may not use the GIVING phrase, and both the ROUNDED and ON SIZE ERROR phrases are available. Of course, these two phrases are more likely to be used in the MULTIPLY statement than they are in ADD and SUBTRACT because the mul-

ADD $\begin{Bmatrix} \text{identifier-1} \\ \text{literal-1} \end{Bmatrix}$ $\begin{bmatrix} \text{, identifier-2} \\ \text{, literal-2} \end{bmatrix}$ ... TO identifier-m [ROUNDED]

[, identifier-n [ROUNDED]] ... [; ON SIZE ERROR imperative-statement]

ADD $\begin{Bmatrix} \text{identifier-1} \\ \text{literal-1} \end{Bmatrix}$, $\begin{Bmatrix} \text{identifier-2} \\ \text{literal-2} \end{Bmatrix}$ $\begin{bmatrix} \text{, identifier-3} \\ \text{, literal-3} \end{bmatrix}$ ...

GIVING identifier-m [ROUNDED] [, identifier-n [ROUNDED]] ...

[; ON SIZE ERROR imperative-statement]

ADD $\begin{Bmatrix} \text{CORRESPONDING} \\ \text{CORR} \end{Bmatrix}$ identifier-1 TO identifier-2 [ROUNDED]

[; ON SIZE ERROR imperative-statement]

COMPUTE identifier-1 [ROUNDED] [, identifier-2 [ROUNDED]] ...

= arithmetic-expression [; ON SIZE ERROR imperative-statement]

DIVIDE $\begin{Bmatrix} \text{identifier-1} \\ \text{literal-1} \end{Bmatrix}$ INTO identifier-2 [ROUNDED]

[, identifier-3 [ROUNDED]] ... [; ON SIZE ERROR imperative-statement]

DIVIDE $\begin{Bmatrix} \text{identifier-1} \\ \text{literal-1} \end{Bmatrix}$ INTO $\begin{Bmatrix} \text{identifier-2} \\ \text{literal-2} \end{Bmatrix}$ GIVING identifier-3 [ROUNDED]

[, identifier-4 [ROUNDED]] ... [; ON SIZE ERROR imperative-statement]

DIVIDE $\begin{Bmatrix} \text{identifier-1} \\ \text{literal-1} \end{Bmatrix}$ BY $\begin{Bmatrix} \text{identifier-2} \\ \text{literal-2} \end{Bmatrix}$ GIVING identifier-3 [ROUNDED]

[, identifier-4 [ROUNDED]] ... [; ON SIZE ERROR imperative-statement]

DIVIDE $\begin{Bmatrix} \text{identifier-1} \\ \text{literal-1} \end{Bmatrix}$ INTO $\begin{Bmatrix} \text{identifier-2} \\ \text{literal-2} \end{Bmatrix}$ GIVING identifier-3 [ROUNDED]

REMAINDER identifier-4 [; ON SIZE ERROR imperative-statement]

DIVIDE $\begin{Bmatrix} \text{identifier-1} \\ \text{literal-1} \end{Bmatrix}$ BY $\begin{Bmatrix} \text{identifier-2} \\ \text{literal-2} \end{Bmatrix}$ GIVING identifier-3 [ROUNDED]

REMAINDER identifier-4 [; ON SIZE ERROR imperative-statement]

(Continued)

MULTIPLY $\left\{\begin{array}{l}\text{identifier-1}\\\text{literal-1}\end{array}\right\}$ BY identifier-2 [ROUNDED]

[, identifier-3 [ROUNDED]] . . . [; ON SIZE ERROR imperative-statement]

MULTIPLY $\left\{\begin{array}{l}\text{identifier-1}\\\text{literal-1}\end{array}\right\}$ BY $\left\{\begin{array}{l}\text{identifier-2}\\\text{literal-2}\end{array}\right\}$ GIVING identifier-3 [ROUNDED]

[, identifier-4 [ROUNDED]] . . . [; ON SIZE ERROR imperative-statement]

SUBTRACT $\left\{\begin{array}{l}\text{identifier-1}\\\text{literal-1}\end{array}\right\}$ $\left[\begin{array}{l}\text{, identifier-2}\\\text{, literal-2}\end{array}\right]$ . . . FROM identifier-m [ROUNDED]

[, identifier-n [ROUNDED]] . . . [; ON SIZE ERROR imperative-statement]

SUBTRACT $\left\{\begin{array}{l}\text{identifier-1}\\\text{literal-1}\end{array}\right\}$ $\left[\begin{array}{l}\text{, identifier-2}\\\text{, literal-2}\end{array}\right]$ . . . FROM $\left\{\begin{array}{l}\text{identifier-m}\\\text{literal-m}\end{array}\right\}$

GIVING identifier-n [ROUNDED] [, identifier-o [ROUNDED]] . . .

[; ON SIZE ERROR imperative-statement]

SUBTRACT $\left\{\begin{array}{l}\text{CORRESPONDING}\\\text{CORR}\end{array}\right\}$ identifier-1 FROM identifier-2 [ROUNDED]

[; ON SIZE ERROR imperative-statement]

Figure 5-9 Statements That Perform Arithmetic

tiplication operation is more likely to produce results that need rounding and size checking.

The GIVING phrase would normally be used in the MULTIPLY statement. Otherwise, the product would be placed in the field used as the multiplier. We'll see that in the examples below.

MULTIPLY A BY B.
A is multiplied by B, *and the product is placed in B.*
MULTIPLY BASERT BY HRSWKD GIVING GROSSPAY ROUNDED ON SIZE ERROR GO TO . . .
The base rate of pay is multiplied by the number of hours worked and the product placed in GROSSPAY. Decimal places are rounded off (probably to two) and the total size of the product is checked to make sure it doesn't exceed the size of the GROSSPAY field. If it does, the program goes to an error routine.

The DIVIDE Statement

Last in the series of simple arithmetic statements is the DIVIDE statement. It allows use of the ROUNDED phrase, the ON SIZE ERROR phrase, and the GIVING phrase. It, like the MULTIPLY statement, is likely to use these options in many cases.

Another phrase, called REMAINDER, appears for the first time in the DIVIDE statement. As the reader knows, a remainder may be significant in many cases and therefore must be saved. This is the purpose of the REMAINDER phrase. As the syntax diagram shows, the REMAINDER phrase is used only in DIVIDE statements also using the GIVING phrase, and it must follow the ROUNDED phrase if that phrase is also used.

Now to the specific use of the REMAINDER phrase; *it names the remainder,* nothing more. Once the remainder is named, of course, it can be handled by other steps in the program as the programmer sees fit.

Some examples of the DIVIDE statement follow. Note that two keywords, BY and INTO, are available in the form using the GIVING phrase but only the word INTO is available for the simple form of the statement.

DIVIDE A INTO B.
The value of A is the divisor, B is the dividend, and the result (quotient) is placed in B.
DIVIDE A INTO B GIVING C.
A is divided into B but the quotient is placed in C, leaving B unchanged.
DIVIDE A BY B GIVING C.
In this case, B is the divisor, A the dividend, and C receives the quotient. Neither A or B are changed.
DIVIDE TOTAL-SALES BY NMSLMN GIVING AVGSALES ROUNDED.
The total sales of the company are divided by the number of salesmen employed, giving the average amount sold per salesman. If the remainder was significant, which it would not be in this case, the REMAINDER phrase could follow the word ROUNDED in the form: REMAINDER SALES-LEFT. This says that the value remaining is to be named SALES-LEFT.

The COMPUTE Statement

This is the most powerful arithmetic statement and is used when complex arithmetic must be done. Many programmers would prefer the COMPUTE statement because it allows the operations to be condensed into one statement rather than written out as individual statements. Of course, this makes the coding somewhat harder to read and understand.

Two phrases are available for use in the COMPUTE statement: ROUNDED and ON SIZE ERROR. The GIVING phrase is not available because it is not needed. This is illustrated in the syntax diagram, which is shown in Figure 5-9. Notice that the results of the COMPUTE statement are placed in the data item, whose name immediately follows the verb COMPUTE. Thus, the variable is already named and the GIVING phrase has no application.

Next, we'll examine the body of the COMPUTE statement. The operator symbols and the data items

named are combined to form an expression, and the COMPUTE statement causes the expression to be evaluated and the result produced. Any valid data name may be used, and the five operators mentioned earlier ($-$, $+$, $*$, $/$, and $**$) cause specific arithmetic functions to be performed. Parentheses may also be used to enclose data items and operators that must be treated as a unit. And parentheses within parentheses are permitted.

Because the COMPUTE statement evaluates expressions very much like BASIC and Pascal, we've provided only two examples of COBOL COMPUTE statements. Readers interested in how to write expressions for evaluation should refer to Chapter 1 where the general rules that apply to all three major languages appear.

One rule that might be overlooked is worth mentioning here. Unlike some languages, COBOL operator symbols must have at least one space *before and after* each operator.

Now to the examples of the COMPUTE statement. Since these statements are fairly long and complex, we've followed the common style of writing the basic statement on one line and then indenting the expression itself by four spaces on the following line. Examples are:

COMPUTE FINAL-GRADE-AVG ROUNDED =
 (MATH-GRD + ENG-GRD + PE-GRD
 + TYPING-GRD) / NUM-COURSES.

COMPUTE TRIANGLE-AREA =
 BASE * HEIGHT / 2.

THE ACCEPT AND DISPLAY STATEMENTS

The display screen and keyboard are used very often to provide data to the computer and for the computer to provide information and instructions to the operator. Although the computer terminal is now the most common input-output device for interaction between the computer and operator, older installations may still use a card reader for operator inputs and a printer to provide messages from the computer to the operator. For low-volume inputs and outputs, the ACCEPT statement is intended to acquire the input and the DISPLAY statement to provide the output. High-volume devices are usually handled by the READ and WRITE statements.

```
ACCEPT identifier [FROM mnemonic-name]

                             ⎧ DATE ⎫
ACCEPT identifier FROM     ─⎨ DAY  ⎬
                             ⎩ TIME ⎭


          ⎧ identifier-1 ⎫   ⎡ , identifier-2 ⎤
DISPLAY  ⎨              ⎬   ⎢              ⎥  . . . [UPON mnemonic-name]
          ⎩ literal-1    ⎭   ⎣ , literal-2    ⎦
```

Figure 5-10 The ACCEPT and DISPLAY Statements

Syntax diagrams in Figure 5-10 show the formats of the ACCEPT and DISPLAY statements, and it is clear that they are very similar. The identifier portion is one of those data items defined in the data division and, of course, the literal is the actual information to be displayed.

Often, a DISPLAY statement gives instructions to an operator and an ACCEPT statement acquires the material that the operator provides. For example:

DISPLAY 'ENTER EMPLOYEE NAME'.
ACCEPT EMPLOYEE-NAME.

In this case, the DISPLAY statement provides a literal, the instruction ENTER EMPLOYEE NAME. The operator types in a specific name and the ACCEPT statement takes it, assigning it to the data item entitled EMPLOYEE-NAME. If a DISPLAY statement was now given: DISPLAY EMPLOYEE-NAME., the name that the operator just typed in would be returned to the screen and displayed.

To summarize: The ACCEPT statement takes an input and assigns it to a named data item; the DISPLAY statement may show either a literal (the actual words or numbers given in a statement) or the current contents of a named data item.

THE MOVE STATEMENT

The purpose of this statement is very easy to understand; it *places information in a specific data item*. When we use the term information in this case, it means either a literal or the contents of a data item.

Simplicity of the MOVE statement construction is shown in the syntax diagram in Figure 5-11. If a literal is to be placed in a specific field, that literal is provided in the MOVE statement itself. On the other hand, if the contents of a data item are to be moved, the name of that item appears in the statement.

The data item into which information is to be placed is called the receiving field. More than one receiving field may be named in a MOVE statement. Logically then, the data item from which information is being taken is called the sending field. After the statement is executed the sending field is unchanged but previous contents of the receiving field have been replaced.

A feature called the CORRESPONDING (or CORR) phrase makes it possible to move several data items with only one MOVE statement. Although it takes the same amount of time within the computer, it does make the coding simpler. CORRESPONDING means that there is a group of sending fields that have the same names as the receiving fields. The sending and receiving fields are in different records. Thus, the CORRESPONDING phrase gives the record names, and the fields with the same names are automatically moved.

```
        ⎧ identifier-1 ⎫
MOVE   ⎨             ⎬    TO identifier-2 [, identifier-3] . . .
        ⎩ literal      ⎭

        ⎧ CORRESPONDING ⎫
MOVE   ⎨               ⎬   identifier-1 TO identifier-2
        ⎩ CORR          ⎭
```

Figure 5-11 The MOVE Statement

Branches, Conditions, and Loops

COBOL has a family of statements that test conditions, take branches, and cause loops to be performed. Many of them will be familiar to readers who have completed the BASIC and Pascal chapters. Included in the statements we'll cover in this section are:

GO TO . . . and GO TO . . . DEPENDING
    ON . . .
IF . . . ELSE . . .
PERFORM . . .
PERFORM . . . THRU . . .
PERFORM . . . THRU . . . TIMES
PERFORM . . . THRU . . . UNTIL . . .

After first discussing the relational and logical operators, we'll divide this section into three parts, covering first the IF statement, then the GO TO statement, and finally, since it has the most complex construction, the PERFORM statement.

Relational Operators

As in arithmetic operators, COBOL offers the choice between words and symbols for the relational operators. Six relationships can be tested: equal, not equal, greater than, less than, not greater than, and not less than. While Pascal and BASIC required the programmer to state the relationship in symbols, COBOL provides both the symbols and the words that may be substituted for the symbols, as follows:

Word Form	*Symbol Form*
IS GREATER THAN	>
IS NOT GREATER THAN	NOT >
IS LESS THAN	<
IS NOT LESS THAN	NOT <
IS EQUAL TO	=
IS NOT EQUAL TO	NOT =

The word IS may or may not be used, depending on the programmer's preference. It does make a sentence somewhat easier to read, however.

Logical Operators

AND, OR, and NOT were applied in BASIC, where they're called logical operators, and in Pascal, where the term used is Boolean operators. These same three operators are available in COBOL, but here AND and OR are also referred to as "logical connectors." Of course they serve the same purpose as in other languages: to establish complex relationships to be evaluated. Let's examine two examples of statements using the logical connectors. The first is:

IF ITEM-STOCK IS LESS THAN 25 AND
DELIVERY-TIME IS GREATER THAN 14
PERFORM ORDER-NOW.

Here is a case where an inventory is being checked for items that must be reordered. When the number on hand is less than twenty-five AND the delivery time is greater than fourteen weeks, the item is to

be reordered. Notice how useful the logical connector is in combining conditions to be tested.

The IF Statement

We've seen the IF statement before. If a certain condition exists, take a certain action; if it does not, do something else. The logic of the IF statement is very clear, and the statement itself is easy to use, but coding it so that it is readable and fitting it into the overall program logic require study.

A first step is to examine the syntax diagram in Figure 5-12 to acquire a good understanding of the statement's construction. Of course, the statement begins with the reserved word IF. Next comes the condition to be tested. Following the condition is the statement to be performed if the condition exists, or is "true." Note that the NEXT SENTENCE phrase may be used here. This means that the next sentence in sequence is to be performed if the stated condition is true.

In the second portion of the sentence, we reach the alternative: What to do if the condition does not exist (is "false"). The ELSE clause specifies the alternative action to be taken, and this may range from simple to very complex.

An IF statement may be written without the ELSE alternative under certain circumstances. Assume that the next statement in sequence is to be executed when the condition given in the IF statement proves to be false. The syntax diagram implies that the ELSE clause and the words NEXT SENTENCE or a statement number must be given, but that's not true in many systems. The program will automatically go to the next statement if the conditions set out in the IF statement are not met.

The GO TO Statement

Another in the group of statements that cause branches is the GO TO statement. Note that it is two separate words, not run together as in BASIC. GO is a reserved word, as is TO.

Whenever the GO TO statement is given, the program stops executing statements in sequence and starts at the procedure specified by the GO TO statement. The syntax diagram for the GO TO statement is also shown in Figure 5-12.

Given in its simplest form, the GO TO statement is punctuated as a complete sentence and is unconditional. It may, however, be preceded by an IF

GO TO [procedure-name-1]

GO TO procedure-name-1 [, procedure-name-2] . . .   , procedure-name-n

DEPENDING ON identifier

IF condition; $\left\{ \begin{array}{l} \text{statement-1} \\ \underline{\text{NEXT}} \ \underline{\text{SENTENCE}} \end{array} \right\}$ $\left\{ \begin{array}{l} \text{; } \underline{\text{ELSE}} \ \text{statement-2} \\ \text{; } \underline{\text{ELSE}} \ \underline{\text{NEXT}} \ \underline{\text{SENTENCE}} \end{array} \right\}$

PERFORM procedure-name-1 $\left[\left\{ \begin{array}{l} \underline{\text{THROUGH}} \\ \underline{\text{THRU}} \end{array} \right\} \text{procedure-name-2} \right]$

PERFORM procedure-name-1 $\left[\left\{ \begin{array}{l} \underline{\text{THROUGH}} \\ \underline{\text{THRU}} \end{array} \right\} \text{procedure-name-2} \right]$ $\left\{ \begin{array}{l} \text{identifier-1} \\ \text{integer-1} \end{array} \right\}$ $\underline{\text{TIMES}}$

PERFORM procedure-name-1 $\left[\left\{ \begin{array}{l} \underline{\text{THROUGH}} \\ \underline{\text{THRU}} \end{array} \right\} \text{procedure-name-2} \right]$ $\underline{\text{UNTIL}}$ condition-1

PERFORM procedure-name-1 $\left[\left\{ \begin{array}{l} \underline{\text{THROUGH}} \\ \underline{\text{THRU}} \end{array} \right\} \text{procedure-name-2} \right]$

$\underline{\text{VARYING}}$ $\left\{ \begin{array}{l} \text{identifier-2} \\ \text{index-name-1} \end{array} \right\}$ FROM $\left\{ \begin{array}{l} \text{identifier-3} \\ \text{index-name-2} \\ \text{literal-1} \end{array} \right\}$

BY $\left\{ \begin{array}{l} \text{identifier-4} \\ \text{literal-3} \end{array} \right\}$ $\underline{\text{UNTIL}}$ condition-1

$\left[\underline{\text{AFTER}} \left\{ \begin{array}{l} \text{identifier-5} \\ \text{index-name-3} \end{array} \right\} \text{FROM} \left\{ \begin{array}{l} \text{identifier-6} \\ \text{index-name-4} \\ \text{literal-3} \end{array} \right\} \right.$

BY $\left\{ \begin{array}{l} \text{identifier-7} \\ \text{literal-4} \end{array} \right\}$ $\underline{\text{UNTIL}}$ condition-2

$\left[\underline{\text{AFTER}} \left\{ \begin{array}{l} \text{identifier-8} \\ \text{index-name-5} \end{array} \right\} \text{FROM} \left\{ \begin{array}{l} \text{identifier-9} \\ \text{index-name-6} \\ \text{literal-5} \end{array} \right\} \right.$

BY $\left\{ \begin{array}{l} \text{identifier-10} \\ \text{literal-6} \end{array} \right\}$ $\underline{\text{UNTIL}}$ condition-3 $\Big] \Big]$

Figure 5-12 Statements That Perform Branches and Loops

statement and thus be made conditional. IF A > B GO TO BAL-TOTALS. is an example of such a case.

There is also a phrase DEPENDING ON that may be added to the GO TO statement to establish limited conditions. When written with the DEPENDING ON phrase, the GO TO statement evaluates the contents of the data item whose name follows the words DEPENDING ON. Evaluation is more limited than the syntax diagram may imply, however. The data item is checked for a number and that number selects one of the several procedure names that appears in the body of the GO TO statement. If, for example, four procedure names were given, a 1 in the data item would choose the first procedure, a 2 the second, a 3 the third, and a 4 the fourth. If the data item holds anything other than a number to select one of the procedure names provided, no branch takes place and the program simply continues in sequence.

The PERFORM Statement

Perhaps the most powerful statement in COBOL is PERFORM, for it selects the names of procedures to be executed. After the procedure named by the PERFORM statement is completed, the program returns to the step following where the PERFORM statement appeared and resumes executing instructions in sequence.

The PERFORM statement has several forms, which are shown in Figure 5-12. We'll begin with the simplest format and work toward the most complex.

PERFORM procedure-name. is easy enough to understand. This statement causes the specified procedure to be executed. When it is finished, the program resumes with the sentence following this PERFORM statement. Of course, conditions can be established in the form IF condition PERFORM procedure-name.

Next in complexity is the form that uses the reserved word THROUGH or THRU to select a series of procedures to be executed. It is no different in execution; it simply specifies two or more procedures that are to be executed rather than one. And conditions may be set by the IF just as all PERFORM statements may be made conditional.

So far, we've seen that the PERFORM statement can cause one procedure or a series of procedures to be executed, and that execution of the PER-FORM statement can be made conditional by preceding it by IF. Next, we'll add a word at the end of the PERFORM statement that causes execution of procedure to continue until a certain condition occurs. That word is UNTIL.

The reserved word UNTIL causes a condition to be tested in a manner similar to that of the IF statement. UNTIL A IS GREATER THAN B, or UNTIL BAL-DUE IS LESS THAN 10 are examples. Only when the specified condition is true does the program return to the sentence following the PER-FORM statement.

Another variation of the PERFORM statement establishes in advance the number of times the selected procedures are to be performed. This is accomplished by using the reserved word TIMES rather than UNTIL. PERFORM procedure-name N TIMES is the form this variation takes. As shown in the syntax diagram, the number may be an integer (a literal known in advance, such as 5 TIMES) or the value of a named data item. Suppose, for example, there were a varying number of cars sold and this procedure had to be performed once for each car. CARS-SOLD could be the name of the data item. If seven cars were sold, the procedure would be performed seven times and, likewise, if forty were sold, it would be performed forty times.

Next we move on to even more complex versions of the PERFORM statement. Often, it is necessary to execute the same procedure over and over but operate on different data. If, for example, we had a list of data and had to process every element in that list in exactly the same way, there would have to be some way to change the identification of the element each time a procedure was executed. The PERFORM statement has the ability to do this. The form is generally called PERFORM VARYING.

The most important word to be added is VARYING, which is followed by the name of the data item or index that is to be changed each time the procedure is executed. Next comes the starting value of the item to be changed. Perhaps it starts at one, but this can be specified in the PERFORM statement. (So far we have PERFORM procedure VARYING X FROM starting point.) Next comes the amount by which the X is to be changed, and logically this is preceded by the reserved word BY. Last in the chain is a definition of how long the process is to continue. Again, the word UNTIL is used to set the limit, and a condition that ends the process is given. We'll discuss the PERFORM

VARYING statement further when we reach the section dealing with tables and lists.

STATEMENTS THAT USE FILES

COBOL has a group of four statements that handle files. READ, WRITE, OPEN and CLOSE are the verbs used, and although these are supplemented by other reserved words, these statements are also easy to learn and use.

Describing a File to COBOL

COBOL requires that data items be introduced in the data division, and files, too, must be defined and described before the procedure division can use them. This is done in both the environment division and the data division. Let's review the material that must be provided in the environment division.

One major part of the environment division is the INPUT-OUTPUT SECTION. Included in this section is the FILE-CONTROL paragraph, which is the place where file names are first given.

The file name is preceded by the word SELECT and followed by an ASSIGN clause. One SELECT entry is provided for each file used, so if there are ten files, there are ten SELECT entries.

The purpose of the FILE-CONTROL paragraph is to match the characteristics of the file to the equipment and, in some cases, to inform the operating system of file characteristics. One file, for example, may be assigned to a tape unit, another to a card machine, another to a printer, and a fourth to a disk. Each has certain characteristics that dictate the choice of equipment and method of file access and handling.

Next the file must be named and described in the data division so that the file name, record name, and fields that make up each record will have been identified for use by the procedure division. A part of the data division called the FILE SECTION is where the file description is given. Each file is described in its own paragraph identified by FD (file description). FD is followed by the file name and a description of the records in the file. From this point on, the procedure division can use the files freely. Therefore, the rest of this section is devoted to a discussion of how the READ, WRITE, OPEN, and CLOSE statements are used.

Fundamentals of the File Handling Statements

Rules for using the four file handling statements should be easy to remember:

a. A file must be opened before its contents may be used.
b. A READ statement acquires one record at a time from the file.
c. A WRITE statement places one record at a time in the file.
d. A file must be closed before the program using that file is ended.

Syntax diagrams for the four basic statements used with files are rather complicated because all possible variations are included. We can reduce these statements to the simple form shown below.

$$\text{OPEN} \begin{Bmatrix} \text{INPUT} \\ \text{OUTPUT} \\ \text{I-O} \end{Bmatrix} \text{file-name}.$$

CLOSE file-name.
READ file-name AT END imperative statement.
WRITE record-name.

The OPEN verb must be followed by a word to indicate the direction of data transfer between the computer and the file. INPUT means input to the computer from the file, which is a read operation. OUTPUT means an output from the computer to the file, which is a write operation. Finally, I-O means that both reading (I) and writing (O) may be done in the file by this program. Concluding the OPEN statement is the name of the file to which this statement applies; this is the same name provided in the environment and data divisions.

Actually, one OPEN statement may select files. It can be written:

OPEN INPUT file-name, file-name . . .
OPEN I-O file-name, file-name . . .
OPEN OUTPUT file-name, file-name, INPUT file-name.

This form is very convenient if a series of files is to be opened simultaneously. The programmer should keep the statements simple for easy reading, however.

CLOSE is used in a similar way. The verb CLOSE is followed by the name of the file to which it applies. It, too, may give several file names in one statement, in the form:

CLOSE file-name, file-name . . .

The simplest forms of READ and WRITE each deal with one record, the next record position in the file. We'll see later that variations of these statements can select specific records, but it is necessary to understand the fundamental operation first.

Recall that part of the file description in the data division gave a file name and the name of the data records in that file. This relationship need not be repeated in the READ and WRITE statements. If, therefore, a READ statement appears in the form: READ file-name, the computer already knows what the record name is. On the other hand, a WRITE statement can be prepared in the form: WRITE record-name, and the computer knows the name of the file in which the record is to be placed.

The format of the WRITE statement is very simple: WRITE record-name. On the other hand, the READ statement allows an addition. That is the AT END phrase, which describes the action to be taken when the end of the file is reached.

Often, the programmer does not know how many records are in a file that must be read and processed. Thus, he cannot determine in advance how many records must be read. The AT END phrase, which is available in nearly all languages, although the words differ, allows the read operation to continue until a mark designating the end of file is encountered. At EOF, the statement following the AT END phrase is executed. This leads to a part of the program that finishes the processing as the programmer sees fit.

At this point we must divide our discussion into sections dealing with the various types of devices. The characteristics of a printer differ so much from those of a diskette file that, of course, the statements using them must be very different in construction.

Printer Files—Printing a Line

Some languages provide a statement called PRINT in addition to a WRITE statement. This allows the printing operation to be clearly distinguished from the recording operation and simplifies the syntax diagrams for the respective statements. COBOL uses the WRITE statement to print, however, and the statement construction is fairly complex.

Let's begin with the basic steps involved in get-ting one line printed. Step one is to review where the material we want to print is located. It is organized into lines by entries in the WORKING-STORAGE SECTION. Perhaps one line is called CURRENT-ORDER-TOTAL-LN and represents the last line to be printed in a customer order form.

Step two is to recall that the FILE SECTION of the data division describes print records and that the environment division matched the print file characteristics to the printer available. So, printing must be done, not from the CURRENT-ORDER-TOTAL-LN but from whatever name is given to the print record. For the sake of simplicity, let's say it is called PRINT-RECORD. Thus, CURRENT-ORDER-TOTAL-LN must be moved to PRINT-RECORD before the WRITE statement is given to print it.

The third step then is to move the line to be printed into the PRINT-RECORD and then print the material. This can be accomplished in either of two ways. A MOVE statement (MOVE CURRENT-ORDER-TOTAL-LN to PRINT-RECORD) followed by a WRITE statement (WRITE PRINT-RECORD) gets the job done, but there is a simpler way. That way is to use the FROM phrase in the WRITE statement. For example, a WRITE statement in the form: WRITE PRINT-RECORD FROM CUSTOMER-ORDER-TOTAL-LN accomplishes both the move and the printing.

The fourth and last step in getting our line printed is to determine where the information must be shown on the form in the printer. The vertical position of the line on the page must be chosen. This is done by more of the phrases and clauses available in the WRITE statement.

We have three possibilities to examine: BEFORE ADVANCING, ADVANCING, and AFTER ADVANCING. The BEFORE and AFTER indicate when the movement should take place with respect to the printing. In English they read: WRITE line BEFORE ADVANCING and WRITE line AFTER ADVANCING. If the ADVANCING phrase appears by itself (without the before or after), the movement takes place *after* the line is printed.

The next thing that must be considered is how many lines to advance. The ADVANCING phrase may be followed by an indication of how many lines are to be skipped, and the indication may be given as a literal (7 lines) or by the name of a data item that holds a number. For example, WRITE line AFTER ADVANCING BLNK-ODR LINES.

A PAGE clause may also be used to control the advance. It means new page or top of next page. Thus, the PAGE clause causes the next page to be moved into position for printing. A statement WRITE line AFTER ADVANCING PAGE would place the line in the first position of a new page.

Handling Tape Files

The nature of tape is such that all files are of the sequential access type. This reduces the number of optional phrases and clauses that may be used with the file handling statements.

The four basic statements OPEN, CLOSE, READ, and WRITE are available for use with tape files. As usual, the characteristics of the file are established in the environment and data divisions.

A file is made accessible to the program when an OPEN statement is issued. The INPUT, OUTPUT, or I-O words then determine whether the file will be read, written, or both. And, of course, more than one file may be opened by one statement.

The OPEN statement also handles the tape header label, if one is to be used, according to the information provided in the environment division. A label is either written, if this is a file to be created, or read if this is an existing file that is to be located.

After the desired tape file is located, the program may either read its previous contents, create a new file of data, or both read data from an existing file and add data to it. Each READ statement acquires one record or a group of records that have been blocked.

Since the name of the data records in the file was given in the data division, the program places the record it read in the area bearing the name of the data record. This is not the only arrangement possible, however. The programmer may use the word INTO to select a different place for the record he reads. READ file-name RECORD INTO data-name is the form in which this would appear. Now, the record just read is placed in the data item whose name follows INTO.

Tape files have the end of file mark we discussed earlier. So, the READ statement may include the AT END phrase, which is followed by a statement of what action is to be taken when the end of the file is reached.

Next, the entry of information into a tape file must be considered. This is done by the WRITE statement. Writing takes place one record at a time or in blocks, if a blocking feature has been specified.

If the programmer wishes, he may use a WRITE statement with the FROM phrase to simplify the operation. WRITE record-name FROM data-name is the form this takes. Of course, the statement may also be used in the form WRITE record-name but in this case the data to be written must have been moved into the record-name area before the WRITE statement is issued. This step can be skipped if the FROM phrase is used, the data being provided directly from the data-name area.

After work with the file is finished, it is closed because there are several things that must be done to it by the system. If, for example, a new file was created, the end of file mark and whatever trailer label is needed must be written. On the other hand, a file that was only read by a program is normally rewound to the load point when work is finished. The CLOSE statement does all these things automatically. However, the programmer does have some options. A NO REWIND clause may be given, and a LOCK clause is available. The LOCK does not involve anything physical; it simply prevents this file from being opened again during execution of the current program.

Disk and Diskette Files

By their physical nature, disks and diskettes make it easy to gain access to data. Tape units must move all the tape preceding the desired record past the read/write head in order to reach a specific record. Disks can move the head, however. This allows access to data without having to pass by everything that has come before.

Most operating systems include a program to manage the storage space on disks and diskettes. It's important that the space be used to the maximum extent possible because it is fairly expensive. In addition, the space must be managed so as to keep access time to the minimum.

This combination of the disk and the storage space manager is usually designed to provide three types of access to records in a file: sequential, direct (or relative), and indexed. We described the access methods in Chapter 2.

COBOL statements can handle files providing any of these access methods. Although the statements used are the same four (OPEN, CLOSE, READ, WRITE) as we discussed earlier for tape and printer files, they are supplemented by additional clauses for disk access. In addition, three more statements are provided for the indexed access mode.

Indexed Access Files

In sequential disk files, the READ and WRITE statements deal with the records in sequential order. In keyed (indexed) files, however, the READ statement provides the key of the record it wants to read. That specific record is then found and read. On the other hand, the WRITE statement provides the key as part of the record to be written and the storage manager places the record in the file in order by the value of its key.

Both the READ and WRITE statements provide an INVALID KEY clause, which is followed by the action to be taken if the key is invalid. In reading, the key is invalid if no record with such a key can be located. In writing, the key is invalid if it is not within the range specified when the file was established or duplicates a key already present.

Now to the DELETE and REWRITE statements, which supplement READ and WRITE. Both operate with indexed files, the objective being to edit the files as data changes. DELETE deals with a specific record, either the record just read or the record whose key is provided, depending upon the mode of file access being used.

REWRITE is used to revise the contents of a specific record. Again the access mode has an effect on how the REWRITE statement works. Either the record just read or the record whose key is given is replaced with new information.

Twice in the previous two paragraphs we've mentioned access mode for indexed files without explaining it further. That was a deliberate omission. Indexed files can also be used in a sequential access mode. If they are, a READ statement takes the next record rather than specifying a key.

A START statement is required to establish the beginning position in an indexed file from which sequential reading is to be done. Two basic forms are available. If only the START file-name form is used, access begins at whatever value is now held by the variable named as the record key.

The second form of the START statement provides the key to be used in locating the starting point. This is done by giving the name of the variable in which the key value can be found.

It should be noted that no actual data exchange with the file takes place as a result of the START statement. A READ statement is required to acquire a record, then a DELETE or REWRITE statement may be issued to remove or modify that record.

Relative Access Files

Very little mention of relative access has been made up to now. It's essentially a simple technique. Records are numbered according to the sequence in which they are written. The storage manager program maintains a list of the locations in which records are placed. Records can thus be read in sequence or randomly. A record number must be provided, and it is treated like a key in the indexed files we've discussed.

The organization of the file and method of access are defined in the environment division. Some systems describe the record number to be given as NOMINAL KEY or RELATIVE KEY in that it differs somewhat from the "real" key used in indexed files. The key is then given a name and a description in the data division. From that point on, the programmer may use the form of the READ statement in which he provides a key. The key being the name of a data item that holds a record number.

STATEMENTS THAT HANDLE TABLES

Whether you call them lists, tables, arrays, or matrices, the subject is basically the same: a collection of data items arranged in order. Let's begin with a list of seven items and organize it using COBOL methods.

The subject is a list of SALESMEN. In the list will appear the names of the seven salesmen on the staff of a small company. This list, or "table," is defined in the WORKING-STORAGE SECTION of the data division in the following manner:

```
01 SALESMEN.
   05 SLSMAN-NAME OCCURS 7 TIMES
      PICTURE X(20).
```

This statement establishes a table named SALESMEN and says that the data items in it are called SLSMAN-NAME. The OCCURS clause is the way COBOL sets the table size; in this case, there are seven data items, all called SLSMAN-NAME, in the table. The first is SLSMAN-NAME (1), the second SLSMAN-NAME (2), etc.

By now, use of the PICTURE clause should be familiar to most readers. Here, the PICTURE clause says that each SLSMAN-NAME may hold alphanumeric data and be twenty characters long.

After the OCCURS clause is given, a table framework is established but it does not have any data in it. Our SALESMEN table, for example, has no names in any of its seven positions. We'll see how data is loaded into a table later.

Thus, it is the OCCURS clause that the programmer must use to establish the dimensions of a table. The SALESMEN table is a one-dimension table; each element in it can therefore be distinguished from the others by the addition of a single number in the form of subscripts: (1), (2), (3), (4), (5), (6), and (7). Subscripts may be words, numbers, or even simple arithmetic expressions.

For the moment, however, we'll stick to numbers. If then, a programmer wishes to use the contents of a specific location in our SALESMEN table, he can select the location by giving the name of the data item, SLSMAN-NAME and its subscript. SLSMAN-NAME (6), for example, gains access to the contents of the sixth location. The contents can then be used, or new information can be stored.

Up to this point, most readers who have completed the BASIC and Pascal chapters should recognize the similarities between BASIC, Pascal, and COBOL tables. The principles are that a table with certain dimensions is named and its framework established; elements within the table are then individually identified by a subscript. And, of course, the fact that a table must be loaded with data even though its framework is in place is common to the three languages.

COBOL allows tables to have one, two, or three dimensions. Each dimension is set by an OCCURS clause. Each element in the table is set to the same size, however, by a common PICTURE clause that follows the last OCCURS clause.

The next idea is not easy to grasp: Each use of the OCCURS clause to define a dimension of a table provides a different name for each level. Let's use an example of a table in which a large company is keeping track of its inventory of TV receivers, ranging all the way from the total held by the company down to those held in a dealer's stock. Three OCCURS clauses might set up a table in the following manner:

```
01 TV-RCVR-INV.
   03 REGION-STK OCCURS 12 TIMES.
      05 DISTRBTR-STK OCCURS 10 TIMES.
         07 DLRS-STK OCCURS 10 TIMES.
            PICTURE 9(6).
```

The basic element in this table is a six-position number. Thus, up to 999,999 TV receivers can be accounted for in each element. There are twelve regions, which are designated REGION-STK (1), REGION-STK (2), etc. Each of those data items will, when the table is filled, hold the number of TV receivers in stock in that region.

Within each region, there may be as many as ten distributors, and each is designated DISTRBTR-STK (1), DISTRBTR-STK (2), etc. When the table is filled, each of these locations will hold the number of TV receivers available at the respective distributor.

Last, each distributor has up to ten dealers that he supplies, designated as DLRS-STK (1), DLRS-STK (2), etc. Of course, the number of TV receivers held by each dealer is placed in the proper position.

Note that this table has a great many locations: Twelve regions times ten distributors is 120, and each distributor may have up to ten dealers, for a total of 1,200 locations, or elements.

Next to be discussed is how an element at the second or third levels, or dimensions, is chosen. This must be done by stating that they are part of a larger group. Suppose, for example, we wished to gain access to the fourth dealer in the second distributor's chain in the tenth region. We would specify it this way: DLRS-STK (10, 2, 4). The 10 chooses the tenth region, the 2 chooses the second distributor in that region, and finally, the 4 chooses the fourth dealer in that distributor's chain.

Loading Data into Tables

Data to be placed into a table may be provided in the data division of the program in which the table is used, and the table may also be filled as a result of program calculations or the reading of external data. Soon we'll examine tables whose contents are provided by entries in the data division of the program in which they are used. While this method may be employed in some cases, it is not practical for large tables, nor is it practical where data in the table changes often. The program has to be recompiled in order to change data in the table.

A more common method of placing data into a table is to load it from an external source. This means that the data is available from a file. The program containing the table must acquire the data from the file and place it in the table before using the contents of the table. Of course, this allows the table to be updated with new data easily.

When a table must be loaded from an external source, its framework is set up in the data division by OCCURS clauses in the normal manner. The procedure division, however, includes a table loading routine.

Now let's discuss how data for tables can be provided in the data division. We'll go back a bit to our table named SALESMEN in which the names of seven salesmen were to be placed in a list. We used an OCCURS clause to establish the framework of a table but never did fill in the names.

Beginning with a clean slate, we'll assume that the OCCURS clause has never been given and that we simply want to give a list of the actual names for the salesmen. This is done in the form:

```
01 SALESMAN-NAME-LIST
   03 FILLER PIC X(20) VALUE 'BROWN
      A.J.'
   03 FILLER PIC X(20) VALUE 'SMITH
      B.M.'
         •
         •
         •
         •
   03 FILLER PIC X(20) VALUE 'TWEILLER
      C.H.'
```

Next, the information must be placed in a table framework with an OCCURS clause, but it requires something to connect the values given above to the framework. That something is the REDEFINES clause, and it is used in the following manner:

```
01 SALESMEN-TABLE REDEFINES SALES-
   MAN-NAME-LIST.
   05 SLSMAN-NAME OCCURS 7 TIMES
      PICTURE X(20).
```

Now the SALESMEN-TABLE is filled with the seven names provided. If the reference SLSMAN-NAME (2) is used to select an item to be printed or displayed it brings forth "SMITH B.M."

The INDEXED BY Clause

So far we've seen only cases in which the program-mer must write out the subscript needed to select a specific element in a table. There are times, however, in which a table is to be handled one element after another in sequence. Therefore, there must be a simple way of producing a series of numbers that select the elements in sequence. That method is to use the INDEXED BY clause.

When a table framework is set up by an OC-CURS clause (or a series of OCCURS clauses), an INDEXED BY clause may be added to each OC-CURS clause. This is done in the form:

```
SLSMAN-NAME OCCURS 7 TIMES
         INDEXED BY index-name.
```

This establishes a pointer, the name given in "in-dex-name," that can be set and stepped up or down to select one element after another in the table.

The SET Statement

The SET statement controls the value of the pointer. It can establish the contents of the index and cause it to count up or down by any value.

By itself, the SET statement is of no use; it simply sets the pointer, and other statements must use the pointer contents to select an element to operate on. One of these statements is the SEARCH statement, which is discussed next.

The SEARCH Statement

One very useful task that a computer can perform is to look up data. If we use an unknown catalog number (named CAT-NUMBER-IN), the computer can compare it against all the catalog numbers in a table, and, when it finds a match, extract the descriptive information from the table for display, printing, or recording. The SEARCH statement performs this operation.

It first names the table to be searched, and a WHEN phrase establishes the search conditions. The name of the unknown data item follows WHEN. Finally, the portion of the table with which the unknown is to be compared is given, perhaps CATALOG-NUMBER in our case. So the WHEN phrase would read: WHEN CAT-NUMBER-IN = CATALOG-NUMBER (index-name) Statement.

The value of the index, which sets the starting point of the search, is increased by one each time the unknown fails to match a catalog number in the table. Thus, the SEARCH statement steps its way through the table, examining all entries automatically.

When a match is found, the statement following the WHEN phrase is executed and the search is concluded. If the end of the table is reached before a match is found, the statement following an AT END phrase is executed. It would take whatever action the programmer chose to take when a matching catalog number could not be found, perhaps displaying a message "INVALID CATALOG NUMBER" to an operator.

To summarize the SEARCH statement:

1. A SET statement establishes the index value first.
2. SEARCH automatically steps through the table.
3. SEARCH compares items named in the WHEN phrase, seeking a certain condition.
4. When the condition is found, the statement following the WHEN phrase is performed.
5. If the condition is not found, the statement following the AT END phrase is performed.

The SEARCH ALL Statement

It should have occurred to some readers that searching a large table may take a long time even for a computer. It does if the program starts searching from the first entry and examines every entry. There is a more efficient way, but the table to be searched must be in sequence by some identifier, which is called the "key." In our example of the catalog number table it would be easy to select the catalog number as the key and place the items in order by the value of the catalog number.

After a table is made sequential by key, in either ascending or descending order, the SEARCH ALL statement can be used. It performs what is called a "binary search." The SET statement is not required because the SEARCH ALL statement establishes its own index, starting at the middle of the table. It checks the value of the middle entry with respect to the value of the unknown item. Obviously then, the SEARCH ALL statement can determine whether the unknown item is within the upper half or the lower half of the table. Again, the SEARCH ALL statement divides the table, going this time to the middle of the remaining half. After repeatedly halving the table, the SEARCH ALL statement either finds the matching entry or determines that it is not present. The statement following the WHEN phrase

or the AT END phrase is then performed, depending of course on the SEARCH results.

The PERFORM VARYING Statement

While the SEARCH statement is obviously a very useful tool, it is limited in what it does. This makes it desirable to have a more versatile statement to process tables, and that is the PERFORM VARYING statement.

The basic function of the PERFORM statement was discussed earlier. To review: The PERFORM statement gives the names of procedures that are to be executed for a specific number of times, or until a certain condition exists. When the word VARYING is added, the PERFORM statement can be made to apply to a sequence of elements in tables.

Figure 5-12 (see page 113) shows the syntax of the PERFORM VARYING statement. Let's examine it. The first line gives the name of the procedure or procedures to be performed, and the next two lines give the name of a data item whose value will be controlled. In the case of tables being processed by the PERFORM VARYING statement, this data item is the name of one of the levels in the table. FROM sets the starting value of the subscript, and BY determines the increment value, which would normally be one. This sequence is ended when the condition given by UNTIL is present. To summarize: The procedures are performed on every element in the table selected by the named level and its subscript. The subscript beginning value is set, and it is then stepped by the value specified each time the procedure (or procedures) is performed.

Notice that there are two more sections that are optional in the PERFORM VARYING statement. These allow the statement to handle two- and three-dimension tables, naming the second and third levels and varying subscripts just as it does for a one-dimension table.

We need not assume that all elements in a table are processed in sequence. The subscripts can be set to any starting value and ending conditions established. Thus it is possible to choose one small area of a complex table and work only with it.

THE SORT STATEMENT

Sorting means to examine a collection of data and to place it in order. The SORT statement, which does this, is a very powerful tool. When this statement is given, a file chosen by the programmer is reorganized to produce a new file.

Of course, the programmer must provide the criterion for sorting. Is it employee number in ascending order or is it salary in descending order? Perhaps there is more than one criterion. Once employees are sorted into order by their work unit number, they are then to be ranked by employee number or salary. The criterion is called a "key," and there may be more than one key given in the SORT statement.

Now it's time to examine the syntax of the SORT statement. SORT is immediately followed by the name of a temporary file, one in which the sorted data will be accumulated. Next in the SORT statement, the programmer names the key or keys that are to be used as a basis for the sorting. The first key is the major key; it establishes the overall sorting scheme. The second key (and subsequent keys) are minor keys; they determine how data is further sorted.

USING appears next, and it is followed by the name of the raw data file, the input file. The word GIVING names the finished file, the output file. All files are opened, closed, read, and written automatically by the SORT statement. The programmer does not have to provide separate statements for these functions.

Everything about the SORT statement seems simple, but there is a complication as to the type of files that can be sorted: They must be *sequential*. If this is not stated in the environment division, the SORT statement assumes it to be true.

STATEMENTS THAT PROCESS CHARACTER STRINGS

We'll begin this section by refreshing our definition of character strings. "J. L. SMITH" is a character string, as are "9N4W744" and "ERROR 101." Although character strings may contain numbers, these numbers are not intended to be used in arithmetic. Most programming languages provide statements and operators that allow a programmer to combine strings, separate strings, and edit strings. In COBOL, these statements, which we'll cover in this section, are:

INSPECT . . . REPLACING . . .
INSPECT . . . TALLYING . . .
STRING . . .
UNSTRING . . .

A few examples of the use of the statements may serve to illustrate their purpose. Suppose that a standard error message was available, which reads, "YOUR ERROR CODE IS NNN." However, the error code varies, depending upon the conditions, and the message must include the correct code for the situation. Either the INSPECT . . . REPLACING . . . statement or the STRING statement could be used to compose a message in this case. The former would replace the "NNN" with the code given for these circumstances, and the latter, the STRING statement, would combine the "YOUR ERROR CODE IS" with the current error code for the situation. This would form: "YOUR ERROR CODE IS 701."

The UNSTRING statement separates data items that are in a string. It can take each selected section of the string and assign it to a specific data item name. If, for example, all the information in a customer order from a clothing catalog is in one character string, the UNSTRING statement can separate them, assigning one portion to CAT-NMR, another to DESCRIPTION, etc.

Some character strings may be variable in length. Despite the fact that a PICTURE clause has set the field size, the field may not be full, and it's sometimes necessary to know the size before acting on the string for printing or display. The INSPECT . . . TALLYING . . . statement can determine the size of the character string.

The four statements in this group permit many added phrases in a wide variety of combinations. We'll limit ourselves to the basic principles involved, however. And we'll start the discussion with the simplest statements.

The STRING and UNSTRING Statements

The purpose of a STRING statement is to join two or more strings together. This is often necessary to form messages for printing or display, as mentioned above.

The first section of a STRING statement gives the name of the strings that are to be joined. A literal may also be joined to another string; it is provided by the STRING statement itself. The last section of the STRING statement names the receiving field in which the combined string will be formed.

A simple STRING statement would appear: STRING data-item-1, data-item-2 INTO data-item-3.

UNSTRING is essentially the reverse of STRING. It separates a string of characters, the name of which follows the verb "UNSTRING." In this case, however, we have one sending field and multiple receiving fields.

The INSPECT Statement

The INSPECT statement examines a specific string, looking for characters and character combinations defined by the programmer. Some COBOL users may find that their system uses the verb EXAMINE rather than INSPECT; that is an older form of the statement.

What is to be done after the string has been examined? There are two basic actions that may be selected. The first is a TALLYING phrase, which counts the occurrences of the character or character combinations specified by the programmer and records this count in the data item named. The second action is to replace; it is selected by the REPLACING phrase. In this case, the character or character combinations listed are replaced by others given in the statement.

An INSPECT . . . TALLYING statement can, for example, check for specific characters and count the number of occurrences. Of course, INSPECT . . . REPLACING could change invalid characters to those that are acceptable.

STATEMENTS THAT USE OTHER PROGRAMS

Now that we've finished our discussion of most statements that go to make up a COBOL program, we have to consider the possibility of one COBOL program using another COBOL program. This is done by two statements: CALL and EXIT.

A third statement we'll also discuss in this section is ENTER. This statement allows COBOL to go to another program but provides that the program may be in another language.

The CALL Statement

A part of COBOL called the Interprogram Communication Module makes it possible for two pro-

grams to communicate with one another. It would certainly be foolish for a programmer to write a new program if there was one already available that did exactly what needed to be done. The existing program can be "called" into operation. It is then executed, and it ends with an EXIT statement. This returns control to the "calling" program.

The "called" program provides a LINKAGE SECTION in its data division. Here, a description of the data to be shared by the calling and called programs is given.

A syntax diagram of the CALL statement appears in Figure 5-13. Immediately following the word CALL is the name of the program to be called, or the definition of an entry point. (An ENTRY clause in the called program is required in the latter case.) The called program begins execution at the beginning of the procedure division unless a different entry point has been provided.

The USING phrase in the CALL statement gives the names of the data that is to be passed to the called program. There is also a USING phrase in the called program. The first data name given by the calling program is related to the first data name given in the USING phrase in the called program, the second to the second, etc. The number of data items in the USING phrases must be the same, although they do not have to be identical in name.

CALL $\left\{ \begin{array}{l} \text{identifier-1} \\ \text{literal-1} \end{array} \right\}$

[USING data-name-1 [, data-name-2] . . .]

[; ON OVERFLOW imperative-statement]

ENTER language-name [routine-name] .

EXIT [PROGRAM] .

Figure 5-13 Statements That Use Other Programs

The called program is then executed. When it encounters the EXIT statement, it returns control to the calling program.

The EXIT or EXIT PROGRAM Statement

This statement, which may be written simply EXIT, causes the program to return control to a calling program. It must be the only statement in its paragraph. For example:

F499-RETURN. EXIT.
G999-RTN. EXIT PROGRAM.

Another use of the EXIT statement is to provide a common ending point for a series of paragraphs in the procedure division.

The ENTER Statement

This statement, whose construction is very simple, causes COBOL to go to a mode and program that uses another language. Most likely this would be the computer's assembler language and it would be used for debugging programs or operating diagnostic programs. Return to the COBOL program depends upon how this feature is implemented, but a statement called ENTER COBOL is defined in the ANSI Standard. It would follow the last statement of the other language.

THE STOP STATEMENT

This statement stops the program in progress. As its syntax diagram in Figure 5-14 shows, two versions are possible: (1) STOP RUN is an unqualified stop and would be used to end a successful run, and (2) STOP literal provides a code in the literal position and allows the program to be restarted. The code provided in the STOP literal version could indicate an error or a successful run, depending on the programmer's choice.

STOP $\left\{ \begin{array}{l} \text{RUN} \\ \text{literal} \end{array} \right\}$ •

Figure 5-14 The STOP Statement

COBOL MODULES AND LEVELS

Each time a programming language is applied to a specific computer system it is said to have been "implemented," and the implementor has some choice in the complexity level and features to be offered. COBOL is organized so that the choice may be simpler than in some of the other languages. In this section we'll discuss the overall organization

and complexity levels established by the 1974 ANSI Standard.

There are twelve parts defined by this standard, consisting of a nucleus and eleven modules:

Nucleus	Sort-Merge
Table Handling	Report Writer
Sequential Input- Output	Segmentation Library
Relative Input- Output	Interprogram Communication
Indexed Input- Output	Debug Communication

In addition, there are two levels of complexity in the modules; level one being less complex than level two. A system that implements level one of the nucleus, the table handling, and the sequential input-output modules is called minimum standard COBOL. Logically then, one that implements level two of all modules is called "full COBOL." Since level one is a subset of level two, programs prepared with a minimum system can be used in a full system.

SAMPLE PROGRAM—USE OF AN INVENTORY FILE ON TAPE

The sample program in this chapter illustrates how COBOL uses tape files. It also has a procedure division that shows how several procedures can be called into use, including procedures that call other procedures.

Figure 5-15 provides some of the source list. Parts have been cut away in order to simplify the explanation and focus attention on the most important features.

This program deals with the parts inventory of a small manufacturer. It reads a file stored on tape and prints out the contents, computing the total value of each type of part in stock and then the value of the entire inventory. A program such as this is unlikely to "stand alone," however. It would normally be part of a system of inventory maintenance programs that allow changes to be made to the inventory file, as well as answering inquiries concerning file contents.

If we jump immediately to the procedure division we find the following four sections:

a. MAIN-CONTROL SECTION, which is the

```
IDENTIFICATION DIVISION.
PROGRAM-ID. STORE-INVENTORY-II.
     .
     .
     .
ENVIRONMENT DIVISION.
CONFIGURATION SECTION.
SOURCE-COMPUTER. Model....
OBJECT-COMPUTER. Model....
     .
     .
     .
INPUT-OUTPUT SECTION.
FILE-CONTROL.
     SELECT INVENTORY-FILE,ASSIGN TO System Model Tape Unit.
     SELECT PRINT-FILE,ASSIGN TO System High-Speed Printer.
DATA DIVISION.
FILE SECTION.
FD   INVENTORY-FILE
     LABEL RECORDS ARE OMITTED
     DATA RECORD IS INVT-RECORD.
01   INVT-RECORD.
     03   STOCK-IN                   PIC X(5).
     03   QTY-IN                     PIC 999.
     03   UNCOST-IN                  PIC 999V99.
     03   DESCRIP-IN                 PIC X(20).
     03   FILLER                     PIC X(30).
FD   PRINT-FILE
     LABEL RECORDS ARE OMITTED
     DATA RECORD IS PRINT-RECORD     PIC X(132).
WORKING-STORAGE SECTION.
77   EOF-FLAG                        PIC X(3)        VALUE ' '.
     88 END-FILE                                     VALUE 'END'.
```

~~~~~~~~~~~~~~~~~~~~~~~~~~~~~~~~~~~~~~

~~~~~~~~~~~~~~~~~~~~~~~~~~~~~~~~~~~~~~

```
77   INVT-VALUE                      PIC 9(5)V99     VALUE +0.
77   TOTAL-VALUE                     PIC 9(7)V99     VALUE +0.
01   HEADING-LINE.
     03   FILLER                     PIC X(15)       VALUE ' '.
     03   FILLER                     PIC X(10)       VALUE 'STOCK NO.'.
     03   FILLER                     PIC X(24)       VALUE 'DESCRIPTION'.
     03   FILLER                     PIC X(23)       VALUE 'QTY    UNCOST'.
     03   FILLER                     PIC X(10)       VALUE 'VALUE'.
     03   FILLER                     PIC X(28)       VALUE 'PAGE'.
     03   PAGE-PR                    PIC Z9.
01   DETAIL-LINE.
     03   FILLER                     PIC X(15)       VALUE ' '.
     03   STOCK-PR                   PIC X(5).
     03   FILLER                     PIC X(5)        VALUE ' '.
     03   DESCRIP-PR                 PIC X(24).
     03   QTY-PR                     PIC ZZ9.
     03   FILLER                     PIC X(5)        VALUE ' '.
     03   UNCOST-PR                  PIC ZZ9.99.
     03   FILLER                     PIC X(5)        VALUE ' '.
     03   VALUE-PR                   PIC ZZ,ZZ9.99.
     03   FILLER                     PIC X(53)       VALUE ' '.
01   TOTAL-LINE.
     03   FILLER                     PIC X(52)       VALUE ' '.
     03   FILLER                     PIC X(14)       VALUE 'TOTAL VALUE = '.
     03   TOTAL-VALUE-PR             PIC Z,ZZZ,ZZ9.99.
     03   FILLER                     PIC X(54)       VALUE ' '.
```

(Continued)

```
                    PROCEDURE DIVISION.
                    MAIN-CONTROL SECTION.
                        OPEN INPUT INVENTORY-FILE,OUTPUT PRINT-FILE.
                        PERFORM HEADING-LINE SECTION.
                        READ INVENTORY-FILE,AT END MOVE 'END' TO EOF-FLAG.
                        PERFORM PROCESSING SECTION UNTIL END-FILE.
                        PERFORM TOTAL-LINE SECTION.
                        CLOSE INVENTORY-FILE,PRINT-FILE.
                        STOP RUN.
                    PROCESSING SECTION.
                        IF END-PAGE PERFORM HEADING-LINE SECTION.
                        MOVE QTY-IN TO QTY-PR.
                        MOVE UNCOST-IN TO UNCOST-PR.
                        COMPUTE INVT-VALUE = QTY-IN * UNCOST-IN.
                        MOVE INVT-VALUE TO VALUE-PR.
                        ADD INVT-VALUE TO TOTAL-VALUE.
                        MOVE STOCK-IN TO STOCK-PR.
                        MOVE DETAIL-LINE TO PRINT-RECORD.
                        WRITE PRINT-RECORD AFTER ADVANCING 1 LINES.
                        ADD 1 TO LINE-CTR.
                        MOVE SPACES TO DETAIL-LINE.
                        READ INVENTORY-FILE,AT END MOVE 'END' TO EOF-FLAG.
                    HEADING-LINE SECTION.
                        MOVE PAGE-CTR TO PAGE-PR.
                        MOVE HEADING-LINE TO PRINT-RECORD.
LINE 00113 ───►         WRITE PRINT-RECORD AFTER ADVANCING TOP-PAGE.
                        MOVE 3 TO LINE-CTR.
                        ADD 1 TO PAGE-CTR.
                        MOVE SPACES TO PRINT-RECORD.
                        WRITE PRINT-RECORD AFTER ADVANCING 2 LINES.
                    TOTAL-LINE SECTION.
                        MOVE TOTAL-VALUE TO TOTAL-VALUE-PR.
                        MOVE TOTAL-LINE TO PRINT-RECORD.
                        WRITE PRINT-RECORD AFTER ADVANCING 2 LINES.
```

Figure 5-15 Sample Program

complete logic of the program. It opens and closes the files involved and issues PER-FORM statements to cause procedures to be executed.

b. PROCESSING SECTION, which reads the file contents, does the computations necessary, and prints the detailed lines of the report.

c. HEADING-LINE SECTION, which places the headings on each page of the printed report.

d. TOTAL-LINE SECTION, which prints the total line on the printed report.

Now we'll move up to the environment and data divisions. In the environment division, the INVENTORY-FILE is assigned to a tape unit; since access method is not specified, it defaults to sequential. And the PRINT-FILE is assigned to a high-speed printer.

In the file description (FD) paragraphs of the data division, the records in the inventory file are described in detail. Each field is named and its picture given. The print file is described only in a general way, however, in that it is said to be 132 characters

long and named PRINT-RECORD. This allows a variety of different lines to be moved into the PRINT-RECORD before the printing is actually done. We'll examine the format of some of those lines shortly.

The WORKING-STORAGE SECTION of the data division comes next. Here some independent data items are named and described; we've cut away part of those to shorten the program listing. Next comes the format of the heading line, the detail line, and the total line. Except for the page number, the actual information to be printed is provided in the heading line description, and a similar arrangement is used in the description of the total line. The detail line must be filled in by the information pertaining to a specific inventory item, so it has no permanent contents.

Before moving on to the logic of the program itself, let's summarize what has been said:

a. The INVENTORY-FILE has been assigned to a tape unit and the PRINT-FILE to a high-speed printer.

b. The record in the INVENTORY-FILE is named INVT-RECORD. It consists of five fields.

c. The record in the PRINT-FILE is named PRINT-RECORD. It consists of one 132-character field.

d. Lines to be moved into PRINT-RECORD are defined in the WORKING-STORAGE SECTION.

As we already know, the procedure division consists of four parts. First is the MAIN-CONTROL SECTION which lays out the logic of the program. The two files involved are opened by the first statement, and the second statement performs the heading procedure for the printer. This starts a new page and titles it. Thus the first two statements "set the stage" for the rest of the program.

Now the first record is read from the inventory file. This is done by the third statement. Ordinarily, the AT END phrase would not come into play in this statement because the file would be at the starting point. Therefore, the normal action of this line is to acquire the first inventory record.

The next step is to start the processing procedure. This is ordered by the statement PERFORM PROCESSING SECTION UNTIL END-FILE. This means that the entire inventory file is to be processed and the related material printed. We'll examine the PROCESSING procedure in detail later, but for now let's move on through the MAIN-CONTROL SECTION.

We know that the PERFORM statement will continue until the inventory file is exhausted, so the program doesn't move to the next line until this is done. When it does, another PERFORM statement orders the TOTAL-LINE procedure to be executed. It provides the total value of the inventory and prints the total line on the printer.

The program then resumes with the CLOSE statement. Both the input and output files are closed, and the STOP RUN statement ends the program.

The next thing to do is to inspect each of the procedures line-by-line. We'll begin with the procedure that prepares headings. It first moves a page number into the line to be printed. Next, the heading procedure moves the heading line into the print record. Thus, the material to be printed is ready.

A statement in line 113 writes the contents of the print record after moving the form to the top of a new page. It then moves a three into the line counter and adds a one to the page count. Consequently, the page count is increased by one each time a new page is started.

The print record is then cleared by the MOVE SPACES TO PRINT-RECORD statement. Following this, a blank is produced (after the printer is advanced two lines). A space between the headings and the first line of the report to be printed next is thus created.

While we're on the subject of printing, let's go on to the TOTAL-LINE SECTION and see what is done when the total line is to be printed. The TOTAL-VALUE accumulated by the PROCESSING procedure is moved to TOTAL-VALUE-PR, which is to be printed as part of the total line. Then the entire total line (prepared in advance by the data division except for the total value) is moved to the print record. The following statement prints the line, after advancing the printer two lines and thus skipping one line before the total is printed.

We'll now examine the details of the PROCESSING SECTION, which has the following tasks to perform:

a. Maintain page control. When the printed page is filled with detailed lines, a new page must be started.

b. Prepare each detailed line to be printed.

c. Compute the extended value of each item.

d. Compute the total value of the inventory.

e. Read records from the inventory file.

When the PROCESSING SECTION begins for the first time, the first record is available from the INVENTORY-FILE and the printer is ready with a new page. These conditions were set up by the MAIN-CONTROL statements. The END-PAGE condition will not be true and the PROCESSING SECTION will begin manipulating data. When the end of a page is reached, however, the HEADING-LINE SECTION is performed before work on the data begins.

MOVE statements take some fields from the tape record and place them in the detail line to be printed. Extended value for this item is calculated, and it too is moved to the output line. After extended value is available, it is added to the total value of the inventory, a running total used only when the processing is finished.

Next, the fully composed detail line is moved to the PRINT-RECORD and printed. The line counter is stepped, and the detail line is cleared out in preparation for the next record.

The last line of the PROCESSING SECTION reads the next record from the INVENTORY-FILE and returns to the first statement in the section. When the end of the file is reached, the PROCESSING SECTION sets a condition that the PERFORM statement in the MAIN-CONTROL SECTION senses. The program then returns to the MAIN-CONTROL SECTION and the PROCESSING SECTION is no longer performed.

SELF-TEST FOR CHAPTER 5

1. There are four divisions in a COBOL program: identification, environment, data, and procedure. Briefly describe the purpose of each.
2. COBOL coding forms provide the first six columns for line identification and columns 8–72 for coding. What is the purpose of column 7, and what symbols may be used there?
3. Data item names (identifiers) used in COBOL must comply with several rules. Which of the following identifiers are invalid, and why?

      7-COUNTED
      FAMILY-ONE
      EMPLOYEE-PAY-RATE
      TOTAL OF FIRST
      CUSTOMER'S-ACCT
      ACCEPT
      4TH GRADE STUDENT AVG
      TV-INVENTORY

4. What is the maximum number of characters permitted in an identifier?
5. The PICTURE clause defines the format of a data item, or field. A, X, and 9 define the type of characters that may be placed in that field. What does each mean?
6. Using the style required in the data division for the definition of a record, provide a description of a record named CUST-ORDER with the following fields: positions 1–10 are customer order number, positions 11 and 12 are unused, positions 13–40 are the customer name, positions 41–46 are order date, positions 47–55 are the total amount of the order, and positions 56–64 are unused.
7. Write a statement to show on a display screen an instruction that requires the operator to type in an employee name.

8. Level numbers in the data division are very important. What does each of the following level numbers mean: 01, 02–49, 77?
9. Describe briefly what each of the following PICTURE clauses mean.

    a. PIC 99V99   d. PIC 999
    b. PIC X(7)   e. PIC XXXXX
    c. PIC A(20)   f. PIC 9(5)V9(2)

10. Add the capability of the number in d. above to carry a sign with it.
11. What is the purpose of the MOVE statement? Write one to take the CUST-TOTAL just calculated and place it in the BAL-DUE.
12. Write statements to perform the following calculations:

    a. DEPOSIT + BALANCE (total to replace current balance)
    b. DEPOSIT + BALANCE = NEW-BALANCE
    c. AMT-DUE − PAYMENT (difference to replace current amount due)
    d. INT-RATE × AMT-BORROWED = INT-CHGS (round the product)
    e. INT-CHGS + AMT-BORROWED = TOTAL-DUE
    f. TOTAL-DUE ÷ REPAY-PERIOD = MONTHLY-PAYMENT (round the quotient)
    g. A = BH/2

13. It's very important that the programmer knows how to read COBOL syntax diagrams so that his statements and sentences are constructed properly. Explain the meaning of each of the following: (a) capitalized words without an underline, (b) capitalized words that are underlined, (c) phrases and clauses within square brackets, (d) phrases and clauses within braces, (e) lowercase words, and (f) ellipsis points.
14. COBOL allows relational operators to be expressed with symbols or words. Write out the words for: NOT =, >, and NOT <.
15. In the statements that perform arithmetic, the COMPUTE statement allows the use of symbols called arithmetic operators similar to those in other languages. There are five symbols (+, −, *, /, and **). Describe the operation that each causes. List the symbols in the order in which they are applied when an expression is evaluated (the arithmetic actually done).
16. ACCEPT and DISPLAY statements take in-

puts and provide outputs; so do READ and WRITE. Briefly summarize where the first pair would be used, then do the same for the latter pair.

17. We discussed three statements that cause branches, make decisions, and cause loops to be executed. What were they?

18. The IF statement can evaluate several kinds of conditions. Write a statement to examine CURRENT-BALANCE, and if it is less than MIN-ACC-BAL, display a message "BALANCE TOO LOW." Otherwise continue with the next sentence.

19. A GO TO statement that uses the DEPENDING ON phrase allows multiple branches based upon the value of the data item following that phrase. Briefly describe how this feature can be used.

20. Write a simple PERFORM statement that unconditionally causes the paragraph FINISH-CHECK-PAYMENTS to be executed.

21. One form of the PERFORM statement allows the programmer to select the number of times a procedure is to be executed. Write a simple, unconditional PERFORM statement that executes SALESMAN-COMM-CALC seven times.

22. File handling statements include OPEN, CLOSE, READ, WRITE, DELETE, START, and REWRITE, which are used in the procedure division. Two other divisions include material that is closely related to the use of files, however. Which divisions are they, and what information is provided in each?

23. Which division, section, and paragraph gives the file organization and type of access information?

24. Which division, section, and paragraph gives the description of the records in a file?

25. Place the following verbs in the order they must be given in dealing with a file: READ, CLOSE, OPEN.

26. What is the result produced by giving a READ statement and a WRITE statement?

27. Write a statement to open a file named FORMER-EMPLOYEES from which you intend only to read. Now change the statement so that you may write as well.

28. Lists and tables are an important source of data in many COBOL programs. How is the data that is placed in the tables acquired? Name the three basic origins.

29. Tables in COBOL may have up to three dimensions. What clause establishes the dimensions? In what division, section, and paragraph does that clause appear?

6

Other Languages, Old and New

INTRODUCTION

One has only to glance at the collection of names in Figure 6-1 to realize that there are a great many programming languages. Our problem is that of choosing a few subjects that will be of interest to the typical reader and yet which are representative of products available and advances made. We've chosen five subjects. Recent additions to the most popular language, BASIC, is the first.

Programming of graphics in BASIC should be interesting to most readers. All of the material in earlier chapters concentrated on the "core" of each language. Now we'll take BASIC and examine the additions made to it that allow a programmer to create something other than letters and numbers on the display screen.

Next in this chapter, FORTRAN and RPG are introduced and described. We discuss their purpose and history and describe their structure. When a reader has examined this material and the detailed descriptions of BASIC, Pascal, and COBOL, he should have a good general knowledge of the programming languages that are widely used.

Another language we'll discuss is called Logo. Although it has a strong capability to produce graphics, it is a complete language and embodies the latest developments in the ability to create and call procedures.

Concluding Chapter 6 is a subject barely touched thus far—operating systems and their relationship to the programming languages and the user. An operating system called CP/M®, which is now being used by many small computers, is introduced and briefly described.

GRAPHICS AND BASIC

Some fascinating things can be done when a computer is arranged to control a display on a TV screen, as proven by the popularity of video games and the sales of word processors. The ability of the computer to process data extremely fast is the key factor in making these things possible.

Because it is so widely used with small machines, it appears that BASIC is the best language to use as an example of how graphics are programmed. Nearly everyone buying a computer for personal use or small business applications will want to use the ability of his machine to produce graphics on the display screen.

One dictionary defines the word "graphics" as: "The making of drawings in accordance with the rules of mathematics, as in engineering or architecture." That is certainly an excellent definition of the graphics created on a display screen by a computer. The programmer must provide his instructions in very precise mathematical terms when preparing or changing the graphic.

Imagine the display screen layout as a set of very fine horizontal and vertical grid lines, numbered left to right and top to bottom. The programmer selects a horizontal and a vertical line and tells the computer to move his "pencil" to the point at which they intersect. From this point, the pencil can be moved in units defined by the size of the grid. Up five, right ten, down five, and left ten are the commands that would draw a rectangle, for example.

A typical color display screen used with a small computer has 320 of the imaginary grid lines running from top to bottom and 200 running from left

130

ADAM	FORMAC	Pascal
AED	FORTH	Pascal-86
AESOP	FORTH 86	UCSD Pascal
ALGOL	FORTRAN	Tiny Pascal
ALTRAN	FORTRAN IV	PILOT
APL	FORTRAN-80	
APL/V80		PL/1
Assembler	GPSS	PRINT
Autocoder	GRAF	
	GAT	QUICKTRAN
BASIC		
BASIC-80	IPL-V	RPG
Advanced BASIC		RPG II
Business BASIC	JOSS	
Extended BASIC	JOVIAL	Short Code
Tiny BASIC		SNOBOL
	LISP	SIMSCRIPT
Tiny COBOL	LISP 2	Speedcoding
COBOL	LISP 80	
COGO	Logo	Transforth II
COLASL		TREET
COLINGO	MAD	
Commercial Translator	MATHLAB	XPLO-Structured Language
	MOBOL	
EASYCODER	MULISP/MUSTAR-80	
FACT	NEAT	
FLOW-MATIC		

Figure 6-1 The Many Languages

to right. Each is given a number. Because zero is used as the starting number in computer languages, the columns are numbered 0–319 and the rows 0–199, as shown in Figure 6-2. A programmer can thus choose any one of the 64,000 points on the screen by giving its column number, called the X coordinate, and its row number, called its Y coordinate.

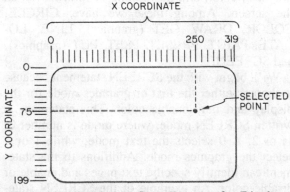

Figure 6-2 X and Y Coordinates of a Display Screen

Next to be determined is whether the beam is to be on or off at the chosen point. Of course, a color must be selected if the display screen handles color.

Color is also given a number. In a black and white display, the choice is simple, but a range of color numbers is available in color displays. Both the background color and the information (the data to be shown) color must be chosen. Thus the programmer must choose a point, define its color, and state what color the unused area must be.

Now, as to how shapes are formed: They are composed of a collection of points, or "dots." In our typical display of 320 columns and 200 rows, we have 64,000 points. If a programmer was to construct a small square in red 8 points wide and high and select column 150 (the X coordinate) and row 100 (the Y coordinate) as the starting point for the upper left corner of the square, 64 points illuminated in red would appear in about the center of the screen. (This is shown in Figure 6-3.) All of the remaining points would be illuminated in whatever color the programmer chose for the background—let's say green.

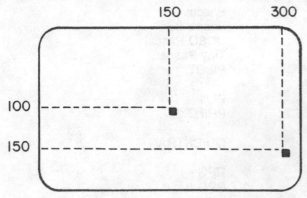

Figure 6-3 Construction and Movement of a Square

How to make the square move is the next question. The answer is to change the coordinates at which it starts. Now we'll give the coordinates as 300, 150. This causes our little group of 64 points to begin in column 300 and row 150, which is to the far right and about three fourths of the way down on the screen and also is shown in Figure 6-3. All other 63,936 points are green, so the square appears to have moved quickly.

And to the last question before we reach the statements that prepare graphics: How can the square we've constructed out of 64 red points be made to move smoothly across the screen rather than jump from the center to the lower right corner? The answer is to make the X and Y coordinates variables and change the value of the variables in small increments, perhaps as part of a loop. Of course, large increments would produce rapid movement.

So now we know the fundamentals of graphics construction and movement. To summarize: (1) the screen is divided into a great many points that can each be distinguished from all the others; (2) the color of each point can be chosen; (3) shapes can be constructed by the points; (4) the starting point of each shape can be chosen; and (5) the starting point can be changed at a rate determined by the programmer.

Statements Available in a Popular BASIC

When most readers casually leaf through the "How to Program in BASIC" books provided with the personal computers now on the market, they'll find that the BASIC offered differs significantly from the simple BASIC we covered in Chapter 3. What has been added? Statements needed to program color graphics is the most obvious addition, but there are

some others. These are generally concerned with controlling special attachments such as joysticks or a cassette recorder.

Although there are a number of ways in which all the versions of "new BASIC" could be handled, we've chosen to use one version as a typical example and ignore the others. This version is the set of statements available in the Advanced BASIC provided for use with the IBM Personal Computer®.

Figure 6-4 summarizes the keywords available. Let's examine the list quickly, searching for both standard statements and new ones, and then move on to a description of what the graphics statements do.

Since our list is in alphabetical order, we'll start with BEEP. Here's a statement we covered in Chapter 3; it causes a brief audible tone from the speaker in the machine, which can be used in a variety of ways to signal the operator.

Among the *C*'s, we have CIRCLE and COLOR, both obviously associated with graphics and selecting screen color. And in the *D*'s we have DRAW, which constructs graphics.

DATA and DIM, standard statements the reader should recognize, along with FIELD, FOR/NEXT, GOTO, GOSUB/RETURN, IF/THEN/ELSE, and PRINT USING show that the fundamental BASIC statements are all here.

MOTOR is an example of a statement added to handle a special attachment, the cassette recorder. And there are also statements to handle other attachments, such as the light pen and joysticks.

How the Graphics Statements Work

Now let's discuss the statements associated with graphics, color, and positioning of information on the screen. Among these we have: CIRCLE, COLOR, DRAW, GET (graphics), LINE, LOCATE, PAINT, PRESET, PSET, PUT (graphics), and SCREEN.

We'll begin with the SCREEN statement because it chooses either the text or graphics mode for the display and may enable color. This statement is written SCREEN mode, where mode is number 0, 1, or 2. A 0 selects the text mode, while 1 or 2 select the graphics mode. Additions to the statement can identify specific text pages and enable or disable color. An example of the SCREEN statement could be:

40 SCREEN 0, 1, 0, 0

BEEP
CALL
CHAIN
• CIRCLE
CLOSE
CLS
• COLOR
COM...ON/OFF/STOP
COMMON
DATA
DATE$
DEF FN
DEF SEG
DEF USR
DIM
• DRAW
END
ERASE
ERROR
FIELD
FOR...TO...STEP
GET
• GET (graphics)
GOSUB
GOTO
IF...THEN...ELSE
INPUT
KEY ON/OFF
KEY
KEY...ON/OFF
LET

• LINE
LINE INPUT
LOCATE
LPRINT
LPRINT USING
LSET
MID$
MOTOR
NEXT
ON COM/KEY/PEN
   STRIG...GOSUB
ON ERROR GOTO
ON...GOSUB
ON...GOTO
OPEN
OPTION BASE
OUT
• PAINT
PEN ON/OFF/STOP
POKE
PRINT
PRINT USING
• PRESET
• PSET
PUT
• PUT (graphics)
RANDOMIZE
READ
REM
RESTORE
RESUME

RETURN
RSET
• SCREEN
SOUND
STOP
STRIG ON/OFF
STRING...ON/OFF
SWAP
TIME$
WAIT
WEND
WHILE
WRITE

The Draw Statement Commands

U – UP
D – DOWN
L – LEFT
R – RIGHT
E – UP AND RIGHT
F – DOWN AND RIGHT
G – DOWN AND LEFT
H – UP AND LEFT
M – MOVE AND PLOT
B – MOVE AND NO PLOT
N – MOVE, PLOT, RETURN
A – SET ANGLE OF ROTATION
C – SET COLOR
S – SET SCALE
X – EXECUTE SUBSTRING

•—Graphics Statements

Figure 6-4 Keywords in a Popular Modern BASIC

This selects the text mode (the first zero), allows color (the one) and sets the two possible page selections to zero (the two zeros on the right). The "40" we've included is nothing more than a line number, and we'll use it throughout this section.

The COLOR statement applies to both the text and graphics modes. In the text mode, it can select the character and background colors by providing numbers corresponding to those colors. For example, the COLOR statement could appear: 40 COLOR 7, 1. This would choose white characters (7) on a blue background (1). The effect of the COLOR statement in the text mode is shown in Figure 6-5.

In the graphics mode, the effect of the COLOR statement is slightly different, as shown in Figure 6-6. The background color is chosen in the same manner, but the foreground is not chosen to be a

specific color but rather a group, called a palette, from which other graphics statements may select. In this case, the COLOR statement could read: 40

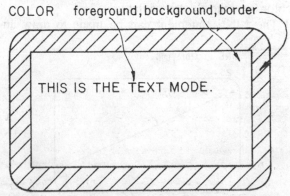

Figure 6-5 Effect of the COLOR Statement in the Text Mode

COLOR   background, palette

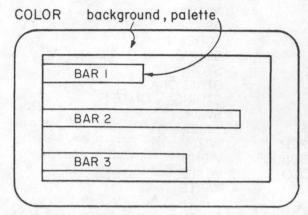

Figure 6-6 Effect of the COLOR Statement in the Graphics Mode

COLOR 8, 0. This would choose gray as the background and the even palette (0) from which the graphics statements can choose a foreground color.

After the programmer has selected the graphics mode, he is ready to use the statements dealing with the construction of graphics. Because the LINE statement is the simplest of this group, that's where we'll begin.

The LINE statement has more than one form. First, it can draw a line starting from the current point to the point whose coordinates are given. This would appear: 40 LINE (X2, Y2). The X2 and Y2 are the coordinates of the ending point, and, of course, the line starts from the current point. Another form gives both the starting and ending points: 40 LINE (X1, Y1) (X2, Y2). This, too, draws a straight line. Figure 6-7 shows how the LINE statement works.

Color of the line to be drawn is given by the number following the last parenthesis. 40 LINE (X1, Y1) (X2, Y2), 1, for example, chooses the first color from the palette available.

The LINE statement can be made to draw an

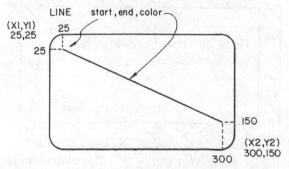

Figure 6-7 Use of the LINE Statement

empty box or a filled box by the addition of letters B or BF, respectively, at the end of the statement. B causes the two coordinates given to become the opposite corners of the box, thus the remaining two corners are known and do not need to be provided. BF does the same thing but fills the box in the color specified by the color number. A solid rectangle could thus be drawn by: 40 LINE (X1, Y1) (X2, Y2), 1, BF. This action is shown in Figure 6-8.

LINE   start, end, color, box

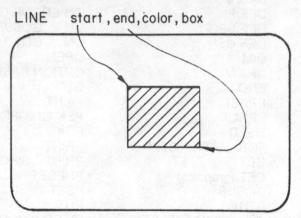

Figure 6-8 Use of the LINE Statement to Draw a Box

Curved shapes are produced by the CIRCLE statement. Visualize this statement as a drawing compass. First, the coordinates of the center must be given, then the radius established. The next item to be given is the color, and this is followed by the start and end angle parameters, which are given in radians.

40 CIRCLE (X,Y), R, N, A1, A2 is the format of the CIRCLE statement. The center point is selected by coordinates X and Y, the radius by the value of R, the color by N, and the start and end angles by A1 and A2. (Figure 6-9 illustrates this.) After the circle is drawn, the reference point (the current point) for additional graphics work is the circle center. Of course, the figure need not be a full circle; it could be an arc, depending upon the values provided.

PAINT is the next statement we'll discuss. Its purpose is to fill in a specific area with color, and perhaps it would be used most often after a figure is drawn. Let's assume the programmer just drew a circle and wishes to fill it in. He does so by issuing the PAINT statement giving a coordinate within the circle, the color he wants for the interior of the circle (the paint color), and the color of the boundary.

A PAINT statement has the form:

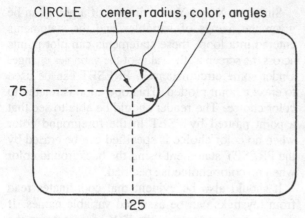

Figure 6-9 Use of the CIRCLE Statement

40 PAINT (X,Y), N, N

The X and Y are the coordinates, the first N is the number of the paint color, and the second N is the number of the boundary color. The statement 40 PAINT (250, 75), 2, 3 selects the figure in which the point chosen by X and Y coordinates 250 and 75 falls. That figure will be painted color number two from the palette out to the boundary color number three. (A PAINT statement and the results it produces appear in Figure 6-10.)

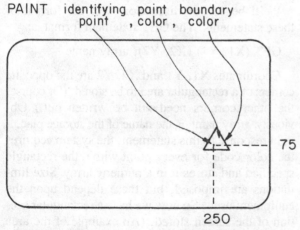

Figure 6-10 Use of the PAINT Statement

A more complex statement is DRAW, which allows the programmer to give the instruction to draw a graphic that is defined by a string of commands. (The commands are listed in Figure 6-4.) The first command given in a string starts its movement from the current position; after that each moves from where the previous command stopped. Included in the list of commands is one that sets the color of the lines being drawn, and it does so by selecting a

color number as we've shown earlier. An example of how DRAW can be used is shown in Figure 6-11.

The N in most of the DRAW commands may be either a literal or the name of a variable from which a number will be obtained when the DRAW statement is executed. Of course, this gives the DRAW statement the power to produce a graphic that represents the results of active calculations. The size of a bar in a bar chart, for example, can be made to depend upon the value of a variable.

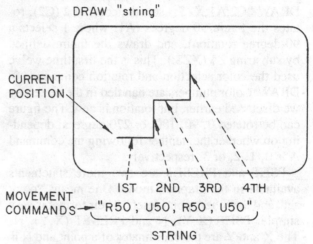

Figure 6-11 Use of the DRAW Statement

First we'll examine a simple DRAW statement. (Note that the semicolons are optional in this case but are required when variables are used, so we've used them in both cases.) The following statement draws a rectangle:

40 DRAW "U10;R20;D10;L20"

If the width of the rectangle is to depend upon a variable, as in a horizontal bar chart, the height of the bar is specified by constants but the width by a variable, in the form:

40 DRAW "U10;R=A;D10;L=A"

Now the height stays at ten units but the width depends on variable A. Of course, variable A results from the evaluation of an expression, so the width of the bar shows the value of A in graphic form.

This statement is extremely interesting, and we could spend a great deal of space on it. However, we'll cover the two most important features and then move on to the next statements. Most important is the command XSTRING$, which means execute the following substring. XZ$ is the form in which this is written, and substring Z$ can be a figure constructed by the commands available to DRAW.

For example Z$="U10;R20;D10;L20" defines a rectangle but doesn't draw it. Think of this as a character string being defined by the simple BASIC statements. The string is first defined but it doesn't actually appear until used by one of the active statements.

Now the DRAW statement is free to use the substring Z$ whenever the programmer wishes. DRAW "C2;A1;XZ$;" sets the color at 2 (C2), rotates the figure 90 degrees (A1, where 1 selects a 90-degree rotation), and draws the figure defined by substring Z$ (XZ$;). This is the first time we've used the color selection and rotation commands in DRAW. Color numbers are handled in the same way we discussed earlier, but rotation is new. The figure can be rotated 0, 90, 180, or 270 degrees, depending on whether the number following the command A is 0, 1, 2, or 3, respectively.

PSET and PRESET are two more statements available in the graphics mode. One means "point set" and the other "point reset." Their format is very simple: PSET (X,Y), N and PRESET (X,Y), N. The X and Y are the coordinates of a point and N is the color number for that point. This is shown in Figure 6-12.

These statements are nearly identical in operation, but there is one difference that affects their use. That is the choice of color if no color number is provided in the statement. PSET chooses the foreground color, meaning that the point is visible, and PRESET chooses the background color, meaning that the point is invisible.

Since the X and Y coordinates of a point can be given the names of variables and the statements entered in a loop, these statements can plot points across the screen as the value of the variables change. Under some circumstances, PRESET can be used to erase a point plotted. This operation is related to color choice. The reader should be able to see that a point plotted by PSET in the foreground color when no color choice is specified can be erased by the PRESET statement using the background color when no color choice is specified.

It should also be evident that coordinates read from joysticks can be assigned variable names. If these names are given as the X-Y coordinates to the PSET statement set in a loop, the joystick can draw a line on the screen.

Another pair of statements available in the graphics mode is GET and PUT. Their action is far different than statements by the same name used with records and files, however, and their names appear to be opposite to their actions if your viewpoint is the display screen. GET takes an image from the screen and places it in an array. Opposite in action, PUT takes an image from an array and places it on the screen. From the viewpoint of the program, however, it is getting an image for an array and putting an image on the screen.

We'll begin our discussion with the format of these statements. The GET statement format is:

GET (X1, Y1) (X2, Y2), array name

Coordinates X1, Y1 and X2, Y2 are the opposite corners of a rectangular area to be stored. (Of course, the other corners need not be written out.) Obviously, array name is the name of the storage place.

In response to this statement, the system acquires the color code for every point within the rectangle specified and stores it in a numeric array. Size limitations are imposed, but these depend upon the equipment used. So now we have a rectangular section of the screen stored. (An example of the area is shown in Figure 6-13.)

The PUT statement, which reclaims the stored image, is somewhat more complex in format and operation. It appears in the form:

PUT (X1, Y1), array name, action

At first glance, this doesn't appear complex. X1, Y1 are the coordinates of the upper left corner of the rectangular area in which the image is to be placed. Already some complexity appears, however. These coordinates can be different from the

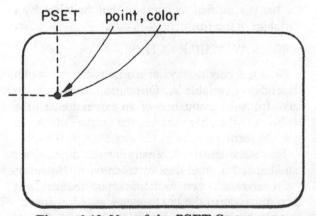

Figure 6-12 Use of the PSET Statement

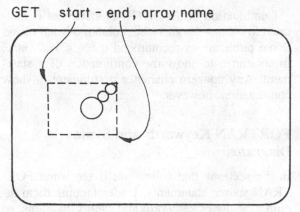

GET   start - end, array name

Figure 6-13 Use of the GET Statement

coordinates of the area stored. Thus, the image can appear in a different area on the screen, as shown by the contrast between Figures 6-13 and 6-14. If the coordinates were variables, the image would move as the value of the variables changed.

The array name is simple enough. It is the name of the array in which the original rectangle was stored.

ACTION is where the complication comes in. There are five words that may be used here: PSET and PRESET, which we discussed earlier as statements, and XOR, OR, and AND. One of these words is always provided to select the relationship between the incoming image and the one currently on the screen. XOR is the standard relationship if the programmer makes no selection.

PSET and PRESET produce the simplest results. PSET places the incoming image on the screen, replacing the existing image while PRESET places it on the screen in negative form, also replacing the existing image.

AND and OR impose some conditions. If AND is used, the incoming image is transferred *only* where

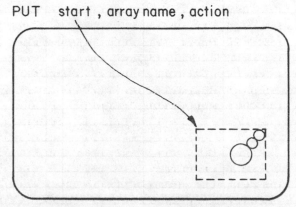

PUT   start , array name , action

Figure 6-14 Use of the PUT Statement

there is an existing image in place, using the existing image like a mask. The OR, on the other hand, superimposes the incoming image on whatever exists.

The standard selection XOR, which means exclusive OR in computer language, superimposes the incoming image onto the existing image (like OR) but inverts each point in the existing image where there is an identical point in the incoming image. This, of course, makes the incoming image fully visible wherever it is placed. Two successive PUT statements with XOR specified at the same coordinates restore the existing screen. This feature allows the incoming image to be moved without leaving a trail destroying the existing display.

FORTRAN—FORmula TRANslator

One of the first high-level languages available was FORTRAN, which was developed by IBM and released in 1957. Intended primarily for engineering and scientific use, rather than business, it became widely used. This, of course, led to the need for standardization.

The first FORTRAN standards were completed and published in 1966, but a 1977 standard is now available. Changes from the 1966 to the 1977 standard were nearly all additions, thus most programs conforming to the earlier standard are compatible with the newer one.

The 1977 standard defines two versions of FORTRAN, full FORTRAN and subset FORTRAN. Some of the additions mentioned above are not available in subset FORTRAN. Among the other features not provided in the limited version are double precision and complex data types.

Most readers will find FORTRAN more similar to BASIC than it is to Pascal or COBOL. For example, the overall organization is not sectionalized, and a program does not even need to be named, although it can be and would normally be.

Since FORTRAN is widely used for scientific and engineering applications, one would expect to find a great many intrinsic functions available, and this is the case.

As the reader makes his way through this section, he will see other similarities and differences between FORTRAN and the three major languages covered in detail. Arithmetic operators, for example, are generally the same (+ , − , *, /, and **) while relational operators are totally different.

FORTRAN uses a two-letter operator bounded by periods. Less than is .LT., while equal is .EQ.

The Coding Form

A FORTRAN coding form is shown in Figure 6-15. It appears to be very similar to those we've used in other languages; however, there are some differences that deserve attention. Columns 1 through 5 are allocated for the source statement number, but column 1 is also used to identify comments and special options. An asterisk (*) in this column identifies the line as one that is not translated by the compiler. As in other languages, FORTRAN accepts and lists comments but doesn't act on them.

Columns 7 through 72 are where the statements are entered. A statement may begin in any of these columns, so indentation schemes can be used to make the coding easy to understand. Like COBOL, columns 73–80 of FORTRAN forms are reserved for program identification and are not used for source statements.

Continuation of a FORTRAN statement is indicated in column 6; otherwise, column 6 is left blank. Some publications recommend using a 1, 2, etc., in column 6 to show the continuation of a statement. Any nonzero character is sufficient to show continuation, however.

FORTRAN Keywords and Syntax Diagrams

In the sections that follow we'll see some FORTRAN source statements. Understanding them requires the use of keywords and syntax diagrams, so an examination of the basic structure of FORTRAN syntax diagrams is necessary before we begin.

All languages use a series of symbols and abbreviations to keep the diagrams short and readable. When one first sees FORTRAN syntax diagrams (shown in Figure 6-16), they appear to be simple compared to those for Pascal and COBOL. That's true. FORTRAN diagrams are roughly equivalent in complexity to the diagrams used for BASIC.

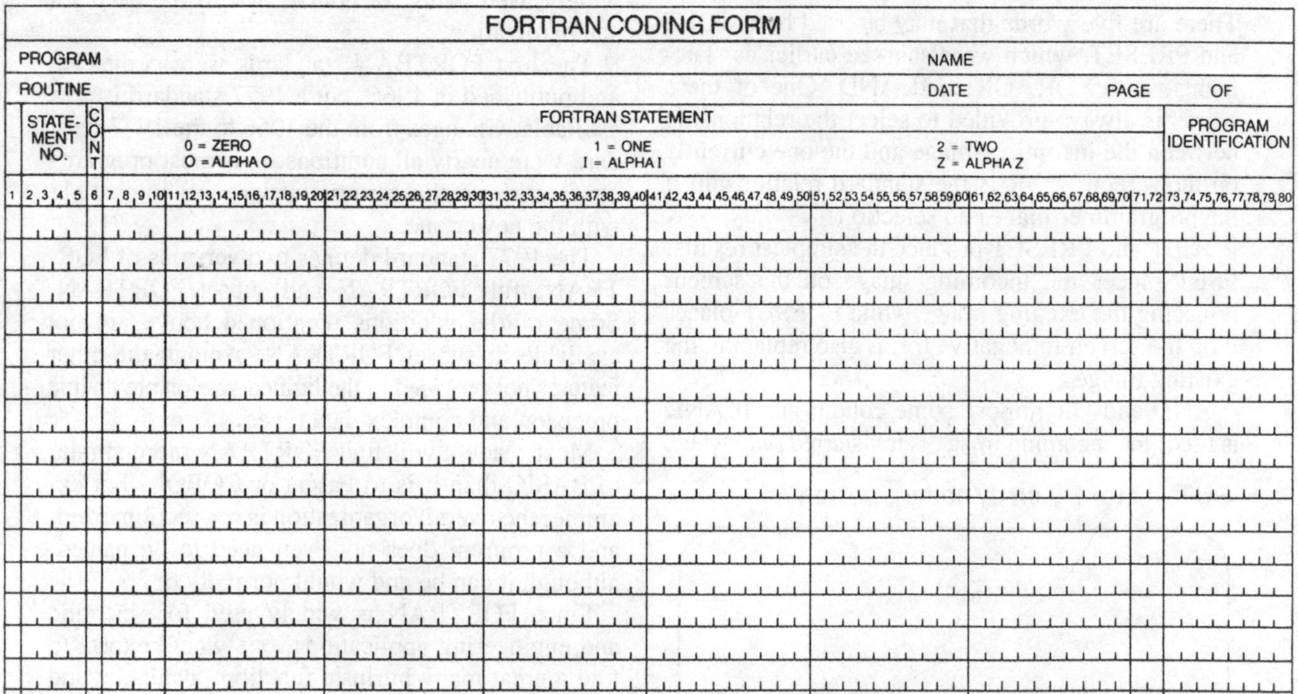
FORTRAN CODING FORM
PROGRAM
NAME
ROUTINE
DATE
PAGE
OF
STATE-MENT NO.
CONT
FORTRAN STATEMENT
0 = ZERO
O = ALPHA O
1 = ONE
I = ALPHA I
2 = TWO
Z = ALPHA Z
PROGRAM IDENTIFICATION
1 2 3 4 5 6 7 8 9 10 11 12 13 14 15 16 17 18 19 20 21 22 23 24 25 26 27 28 29 30 31 32 33 34 35 36 37 38 39 40 41 42 43 44 45 46 47 48 49 50 51 52 53 54 55 56 57 58 59 60 61 62 63 64 65 66 67 68 69 70 71 72 73 74 75 76 77 78 79 80
1 2 3 4 5 6 7 8 9 10 11 12 13 14 15 16 17 18 19 20 21 22 23 24 25 26 27 28 29 30 31 32 33 34 35 36 37 38 39 40 41 42 43 44 45 46 47 48 49 50 51 52 53 54 55 56 57 58 59 60 61 62 63 64 65 66 67 68 69 70 71 72 73 74 75 76 77 78 79 80

Figure 6-15 The FORTRAN Coding Form

Keywords	Typical Syntax Diagrams
ASSIGN, GOTO, IF, THEN,	ASSIGN s TO i
ELSE, ELSEIF, ENDIF	GOTO (s1,s2,. . .,sn) [,]i
DO, CONTINUE	IF (e) s1,s2,s3
STOP, END, PAUSE	STOP [n]
CALL, RETURN, ENTRY	CALL subroutine (parameter list)
READ, PRINT, WRITE,	READ*[,list]
REWIND, BACKSPACE, ENDFILE,	READ fs [,list]
OPEN, CLOSE, INQUIRE, FORMAT	WRITE (u,fs,control specifiers) [list]
DATA, DIMENSION, COMMON,	DATA v1, v2,. . . / c1, c2,. . .
EQUIVALENCE, INTEGER, REAL,	DIMENSION A1 (k1), A2 (k1,k2)
COMPLEX, LOGICAL, CHARACTER	PROGRAM name
DOUBLE PRECISION, IMPLICIT,	
PARAMETER, EXTERNAL, INTRINSIC,	
PROGRAM, FUNCTION, BLOCK DATA,	
SUBROUTINE, SAVE	

Figure 6-16 FORTRAN Keywords and Typical Syntax Diagrams

Let's begin our explanation of the diagrams with the square brackets and then move on to the letters used. Brackets mean that the item or items they enclose are optional. For example, a number may follow the word STOP in the STOP statement to distinguish one stop from another, but that number is not mandatory.

Now let's proceed to the letters that may appear in the diagrams. Some of the most common are listed below:

Symbol	Meaning
A	Name of an array
e	Expression
f	Subprogram name or function name
fs	Format statement number label
i	Integer variable
k	Any type of constant
n	A five-digit integer number or a character constant
s	Statement number label
st	Statement
u	Unit selection (integer constant or variable) in an I/O statement
v	Variable (integer or real)
w	Field width in a FORMAT statement

Operators—Arithmetic, Relational, and Logical

FORTRAN uses arithmetic, relational, and logical operators. Some are the same as those in other languages but others are totally different. We'll summarize the operators quickly because most readers now know what operators are and how they're used.

FORTRAN operators include:

+	addition	.LT.	less than
−	subtraction or negation	.LE.	less than or equal
		.EQ.	equal
*	multiplication	.NE.	not equal
/	division	.GT.	greater than
**	exponentiation	.GE.	greater than or equal
//	concatenation		
		.NOT.	logical negation
		.AND.	logical and
		.OR.	logical or
		.EQV.	equivalent
		.NEQV.	not equivalent

Names for Variables

One of the most difficult parts of learning a new programming language is to become accustomed to the rules for naming variables. The rules in FORTRAN are:

a. The first character in the name must be alphabetic (a letter).
b. Only letters and numbers can be used (no special characters like $). Blanks are ignored; they have no effect.

c. A name must not have more than six characters.

To summarize: Up to six characters (numbers or letters) may be used, but the name must start with a letter.

There is an additional restriction. The names for integer variables must begin with I, J, K, L, M, or N and those for real data with A through H and O through Z. This can be modified as we'll see later.

Construction of Statements

FORTRAN statements have the same general appearance as those in BASIC. Except for comment lines, they are likely to be rather short. A limitation on the size of names and the short operator symbols contribute to this.

Let's examine a few simple statements to see what they look like before moving on. We'll use the following five:

```
A = B+C
X = (A+B)/(C+D)
READ *, X, Y, Z
WRITE (6,750) MTH, DAY, YEAR
IF (X.GT.Y) GOTO 400
```

In our first example, B and C are added and the sum assigned to variable A. The + sign is the arithmetic operator and the equal sign makes the assignment. This is identical to the style used in BASIC. Spaces may be inserted in the expression as necessary to make it easy to read; the FORTRAN compiler ignores spaces before and after the operator symbols and before and after the variable names.

Next we have a somewhat more complex expression. It uses the division operator, the slash (/) and parentheses to group terms that are to be treated as a unit and thus eliminate ambiguity. As in all the programming languages, FORTRAN requires that expressions be written on one line. Everyone should recognize that the expression we've written is:

$$X = \frac{A+B}{C+D}$$

In processing this expression, the computer first removes the parentheses, adding A to B and C to D. Then the sum of A and B is divided by the sum of C and D. Finally, the quotient is assigned to the variable X.

Now we'll examine two of the input-output statements available. READ accepts data and brings it into the computer. In this case, the statement

reads three inputs, most likely from a keyboard, and assigns those inputs to variables X, Y, and Z in the order received. The asterisk shown in this statement is *not a multiply operator;* it simply says that the material to be read has no separate FORMAT statement governing how it should be handled.

The fourth statement in our samples is an output statement, WRITE. It chooses unit number 6 on which to write; this is frequently the unit number assigned to the printer in a FORTRAN system. It also includes the number 750, which is the line number of a FORMAT statement that controls the appearance of the printed material. Concluding the WRITE statement are the names of three variables (MTH, DAY, YEAR) whose current values are to be printed. Thus, the variables will be printed on unit 6 in the format established by line number 750.

Last in the samples is a decision statement. FORTRAN has a variety of such statements. We've chosen only a simple one, primarily to show a relational operator. The statement says: If the relationship specified in the expression in parentheses is true, go to line number 400 for the next instruction. The expression reads "X is greater than Y"; the .GT. being the relational operator greater than.

Data Types

Although integer and real are the only two data types mentioned so far, FORTRAN provides other data types and ways of specifying them. First, the additional data types must be covered. There are four:

a. Character, which is in the same class as string variables in other languages. Character data is any combination of characters in the character set but which is not used in arithmetic. CUSTNM, customer name, for example, would be a variable consisting of character data.
b. Double precision, which increases the positions available for a number. It is needed only in a system with a limited number of digits in the single precision number.
c. Complex, meaning a complex number as used in mathematics.
d. Logical, which means a variable that may only have one of two states, true or false.

This brings us to the way in which variables of

these types are declared to exist. It's done with a type declaration. That type declaration may also include integer and real data types and thus override the rules concerning the first character of the variable's name.

A type declaration must be given before a specific variable is used. Some programmers prefer to provide all type declarations at the beginning of the program. Its format is simple: type v1, v2, . . . vn. The word "type" is replaced by INTEGER, REAL, CHARACTER, DOUBLE PRECISION, COMPLEX, or LOGICAL. V1, v2, etc. are the names of variables, arrays, or functions being declared that data type. An advantage of using this explicit declaration of data type for real and integer data is that it overcomes the naming restrictions mentioned earlier.

Intrinsic Functions Available

As one would expect in a language intended for engineering and scientific applications, FORTRAN has a large number of intrinsic mathematical functions available—the word "intrinsic" meaning in this case "built-in to the language."

Each function is given a short name. When that name is used in a statement, it is followed by the expression to which it is to be applied. The expression, or argument as it is called, is enclosed in parentheses. If a statement such as $A = SQRT(B + C)$ is constructed, A is assigned the value of the square root of the sum of B and C.

This concept was first introduced and explained in Chapter 2 and repeated for each of the major languages. FORTRAN functions are applied in the same basic way. Where they do differ, however, is that the names for the same function may vary depending upon the type of data being operated on. If only the generic name appears in a statement, the compiler examines the data type of the argument and applies the correct function. Thus, the programmer is free to use only the generic name in his statements. In addition, FORTRAN includes some functions used to convert between data types.

Overall Organization of a Program

In COBOL and Pascal the rules concerning the declaration portion of a program are well defined. On the other side of the coin are BASIC and our current subject, FORTRAN, which allow the programmer

a great deal of freedom. Neither of these languages requires a separate declaration section that makes programs easy to read, test, and maintain. The programmer is wise, however, if he uses comments to prepare lists and provide identification as suggested below.

A fact to be considered is that there are really *four kinds of programs that may be prepared*—a main program and three kinds of subprograms. Each has basically the same organization, although the main program is very likely to be the largest. *Each is entered into the system and compiled separately*.

PROGRAM followed by a name assigned by the programmer (in the form: PROGRAM name) identifies the main FORTRAN program. Although the FORTRAN system itself does not require the program to be named by a PROGRAM statement, most implementations and operating systems require that names be assigned.

The three kinds of subprograms are titled in the same manner, as follows:

SUBROUTINE name. A subroutine may be called by the main program, like procedures in other languages. It must be named.
FUNCTION name. A user-defined function is called when its name is used in an expression. It returns a value to the expression.
BLOCK DATA name. The BLOCK DATA subprogram can initialize variables declared to be common to the main program and/or subprograms. It does not require a name.

Figure 6-17 illustrates how a PROGRAM, SUBROUTINE, or FUNCTION might be organized if a programmer was meticulous in describing the program and its components. Some of the information provided is optional and is entered in the form of comments.

We've shown program identification first. This consists of the word, PROGRAM, SUBROUTINE, FUNCTION, or BLOCK DATA, and a name as we discussed above. Following the name, in the form of comment entries, is a description of the program, the author's name, probably dates, and remarks concerning revisions made.

A section is then devoted to listing the items used by the program. This is all in the form of comments, and it has no effect on program execution. Although this listing might seem to be a chore, it is invaluable in testing and maintenance. Our sample list consists of:

a. Variable Identification—all the variables used are listed and the full meaning of their names is given.
b. Array Identification—array names are listed and their full meaning explained.
c. Constant Identification—all constants are listed by name (if used), and their value and the full meaning of the name are given.
d. Functions and Subroutines List—names are given and their full meaning explained.

Up to this point nearly everything entered is for the purpose of documenting the program. Only the title word PROGRAM, SUBROUTINE, FUNCTION, and BLOCK DATA along with the name and any parameter lists provided have any effect on program execution. Now, however, we encounter a set of declaration statements which do determine

the program results. This could logically be called a declarations section, but some publications refer to it by other names. Storage allocation block is one common term.

Whatever we call it, this section includes statements such as PARAMETER, DIMENSION, COMMON, and DATA. In Figure 6-17, the basic function performed by each statement is outlined.

Next the program moves into action. The blocks that execute the logic of the program or subprogram now appear. The END and STOP statements shown might seem to do the same thing; they do not. END defines the end of the program unit in which it appears; it is an instruction to the compiler. On the other hand, STOP causes execution of the object program to be terminated at the point at which it appears.

PROGRAM, SUBROUTINE, FUNCTION, BLOCK DATA   program name

Program Description and History

Variable Identification
Array Identification
Constant Identification

Functions and Subroutines List

PARAMETER ———————— equates a name and a value
IMPLICIT ———————— defines first letter of a name as a data type
INTEGER, REAL, COMPLEX, DOUBLE-PRECISION, LOGICAL, CHARACTER ———————— data type declarations list names belonging to each type
DIMENSION ———————— sets array size
COMMON ———————— data names in common storage
EQUIVALENCE ———————— data names using the same space
EXTERNAL ———————— external functions list
INTRINSIC ———————— internal functions list

Program Body

Groups of Statements

STOP
END

Figure 6-17 Overall Organization of a FORTRAN Program

Ordinarily, there would be only one STOP statement in most simple programs, and it would appear just before the END statement. In complex programs or in programs being tested, however, the programmer may provide several STOP statements, each including an identifying number. This number is printed or displayed when the program halts, so the programmer knows exactly which path the program followed to completion.

A Section of a FORTRAN Program

No description of a FORTRAN program would be complete without at least one example program. We've provided one in Figure 6-18 and, although we won't analyze it, the reader should find several useful examples of statements mentioned earlier.

REPORT PROGRAM GENERATOR—RPG

Here is a language with a name quite different from the others we've discussed. Its structure is different as well. RPG produces programs that prepare reports, hence the name "report program generator."

Let's examine first a very simple program generator to understand some of the ideas involved. Computer manufacturers offer program generators to allow a user to produce an application program that fits his exact needs without having to write the program himself. When the user loads and executes the program generator, it lists options available and allows the user to make selections. The generator then takes the choices made and combines them with the basic logic of the program.

Imagine this basic logic represented in flowchart form. The using programmer writes none of it; he simply chooses whether or not certain parts are executed and if they are what specifications apply.

Of course, the program generator may be used over and over. Each program it produces is unique, based upon the specifications provided by the user, but the basic program logic is the same for all the customized programs.

To summarize: Program generators require the using programmer to provide a set of specifications. These specifications are combined with the existing program logic to produce a program that does a specific job. That's also the nature of RPG.

A question now arises: Where is the "programming language" in RPG? And the answer is that the language is used to prepare the specifications. These are far more complex than simply making the selections, but the principles are similar. RPG requires, however, that the specifications be entered in the form of a source program. A compiler then produces the RPG object program, which is tailored to the user's specifications.

RPG is a fairly old language, having been introduced in the mid-1960s and upgraded to RPG II in 1970. As evident from the preceding paragraphs, RPG is certainly different from the languages we've covered up to now.

RPG is well suited to the preparation of routine business reports and to the establishment and maintenance of files related to these reports. Most people would not want to program complex tasks in RPG, however, because of the great detail that the programmer must provide. Therefore, we'll stay away from complex applications in this discussion, concentrating instead on the strengths of the system.

```
READ *, ID, HRSWRK, WGRATE, DEDUC
PRINT *, 'ECHO CHECK'
PRINT *, ID, HRSWRK, WGRATE, DEDUC
PRINT *, ' '
GRSPAY = HRSWRK * WGRATE
TAXES = GRSPAY * TAXRT
PAYCHK = GRSPAY - TAXES - DEDUC - PNRATE * GRSPAY
PAYRTN = PAYCHK / HRSWK
PRINT *, ' GROSS   TAXES   CHECK   RATE '
PRINT *, GRSPAY, TAXES, PAYCHK, PAYRTN
STOP
END
```

Figure 6-18 A Section of FORTRAN Program

The Five Specifications

RPG accepts data from files, processes it in a certain manner, and provides output files. Thus, we can already see three sets of specifications that the using programmer must provide: the input, the process, and the output specs. These are three of the five most important specifications. Each is provided on a coding form. The form has a very rigid format, is very complex, and is called a specifications form rather than a coding form.

Each type of specification is given a letter to distinguish it from other types, and this letter is entered in every line. We'll cover them in the order in which they must be entered into the system, later enlarging important sections where necessary.

First, we have the "H" specification, called the control card specifications, which provides information concerning the computer and program. For example, it defines memory size to be used and gives the program name. It defines the currency symbol, the character set, the number of printer positions, etc.

Next comes the "F" form, the file description specifications, which names and describes the files the program will use. It gives file name, type, access method, type of device the file is associated with (printer, tape, etc.) and many other details.

The "I" form, the input specifications, is provided next. It describes the organization of the input records. This form gives the file name and defines the layout of the records in each file.

Fourth in appearance is the "C" form, the calculation specifications, which defines the processing to be done. The format of the calculation specifications is similar to coding forms used in low-level languages. It provides areas for operands and operations to be entered, and it also lists conditions on which the calculations depend.

Last in the group is the output specifications form, the "O" form, which describes the layout of the records to be produced by the program. It gives file names, field sizes, output positions and information needed to control the device holding the output file.

A Source Program and Its Compilation

Now we'll jump ahead to the compilation of an RPG program, assuming that the programmer has prepared the specification sheets. Later we'll describe the format of each specification and show what can be entered in each type.

The specifications are handled like source statements in other languages. Columns 1 through 5 of each form provide page and line number, and the information necessary to place all the lines in consecutive order. Column 6 of each form holds a letter indicating the specification type. Specifications must be entered in the order in which they were described above: H, F, I, C, and O.

After the compiler accepts and processes the specifications, combining them with any subroutines called by the programmer from a subroutine library, it produces the object program and a source listing. As usual, diagnostic notes are added.

A Section of a Source Listing

RPG source listings take some "getting used to." A section of one is shown in Figure 6-19, and although it has been greatly reduced in size, the reader should be able to see that we have essentially the contents of the specifications forms after the background has been removed.

On the left, as usual in source listings, is the sequential line number assigned by the compiler. Next appears the page number and line number taken from the forms entered. A letter showing the form type comes next, then the contents of the form. At the far right, occupying columns 75–80, the last five columns, is the program identification.

A "bare" listing like this is hard to use. Obviously, it is possible to improve the appearance of a source listing if the programmer takes the time to prepare comments and separating lines.

The Fixed Program Logic of RPG

Now let's examine the object program. A good way to illustrate the order in which the program logic is executed is to show it in flowchart form as we've done in Figure 6-20. This flowchart is simplified, leaving out details that require great knowledge of the system but retaining all the information needed for the reader to understand the basic cycle.

The primary purpose of these programs is to produce reports based on the contents of data files. Some processing can be done, but RPG does not have a long list of powerful instructions that can be given in the calculation specifications.

The first block encountered is entitled "initialization." It opens files, loads tables and arrays, and sets certain indicators.

Let's talk about indicators briefly. They are ex-

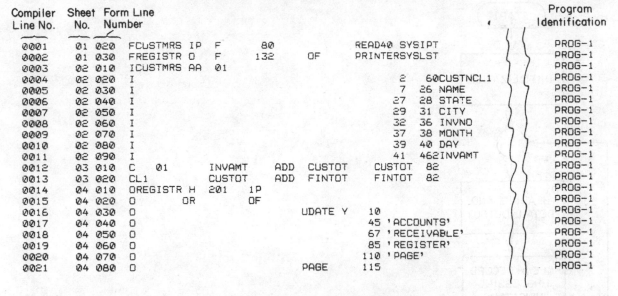

```
Compiler   Sheet  Form Line                                                                    Program
Line No.    No.   Number                                                                       Identification

 0001      01  020    FCUSTMRS IP  F      80                  READ40 SYSIPT                      PROG-1
 0002      01  030    FREGISTR O   F     132       OF         PRINTERSYSLST                      PROG-1
 0003      02  010    ICUSTMRS AA  01                                                           PROG-1
 0004      02  020    I                                               2   60CUSTNCL1            PROG-1
 0005      02  030    I                                               7   26 NAME               PROG-1
 0006      02  040    I                                              27   28 STATE              PROG-1
 0007      02  050    I                                              29   31 CITY               PROG-1
 0008      02  060    I                                              32   36 INVNO              PROG-1
 0009      02  070    I                                              37   38 MONTH              PROG-1
 0010      02  080    I                                              39   40 DAY                PROG-1
 0011      02  090    I                                              41  462INVAMT              PROG-1
 0012      03  010    C    01        INVAMT    ADD   CUSTOT    CUSTOT   82                       PROG-1
 0013      03  020    CL1            CUSTOT    ADD   FINTOT    FINTOT   82                       PROG-1
 0014      04  010    OREGISTR H   201     1P                                                   PROG-1
 0015      04  020    O            OR        OF                                                 PROG-1
 0016      04  030    O                                 UDATE Y    10                           PROG-1
 0017      04  040    O                                            45 'ACCOUNTS'                PROG-1
 0018      04  050    O                                            67 'RECEIVABLE'              PROG-1
 0019      04  060    O                                            85 'REGISTER'                PROG-1
 0020      04  070    O                                           110 'PAGE'                    PROG-1
 0021      04  080    O                                 PAGE     115                            PROG-1
```

Figure 6-19 Section of a Source List

tremely important to RPG. An indicator is a sign that a certain event has occurred or that a certain condition exists. Each is given a two-position designation. Numbers 01 through 99, for example, indicate types of records. Certain calculations should be done on type 01 but not on type 02. In this case, the indicator 01 is set when a record of that type is read and the indicator causes these certain calculations to be executed. Perhaps specific fields of record type 02 are to be placed in the output file. The 02 indicator causes that to take place.

After the operations required by a specific indicator are performed, the indicator is turned off. It is turned on again when the same conditions exist, such as when the next record of the same type is read. Indicators can thus be considered as RPG's way of saying such things as WHILE condition DO statement that the high-level languages can express directly.

Now we'll jump down to rectangle 3, the READ RECORD in Figure 6-20, and move to the main logic of the program. A record is read from an input file and examined to determine its type. A specific record identifying indicator is set as the result of this examination. Thus the record has been identified and the program can execute the steps the programmer has specified for this record type.

If the record is the same type as the previous record and is thus to be processed in the same manner, there is no control break and the logic proceeds to the detail calculations (5) and detail output steps (1). A new cycle then begins with the reading of the next record to be processed. This flow continues until the last record is processed or a control break is indicated.

A control break in RPG means that the programmer has specified that certain fields are to be compared with the same fields of the previous record. When RPG finds that the records differ, certain action specified by the programmer is to be taken. This involves some type of activity by the "total" logic, which is shown on the right side of the flowchart.

There are two basic events that cause the total logic to be executed. We discussed one, the control break; the other is the last record indicator. Action taken by the total logic differs slightly depending upon which event caused it.

In the case of a control break, the total logic executes the total calculations and output steps specified by the programmer for that type of control break. These steps complete the processing for all records of the type being handled prior to the detection of the difference in the records—prior to the control break in other words. After the total logic is executed, the program moves on to the detail logic to process the record in which the difference was detected, the first of a new group.

A last record indicator also causes the total logic to be executed. However, the program does not go on to the detail logic because the detail calculation and output lines for the last record have already been executed. Instead, the program moves to the end of the job.

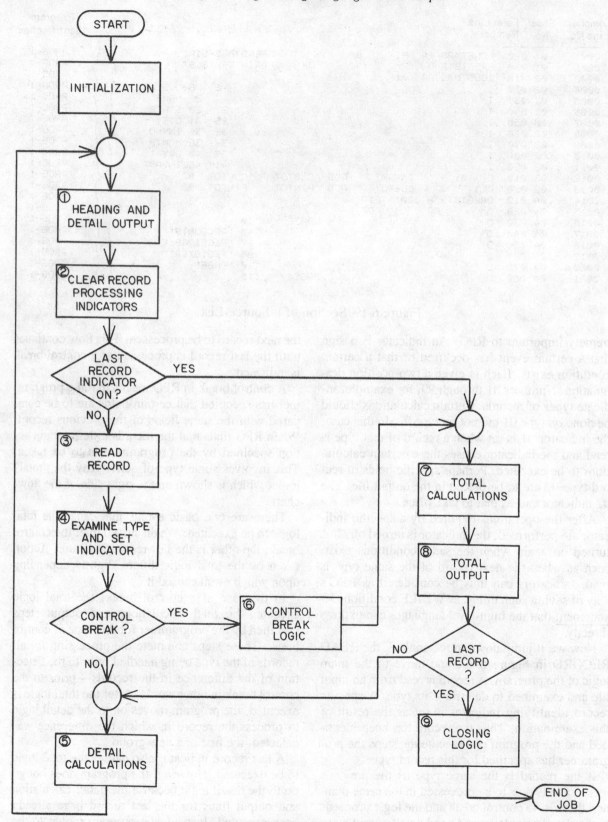

Figure 6-20 Object Program Flowchart

Before we close this discussion of an RPG object program we must make clear that the terms "detail time" and "total time" are significant and the reader should keep their meaning in mind while going through the rest of this section. "Detail time" is basically blocks 1 and 5, while "total time" is blocks 7 and 8. Later, when we discuss lines of instructions given in the specification forms, we see that some are labeled so as to be executed only during total time or only during detail time. These terms are thus important to anyone wishing to develop a good understanding of RPG.

Naming Conventions

There are two basic units that must be named in RPG: (1) files and (2) data items, which include tables, arrays, and fields. Names given to files may be up to eight characters long, although only the first seven are used by many compilers. Characters permitted in a file name vary slightly with the system.

Field names are limited to six positions, as are table and array names. And again there are slight differences in the naming rules from one implementation to another.

Table and array names differ somewhat from field names. The first three characters of a table name must always be "TAB," but the remaining characters may be any letter or number.

Control Card Specifications

This single-line specification, which differs significantly from one system to another, is printed on the same form as the file description specifications. Like the Identification Division in COBOL, the control card specifications in RPG provide only limited information, including program name. Many of the entries take on a standard value if they are not provided.

File Description Specifications

Printed on the same form as the control card specifications are the file description specifications, which list files used by the program and describe their characteristics. We'll concentrate on the most important file characteristics, however, leaving the details to RPG reference books.

Figure 6-21 shows a section of the F form. On the left is the line number entry, which is consecutive within each page but not between pages. The page number itself, which occupies columns 1 and 2, is usually provided at the top of each form. Next is the form type, which is preprinted.

File name, MYFILE in this case, occupies the next few columns. A single letter for file type comes next. We've entered I for input here. Another letter goes in the next column to describe how the file is used: P (primary), S (secondary), C (chain), D (demand), etc.

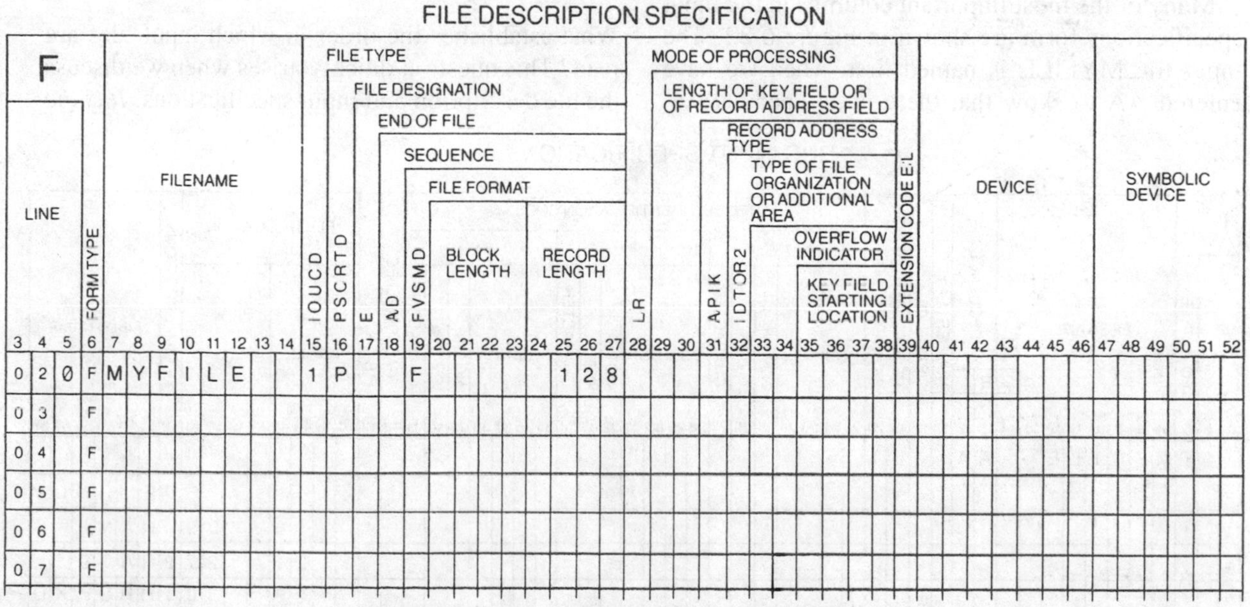

FILE DESCRIPTION SPECIFICATION

Figure 6-21 File Description Details

Skipping to column 19 we enter an F to point out that records in this file are fixed length, and then we state the record length in columns 24 through 27.

The file thus described is to be read first (primary) and the program can expect to find that all records are 128 characters long.

Input Specifications

Readers who remember COBOL's Data Division should find the appearance and content of the RPG input specifications form somewhat familiar. It defines the format of the records that make up each input data file, giving field name, location, and size. It also specifies whether a field is numeric or alphanumeric.

The use of indicators to select the processing to be performed on each record is new, however. Also being encountered for the first time is the possibility that a file may hold more than one record type. A substantial part of the input specifications form is allocated to information RPG needs to identify records of different types and to check their sequence.

First to appear in the specifications is the name of the file whose contents are to be described. It appears in columns 7 through 14 and is the same as that given in the file specifications. The file name is entered on only one line, although the input specifications for a file may occupy many lines. Of course, each file must be fully described before the next file name appears.

Many of the most important columns in the input specifications form are shown in Figure 6-22. The input file MYFILE is named first. Then we have entered AA to show that there is no specified sequence in which the records must appear; they are all the same in this file.

Next comes the number of the indicator that will be turned on when a record from this file is read. Indicator 01 thus signals the program that the fields defined on the right side of the form are available for processing.

Since the name, size, and location of each field is given, the program knows exactly where each field is. Column 52 defines field type. Fields are alphanumeric unless a number appears in this column.

Since all the records in this file are identical, no entries are needed in columns 21 through 41. Let's assume though that the first record was a label and, although it was 128 characters long like the others, it had to be recognized and handled in a different way. The label record would thus have a different indicator number. That indicator would be turned on only when specific characters were recognized in the record read from MYFILE. The distinguishing characters and the positions they occupy are stated in columns 21 through 41, and then the fields of the label record are identified in the same manner described above.

Perhaps the label record is always first. In this case, the sequence columns would state that the label record is first and that the data records are second and all following records read from this file.

Relationship Between Files

What establishes the order in which input files are read? This question quickly arises when we discuss the file description and input specifications. *It is the*

RPG INPUT SPECIFICATIONS

I	LINE	FORM TYPE	FILENAME	OR AND	SEQUENCE	NUMBER (1-N)	OPTION (O)	RECORD IDENTIFYING INDICATOR OR**	POSITION 1	NOT (N)	C Z D	CHARACTER	POSITION 2	NOT (N)	C Z D	CHARACTER	POSITION 3	NOT (N)	C Z D	CHARACTER	STACKER SELECT	P B L R	FROM	TO	DECIMAL POSITIONS	FIELD NAME
	3 4 5	6	7 8 9 10 11 12 13	14		15	16	17 18	19 20	21 22 23 24	25	26	27	28 29 30 31	32	33	34	35 36 37 38	39	40	41	42	43	44 45 46 47	48 49 50 51	52	53 54 55 56 57 58
	0 1	0 I	MYFILE		A A			0 1																		
	0 2	I																					1	5 0		EMPNUM
	0 3	I																					6	2 0		NAME
	0 4	I																					2 1	2 7	2	RATE
	0 5	I																					2 8	3 0	1	HRSWKD

Figure 6-22 Record Description Details

input specifications that defines the order. The first file named on the I form is considered to be the primary file, and it is read first. All other files named are secondary files, and each is read in the order in which the name appears on the I form. Each file is read at one record per cycle of the object program.

With respect to output files, the order of data output is established by the output specifications. This is subject to conditioning indicators and a certain instruction (EXCPT) in the calculation specifications.

There are some special arrangements that may be made for reading input files, however. Included are demand files, chained files, use of the FORCE instruction, and the matching records feature. Each of these processes is fairly complex, and they will have to be left to RPG reference books.

Arrays and Tables

RPG's way of handling tables and arrays is somewhat different than the methods used by the languages we've studied so far. Up to now, we've thought of an array as being a table. In RPG, however, arrays and tables are distinctly different.

Let's go into the description of an array first because it is similar to the arrays used in other languages. RPG allows only one-dimensional arrays.

An array name consists of up to six characters. Each element in the array is then numbered and is selected in the following manner: array name, element number. For example, the entry PYRT, 3 would select the third element in the array named PYRT to be acted on. The element number is called the array index.

Tables are handled much differently. A table is a list and a table by itself is of limited value. We might have a table of employee names, another of part numbers, and still a third of part costs. Each table can be displayed, printed, and updated, so if all we're interested in is a current list, a table by itself satisfies our requirements.

On the other hand, tables can be paired with one another to perform more useful functions. Product part number might be paired with the price of the product, for example, to form two lengthy lists, one holding part numbers and the second holding the price of that part. Of course, the related information must be in corresponding positions. If the part number for Toaster E52A75 is in the twenty-seventh position of the first table, then the price of the toaster must be in the twenty-seventh position of the second table. In RPG, this is done at the time of data entry through the method of naming two tables and alternating the entries in the form: part number, part cost, part number, part cost, etc.

Table names always begin with the characters TAB. These characters distinguish tables from arrays. Both tables and arrays are described on the file extension specifications form, which we haven't covered in this book, and this form establishes the relationship between two tables as well.

Calculation Specifications

A good way to start a discussion of the calculation specifications is to examine the "core" of the form, columns 18 through 42, which is organized into operation and operand fields much like an assembly language coding form. (Figure 6-23 shows this.) Factor 1 and factor 2 are operand areas, and the operation code occupies the operation field. Later in this section we'll discuss some of the instructions that may be entered here.

There are two other major areas on the calculation form. Conditioning indicators occupy most of the left side. When an indicator listed here is active, the related operation line is performed. This is the basic control device that determines whether or not a line in the calculation specifications is executed.

On the right side are listed the indicators that are to be controlled by the action of a line when that line is executed. In this manner, the results of certain operations can be recorded and later acted upon.

Now we can examine the calculation specifications form in detail. Let's use the simple example in Figure 6-23, which shows one line. At the left we have the indicators that must be on to allow this instruction to be performed. Nothing is entered in columns 7 and 8, so this is a detail line. Indicator 01 is the only condition required.

When indicator 01 comes on then, the instruction MULT (multiply) is executed. The fields named in factor 1 and 2 were defined the input specifications, so the program knows their location, type, and size. After multiplication, the product is placed in the result field, and its type and size are defined on the calculation specifications. (Note that column 53 has an H in it; this means half adjust, "round" in other words.)

RPG offers many instructions for use in the calculation specifications. We won't go into the details of each, but we will briefly describe some.

Most of the instructions in the arithmetic group

RPG CALCULATION SPECIFICATIONS

C LINE	FORM TYPE	CONTROL LEVEL (L0-L9, LR, SR, AN OR)	INDICATORS AND / NOT	AND / NOT	AND / NOT	FACTOR 1	OPERATION	FACTOR 2	RESULT FIELD NAME	LENGTH	DECIMAL POSITIONS	HALF ADJUST (H)	RESULTING INDICATORS
0 1 0	C		0 1			RATE	MULT	HRSWKD	GRSPAY	5	2	H	
0 2	C												
0 3	C												
0 4	C												
0 5	C												
0 6	C												
0 7	C												
0 8	C												
0 9	C												

Figure 6-23 A Sample Calculation Line

are easy to understand. They operate on factor 1, factor 2, the result field, and indicators, and naturally the instruction name is placed in the operation field. Some of the instructions in this group are:

ADD Adds factor 2 to factor 1; places the sum in the result field.

COMP (Compare) Compares factor 1 and factor 2; sets indicator(s) specified to show results.

DIV (Divide) Divides factor 1 by factor 2; places quotient in the result field.

MULT (Multiply) Multiplies factor 1 by factor 2; places the product in the result field.

MVR (Move Remainder) Given immediately after DIV, moves the remainder into the result field.

SQRT (Square Root) Takes the square root of factor 2 and places it in the result field.

SUB (Subtract) Subtracts factor 2 from factor 1, places the difference in the result field.

Next, we have the Lookup (LOKUP) instruction whose purpose is to find an entry in a specific table or array. Factor 2 holds the name of the table or array involved, while factor 1 holds the search information, or argument. For searches involving pairs of tables, the result field holds the name of the second table in the pair.

A limited number of instructions appear in the branches and subroutines group. GOTO is available, as is the ability to create subroutines and link to them.

A subroutine is called by an EXSR (Execute Subroutine) statement; the name of the subroutine is given in factor 2. At the end of the subroutine, control returns to the statement following the EXSR instruction that called it into action.

We have eight instructions in the program control group. Since RPG has a fixed program logic, instructions that force inputs or outputs override the basic logic and are thought of as program control instructions.

The STOP instruction causes the program to halt immediately and to display a two-character code supplied in factor 2. It is not the normal way in which the program stops so the "stop code" is displayed.

Next we'll deal with three instructions that cause reading to take place; they override or supplement the basic logic of RPG. FORCE selects a specific file from which the record used on the next cycle will be read. READ causes a record from a demand file to be made available for processing immediately. And, last, CHAIN retrieves chained records at calculation time.

Now we'll discuss the instructions that produce outputs. There are three of these: EXCPT, DUMP, and DUMPF. The purpose of the EXCPT instruction is to permit an output to take place during calculations, while DUMP and DUMPF are special instructions that are used to record the RPG object program and selected files.

There are six MOVE instructions. All have the same purpose: to move data into the result field. They differ in what information is moved and how it is aligned.

To close our discussion, we have two instructions whose sole purpose is to control indicators and thus give the programmer direct control of indicator status. They are SETON/SETOF, which turn on or off, respectively, the indicator listed in columns 54 through 59.

Output Format Specifications

The purpose of this form is to describe the output records and the conditions under which the output will take place. It is similar in appearance to the input specifications but there are significant differences that make a detailed examination necessary. Part of the form appears in Figure 6-24. In order to keep related functions together we'll have to skip around among the columns rather than discuss them left to right in numerical order.

First to be given is the output file name. This appears in columns 7 through 14; it was related to a specific type of unit (printer, video terminal, etc.) in the file description specification.

Next, in column 15, is a one-character definition of the record type. H and D in this column stand for heading record and detail record, respectively. Both are processed for output at detail time. T means a total record, which is processed during total time, and E designates an exception record, which is processed when the EXCPT instruction in the calculation specifications is obeyed.

Columns 23 through 31 provide the output indicators, which state the conditions that must be satisfied before a particular record or field can be handled for output. The entries and use are very similar to the conditioning indicator columns in the calculation specifications.

Next are the names of the fields involved in output. These are names given in either the input or calculation specifications, or they may be table names, array names, array entry names, or some special names.

Column 38, called edit codes, provides a letter or number to select the editing conventions followed in providing the output. This would apply to printer and display outputs. (Editing can also be done by an edit word provided in the "constant or edit word" area that we discuss later.)

RPG OUTPUT SPECIFICATIONS

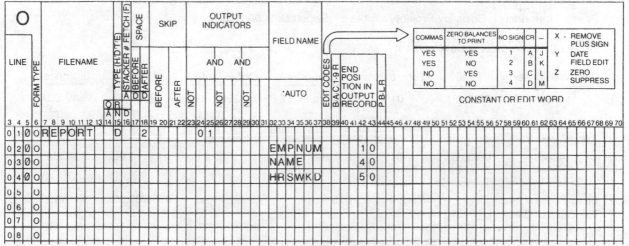

Figure 6-24 Output Description Details

In our example, we have the format of a detail line laid out. Each time indicator 01 comes on, the contents of the three fields named are placed in the output record in the positions given. Since field size and type are known—it has been defined on either the I or C forms—only the position of the field in the output record needs be shown on the O form.

Control of the printer and video terminal screens is provided by entries in several columns, 17 through 22. Entries in these columns control line spacing on the printer and move the cursor symbol on the display screen.

In most printed reports, the programmer needs to insert information such as headings that cannot be obtained from the input records. Special editing of the data fields may also be desired before they are actually printed. Space for the entry of both titles and editing symbols is available on the right side of the output specifications form in columns 45 through 70.

One use of this area is to enter information that is to be displayed or printed. Up to twenty-four characters framed by apostrophes—in the form 'CHARACTERS'—may be entered. When these entries are combined with the ending position stated in columns 40 through 43, the result is that the characters are placed in certain locations along a displayed or printed line.

An edit word may also occupy this area. It applies to the related field given on the same line and gives the specific format for that field's contents. The place of the decimal point, zero suppression, etc., can be specified.

An Ideal Application for RPG

A common and important application of RPG is to derive routine reports from data available in existing files. The calculations required are limited and the output specifications are often the largest portion of the program.

Figure 6-25 shows a small part of a routine project cost report. Most of the body has been eliminated because it is very difficult to reproduce large computer printouts in a book this size. Figure 6-26 does show how the entire report is organized, however.

Our only objective in analyzing this report is to show examples of things a programmer must consider; we are not writing the program itself. A reader should be able to relate these examples to entries in the specification forms, however, and have a general idea how he would go about organizing a program.

The first thing to be printed is the report title,

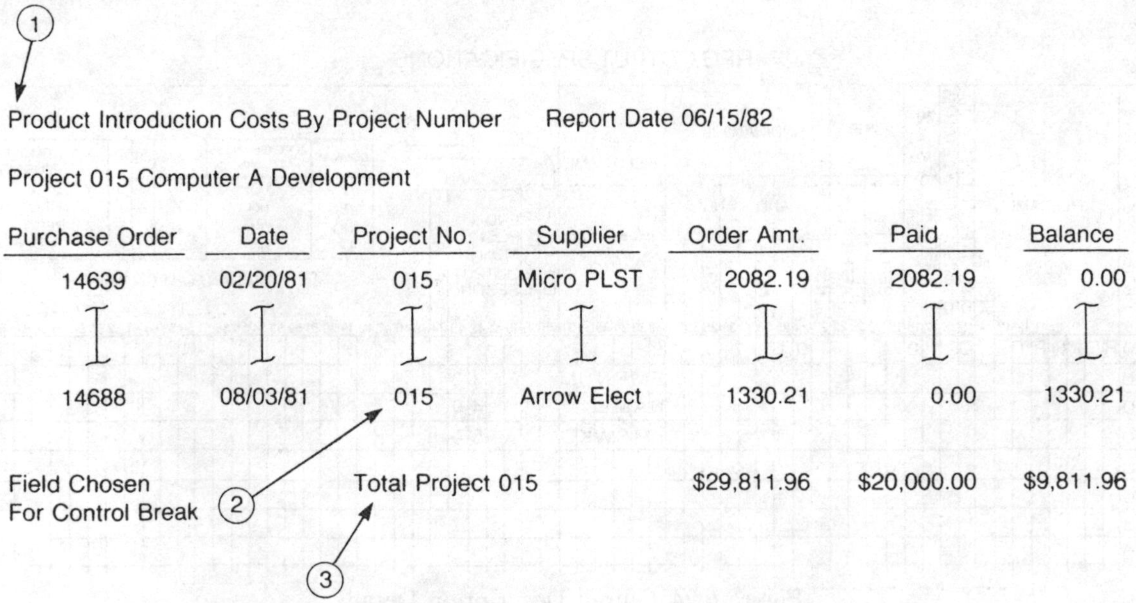

Figure 6-25 Section of a Sample Report

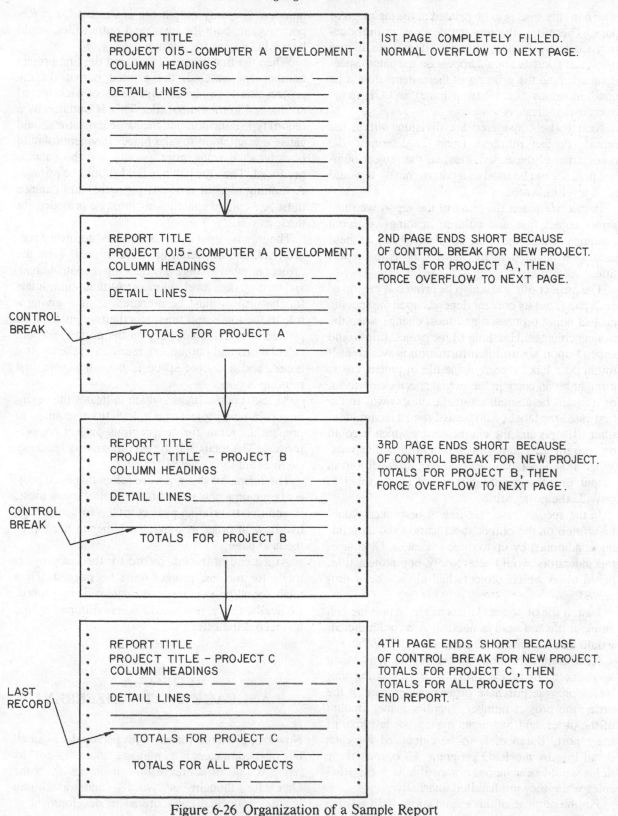

Figure 6-26 Organization of a Sample Report

which in this case is to be printed at the top of every page. Therefore, the report title Product Introduction Costs by Project Number (item 1 on Figure 6-25) and the date should appear on the output specification. And the printing of these items should be conditioned by the 1P (first page) and OF (page overflow) indicators.

Next to be considered are divisions within the report. Project numbers (item 2) determine the boundaries of these divisions, so the project number field should be used as a control break. It would set a level indicator.

Before we reach the body of the report we must print project title and column headings. Column headings remain the same for every sheet, so these would be handled in the same way as the report title.

The project title must also be printed at the top of each page, but its content depends upon the specific project being processed and must change when the project changes. Handling of the project title would depend upon where the information is available. It might be a label record in the file of project costs, it might be an entry in the output specification form, or it might be a small input file on its own. In the first case, the label could be assigned a record identifier (01–99) and the characters by which it could be recognized entered on the input specifications. When that label was read, it would condition an output line that prints part or all of the label to provide the project title.

In the second case, the line to be printed would be written on the output specification and its printing conditioned by up to three indicators. Of course, the indicators would select only one project title, based upon which projects had already been processed.

Last, a file of project labels might be provided on an input file and read as needed. A record indicator would then condition the output.

Next comes the body of the report. It is based upon six fields of each record in an existing file, which provide purchase order number, date of the order, the project number, supplier name, amount of the order, and payments made. The last field of the report, Balance, is to be calculated for each detail line by the RPG program. Of course, these fields would bear names compatible with the RPG rules while they are handled internally.

For the purpose of this explanation, we'll assume that the input file Project Costs is in order by project number. The only output file is Project Costs Report. Again, both the input and output files would bear RPG names for internal use.

When the first record is read and the first project number encountered, the printed output for the project title is produced. Six fields of each record are moved to the output file. This is initiated by a record type indicator, and the same indicator should cause a calculation to take place. Payments should be subtracted from order amount and the balance produced. Then the balance field should be printed. A running total of amount, payment, and balance must be kept, so calculations must be provided for those as well.

The input-output cycle is repeated for every record read, and the detail lines are printed. Then the project number changes, producing a control break and turning on a level indicator. At that point, totals for the project must be prepared. A line giving a title to the totals and the totals themselves must be printed after a double space on the printer. So both calculations and outputs are required at the control break, and a double space is needed before first printing is done.

At each control break, which indicates the beginning of a new project, the calculations required to prepare the totals for the previous project are performed. The totals and the accompanying headings (item 3) are then printed.

The format of this report requires that each project begin on a new page, so the control break must, in addition to printing project totals, force the page overflow in order to move the paper to the top of the next page.

At the end of the last record for the last project, totals for the last project must be printed. Then totals for all projects must be calculated and printed. Logically, this action would be conditioned by the last record indicator.

LOGO—A LANGUAGE THAT'S DIFFERENT

Now being offered for use with personal and small business computers is a language called "Logo." Its name is not an abbreviation—it comes from the Greek for "thought" or "word"—and was chosen by the group that collaborated in development of the language.

The Artificial Intelligence Laboratory at MIT produced Logo, and Dr. Seymour Papert is credited with originating the Logo Project. There is no standard for Logo, however, and there are already significant differences between the "Logos" available.

The ability to easily construct complex graphics and motion on the display screen may be Logo's outstanding feature. This sets the language apart. When we look deeper, however, we find that Logo is a complete language. It has a long list of reserved words, most of the control structures we've seen earlier, arithmetic operators, relational operators, several intrinsic functions, and the ability to perform arithmetic using fairly large numbers.

Logo does have a very different idea when it comes to data structures, however. There are no arrays or records, only "lists." We'll see what they look like later in this section. And there are some other Logo features that justify our title, "A Language That's Different." Remember what procedures are?—miniprograms that are called into action as needed but which are completely independent of one another otherwise. Logo depends on procedures. It provides standard procedures and makes it very easy for the programmer to construct his own.

Remember the extensive declaration section of Pascal and the data division in COBOL? Every item the program used had to be described in detail. Logo doesn't use this method. The programmer need not provide data type information in advance. It was only for the use of the compiler anyway. Making the compiler's job easier is hardly a goal of the computer user. Logo is capable of handling information whose type and size haven't been declared in advance.

Logo is an interpreted language, not a compiled one. In other words, individual source statements go to an interpreter for execution. In the compiler method, all source statements are converted to machine language before execution of the program begins.

Of course, the interpreter method is also used in other languages. BASIC, for example, is often provided with an interpreter rather than a compiler.

An "immediate" mode of interpretation is available in Logo. In this case, each source statement is interpreted and executed as soon as the programmer enters it. While some BASIC's also offer this feature, it is much more valuable in Logo and the results are dramatic in the construction of graphics. The action of a statement is immediately shown. This allows the programmer to watch a graphic being constructed and to modify his statements as needed.

Of course, a normal mode of interpretation can also be used. In this case, the program is complete and is to be executed in its entirety. The interpreter simply executes one statement at a time in the order specified.

Remember the BASIC graphics statements we discussed earlier in this chapter? They were powerful enough to allow a programmer to construct shapes, assign them colors, and move them about. Logo makes this much easier, however. It offers predefined movable objects that can be called by name. The primary object is called the "turtle," and when this symbol is visible, it is a small triangle. Statements such as FORWARD, RIGHT, etc., can move the turtle. (Figure 6-27a shows the turtle and a simple movement.)

The second predefined movable object, called a "sprite," appears in most implementations. One Logo offers thirty sprites. Each is capable of movement, and each can take on a variety of shapes and colors, including shapes that the programmer creates. (One sprite is shown in Figure 6-27b.)

And, if this wasn't enough in the way of graphics, there is still another way to create shapes. It's called a "tile" and can be thought of as a square tile that makes up a floor. Within each tile, we have a grid pattern; some squares can be filled in and others left blank to form shapes, like that shown in Figure 6-27c.

So far, our description makes Logo sound as if it

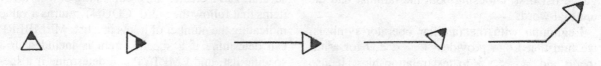

To begin   RIGHT 90   FORWARD :LENGTH   LEFT 45   FORWARD 10

Figure 6-27a The Turtle

A Sprite

Figure 6-27b A Sprite

was easy to use and maybe even fun. Most of the programming rules still apply, however. Use of the reserved word set must be studied, statement syntax rules must be followed, and programs must be organized by flowcharts, pseudocode, and decision tables if useful results are to be produced. In the pages that follow, we'll discuss some of Logo's most interesting features and show how a programmer handles them.

A Tile

Figure 6-27c A Tile

A Sampling of the Reserved Word List

We've said that Logo is a complete language, and a good way to prove this point is to pick samples from the reserved word list to show the range available. There are, however, two such lists, the first providing the base language and the second, the instructions used for graphics. Let's look at the base language list first, choosing both the familiar and the unusual words.

Beginning with the familiar operator symbols, we find that Logo provides +, −, *, / for arithmetic and =, <, > to test relationships. It also includes words that produce arithmetic. For example, DIFFERENCE returns the difference between the two numbers that follow, and SUM, PRODUCT, and QUOTIENT do the same for their respective operations. (Words are also available to test relationships. Included are GREATER, LESS, EQUALP, and NOT.)

One symbol, "dots," deserves special attention. The "dots" are a colon, and the colon is placed before the name of a variable in the form __:DISTANCE. This tells Logo to acquire the value of the variable DISTANCE and use it as the rest of the statement dictates. The "dots" are needed because variable names and procedure names look alike; the dots point out a variable whose value is to be obtained.

Also available are some of the familiar intrinsic functions including ARCTAN, COS, SQRT, and SIN for arithmetic. Several string functions are provided but their names are somewhat different from other languages. As an example, the function CHAR(X) returns the character whose numeric value is given in X.

We know that a set of control structures must be present in any language based on procedures. Logo has them; the IF/THEN/ELSE trio, REPEAT N times, and the less useful GO (for GOTO) are all present.

Inputs and outputs are also handled by a group of words that should be easy to use. "OUTDEV," for instance, selects a specific output unit; of course, the devices available depend upon the computer and version of Logo used. For inputs, we have READLINE, which takes the keyboard input and stores it as a list, and READPICT, which reads a picture file from a disk.

On the other end of things, four words provide outputs. PRINT says "print what follows and begin a new line," while PRINT1 does the same but remains on the same line. SAVE stores data or procedures on a disk (or other device) and SAVEPIC stores the graphic picture.

Twice earlier, we've pointed out that the Logo data structure is the "list." Logically then, one would expect to find a series of instructions needed to create lists and manipulate their contents. There are several. LIST creates a list consisting of a series of items that follow the word. COUNT returns a value indicating the number of items in a list. MEMBERP can determine if a specific item is included in a specific list, and EMPTYP can determine if a specific word or list is empty.

There are also several instructions to get list contents. FIRST and LAST acquire the respective element from a list, while BUTFIRST and BUTLAST get the rest. ITEM N gets the N item from the list. On the other hand, FPUT can place an item in the first position of an existing list.

Enough said about the nongraphics instructions—let's move into the graphics statements. We'll see how some of these are used later when the turtle, sprites, and tiles are discussed.

There are over fifty reserved words commonly available to deal with graphics. A good way to organize them is to place them in four groups: basic screen control, turtle control, sprite control, and use of tiles. Several of the instructions apply to all three elements (the turtle, sprites, and tiles). We'll point out those instructions as we go along.

Among the screen control instructions we have:

a. BACKGROUND, which chooses the background color in some Logos but has a different purpose in others.

b. CLEAN, CLEARSCREEN, CLEARTEXT. The basic purpose of this instruction is to start with a clear screen. It varies somewhat from one Logo to another.

c. CURSOR or SETCURSOR. Moves the cursor to a specific position.

d. DOT. Places a dot at a specific position on the graphics screen.

e. DRAW. Clears the graphics screen, makes the turtle visible, and places it in the center.

f. FULLSCREEN. Allows graphics to occupy the full screen with no text lines at the bottom.

g. NODRAW or TEXTSCREEN. Switches the entire screen to the text mode.

Now to the instructions associated with the turtle, sprites, and tiles. The first of these is TELL. It applies to all objects and is Logo's way of singling out an object that is to respond. TELL TURTLE makes the commands apply to the turtle, and TELL 5 chooses the fifth sprite as the object of commands.

Among the instructions that the turtle can execute, we have:

a. BACK, FORWARD, LEFT, and RIGHT. Of course, these set the basic movement to take place. Each word is followed by a value that tells "how much." (SETHEADING can also determine the direction in which the turtle moves.)

b. PENCOLOR, PENDOWN, PENUP, PEN-

ERASE. These instructions all control the pen at the turtle position. Obviously, they choose color, determine whether or not drawing will take place, and in the case of PENERASE, make the pen ready to erase a line.

c. HIDETURTLE and SHOWTURTLE make the triangular shape disappear and reappear, respectively. HOME returns the turtle to the center of the screen.

Now let's look at the instructions that may be issued to a sprite. Nearly all of the sprite's characteristics are under control of the programmer. Assuming that he isn't satisfied with the standard sprite shapes available, he can create his own through the use of the MAKESHAPE instruction. The shape is given a number and a certain sprite is told to CARRY that shape.

Among the other instructions available to control sprites, we have:

a. EACH, which lists a group of sprites to which instructions apply.

b. FREEZE and THAW. Respectively, these commands stop all sprite movement and allow it to resume.

c. HOME, which causes the selected sprite to move to the center of the screen.

d. LEFT, RIGHT, SETHEADING, SETSPEED, and SETCOLOR, which choose the direction in which sprite is to move, its rate and its color, respectively.

Last among our graphics objects is the tile. Like squares in a tile floor, these can be arranged to form a series of interesting patterns. They can be placed in any position, but they are not movable objects like the sprites and the turtle.

Of course, the appearance of the tile is of great importance. A MAKECHAR instruction allows the programmer to create the pattern the tile will carry, and a SETCOLOR instruction chooses the color. Placement of the tile is controlled by the PUTTILE instruction, which selects the location on the screen for a specific tile.

Recursion and Its Importance

In one popular dictionary, "recursion" has two definitions, both of which relate to mathematics. Its origin in Latin, which translates to "a return" will serve us better for this explanation, however.

In Logo, "recursion" is used to mean the feature that allows a procedure to call itself, to return to itself. This feature is also available in Pascal, although we didn't mention it there. It's important in Pascal, of course, but is a key part of Logo because it is used to construct very complex graphics.

When a procedure calls itself, it may modify the value of the variables involved and thus cause the procedure to be performed with different parameters. We'll discuss how this is done in the description of procedure construction that follows.

Construction of a Procedure in Logo

A Logo program is often a collection of procedures; thus it's important that we quickly find out how procedures are constructed.

First, we'll examine the two reserved words that establish a procedure and set its boundaries. TO is the word that defines the beginning of a procedure; it is used in the form:

TO procedure name.

All statements following this entry now become part of the procedure. END is the word that sets the concluding boundary. It appears by itself.

So now we know that a procedure in Logo has the following format:

TO procedure name

```
Group of Statements
```

END

Next we must discuss how a procedure is called into action. This too is simple, involving nothing more than using the procedure name in a statement. We've seen this method before, so we know it's not unique to Logo.

Let's assume that the purpose of our overall program is to construct a sales chart on the display screen in the form of a bar graph. The program itself would be a procedure named in the form: TO SALESCHART. In turn, it is made up of a series of procedures that construct the graph, add titles, and construct bars for various sales. Thus, the overall program appears:

```
TO SALESCHART
GRAPH
TITLE
SALESBARS
END
```

Now we'll construct a procedure that produces a complex graphic on the screen. We'll name the graphic SPIRAL, so the first line of the procedure would read TO SPIRAL. When the procedure is to be used, all we need to do is give its name, and the entire graphic is constructed.

In order to form the spiral, we must include the movement variables in the procedure. We'll call one ANGLE and the other LENGTH. The variable ANGLE will be the number of degrees that the turtle is to turn and the variable LENGTH will be the distance the turtle is to move. Thus, the simple procedure will be:

```
TO SPIRAL
FORWARD :LENGTH
RIGHT :ANGLE
END
```

When this procedure is performed, the turtle moves forward by the value of the variable LENGTH and then turns right by the value of the variable ANGLE. This movement, shown in Figure 6-28 is the beginning of a complex graphic.

Now we'll add recursion by inserting the procedure's own name. This takes the form:

```
TO SPIRAL
FORWARD :LENGTH
RIGHT :ANGLE
SPIRAL :LENGTH :ANGLE
END
```

Once called, the procedure will be performed over and over, but this is of limited use because the value of the variables is not changed. Assuming that the angle was ninety degrees, this procedure would produce a square whose side was the size of variable LENGTH, as shown in Figure 6-28.

As the final step needed to produce our spiral, we add a modifier to the procedure:

```
TO SPIRAL :LENGTH :ANGLE
FORWARD :LENGTH
RIGHT :ANGLE
SPIRAL :LENGTH + 2 :ANGLE
END
```

Now each time the procedure calls itself, the value of LENGTH is increased. Thus, instead of forming a square, the procedure forms a square spiral like that shown in Figure 6-28.

Of course this could go on even after the graphic exceeded the screen size, so a limiter must be added. Perhaps, a size of fifty is the largest that LENGTH is to become. In this case, we add an IF statement with a relational operator to control how many times the procedure is performed. This takes the form:

```
TO SPIRAL :LENGTH :ANGLE
IF :LENGTH > 50 THEN STOP
FORWARD :LENGTH
RIGHT :ANGLE
SPIRAL :LENGTH +2 :ANGLE
END
```

This procedure will now be performed a number of times but when the value of LENGTH exceeds fifty, it will stop.

Sprites and Tiles

Now that we know how to make the turtle move, let's look at the use of sprites and the construction of shapes on tiles. A simple sprite statement is:

TELL 5 CARRY 7

This selects sprite 5 and tells it to take on (carry) shape 7, whatever that may be. After this statement is executed, sprite 5 has a certain shape, but that's all.

We can also choose its color, direction of movement, and speed with:

TELL 5 SC :ORANGE SH 270 SS 17

Again, the statement selects sprite 5. This time, however, the statement sets its color (SC) to orange, sets its heading (SH) to 270, and its speed (SS) to a rate of 17. Now the sprite moves. If the shape was a truck, it would be moving across the screen at a certain speed.

In one popular Logo, sprites may take on any one of twenty-eight different shapes. Six standard shapes include a turtle, truck, airplane, rocket, ball, and a box. The programmer may create the remaining twenty-two different shapes and assign them to as many sprites as he chooses. (This Logo also allows the programmer to modify the standard shapes.)

A reserved word MAKESHAPE starts the proc-

Step I
The Basic
Movement

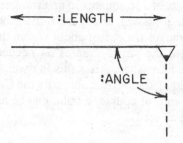

Step 2
Recursion.
The Basic Movement
is Repeated

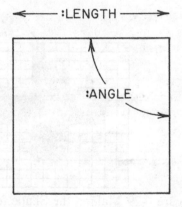

Step 3
Recursion with
a Modified Variable
LENGTH

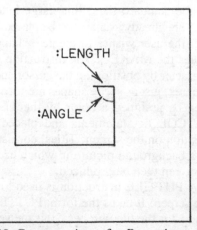

Figure 6-28 Construction of a Procedure

ess of sprite shape construction. It appears in the form MAKESHAPE 12 (the 12 is the shape number) and produces a grid on the screen. The grid consists of 256 squares in an arrangement 16 by 16, like that shown in Figure 6-29. The programmer then moves the cursor about within this grid, blacking out the small squares as needed to form the shape he wishes. After this is done, any sprite can be told to assume that shape by the CARRY instruction, and, of course, a color can be assigned to that sprite as well.

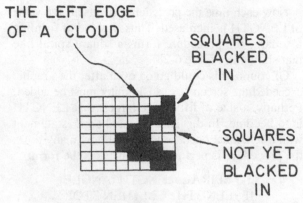

Figure 6-30 Making the Shape for a Tile

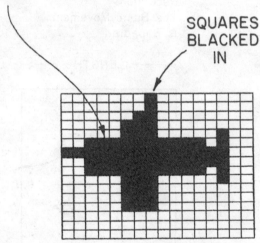

Figure 6-29 Making the Shape for a Sprite

Background graphics can be created by placing tiles on the screen. Each tile consists of 64 small squares, arranged in an 8-by-8 grid, as shown in Figure 6-30. All keyboard characters are available on the standard tiles, thus large letters, numbers, etc., are already available to be placed on the screen.

If the user wishes to create a shape on a tile, he issues the MAKECHAR instruction and forms the character by positioning the cursor and blacking out squares, just as sprite shapes are formed. A tile can then be assigned a color by the TELL TILE and SETCOLOR statements and placed in a specific position on the screen. Titles, consisting of letters, or a background picture in which each tile forms a part, can then be produced.

A PUTTILE instruction is used to place tiles on the screen. It takes the form: PUTTILE 17 20 105. The 17 is the tile number, 20 is the vertical position on the screen, and 105 is the horizontal position.

Obviously, a series of PUTTILE instructions can be placed in a procedure and the overall group given a name. TO CLOUD, for example, would consist of a series of PUTTILE instructions that placed clouds in a picture.

The Appearance of Some Logo Statements

So far, we've seen the statements used to create procedures, move the turtle, create and move sprites, and create and place tiles on the screen. Now let's look at some of the statements used for arithmetic, printing, and control.

Logo statements look different from those in BASIC, Pascal, and COBOL, but those languages also differ from one another in appearance. Shown below are ten Logo statements. A short explanation of them follows.

The first six statements deal with testing and control. Tests are made by statements one and two, and the results recorded as FALSE and TRUE, respectively. These can be checked by the IFFALSE statement, the third in the list, which takes appropriate action. An IF statement can also take action after doing its own tests, as statements four and five show.

Note the symbol " (the left double quotation mark only) is used in some cases. This says: "Don't evaluate what follows." In other words, the following name is not that of a variable whose value is to be inserted into the statement and it is not that of a procedure to be called into action.

A REPEAT statement appears next. It causes the movement given in brackets to be performed six times. The turtle thus moves forward by the value of the variable :LENGTH and turns right sixty degrees six times.

Next we have two assignment statements. The first takes the value of the variable A, adds a three to it, and assigns the total to become the value of the variable X. In the second, the variable named NUM1 is given the value of fourteen.

Some arithmetic is done in the next statement. It adds seven to five and shows the sum.

Last, we have a simple print instruction. It prints the current value of the variable named :VAR1, the colon telling Logo that the value is to be acquired.

Now that we've examined some of the Logo statements, many readers would conclude that they aren't so different after all. That's true; all languages are strangers at first glance and old friends after you've worked with them awhile.

```
IF :FIRST > :SECOND OUTPUT "FALSE
IF D < 20 OUTPUT "TRUE
IFFALSE [PRINT [WRONG ACCOUNT NO.]]
IF :N > 5 [MAKE "N 1]
IF :NUMBER = 0 [STOP]
REPEAT 6 [FORWARD :LENGTH RIGHT 60]
MAKE "X :A + 3
MAKE "NUM1 14
SUM 7 5
PRINT :VAR1
```

The Idea of Lists

Another thing about Logo that takes some "getting used to" is the idea of lists. In most of the languages we discussed, it was necessary to organize data structures, declare their contents to be of a certain type, and even give the size of the expected entries. As we now know, Logo doesn't require this, but until one has actually seen some simple lists, it's hard to visualize their appearance. Several appear below. Note that numbers and characters may be mixed (they are both "words" to Logo) and that lists may be included within lists.

A List of Numbers
[17.5 25.95 18.2]
A List of Character Data
[SMALL MEDIUM LARGE]
A Mixed List
[HARRIS 3.54 THOMPSON 2.95 WILLIAMS 4.0]
Lists Within a List
[SIZE [SMALL MEDIUM LARGE] COLOR [RED BLUE GREEN]]

CP/M—AN OPERATING SYSTEM YOU MAY HEAR ABOUT

Most operating systems are "silent partners" of the application programs, but one called CP/M has become well known among the users of small business and personal computers. Therefore, we've included a brief description of CP/M in this section.

An operating system ties things together. It gets the computer started, loads programs, manages storage space, links programs to one another, and handles the details of input/output operations. These are typical functions. Some systems do less and others more.

Of course, the operating system is itself a program. CP/M means "Control Program/Monitor." One trade magazine estimates that as of mid-1981 there were about 200,000 installations of CP/M. This covered over 3,000 different computer and peripheral equipment arrangements. These are certainly large numbers, and they indicate how popular microcomputers have become. Inexpensive microprocessor chips, semiconductor memories, and floppy disks are three primary reasons for their popularity.

The microprocessor family for which CP/M was developed is the Intel 8080 and 8085 group. It also applies to the Zilog Z-80 processor.

Computers based on these microprocessor chips vary considerably. CP/M is arranged to handle the differences, with one portion of the system remaining the same regardless of the machine on which it is used, and a second section being custom-made to fit a specific computer arrangement. CP/M consists of a fixed portion and a variable portion. When an implementor applies CP/M to a certain computer, he prepares the variable portion. This is illustrated in Figure 6-31.

CP/M is supplied on an 8-inch or 5¼-inch diskette and bears a version number like 1.4 or 2.2. A third digit, related to the computer type, is often added, in the form: 1.42. The first digit is the overall version number, the second indicates a certain revision level within the overall version, and the last digit shows variations of CP/M for a specific machine.

As a first step in getting started, the computer user places the CP/M diskette in his machine and turns power on. A loading program is then automatically moved from the diskette into the computer and executed. In turn, the loader transfers

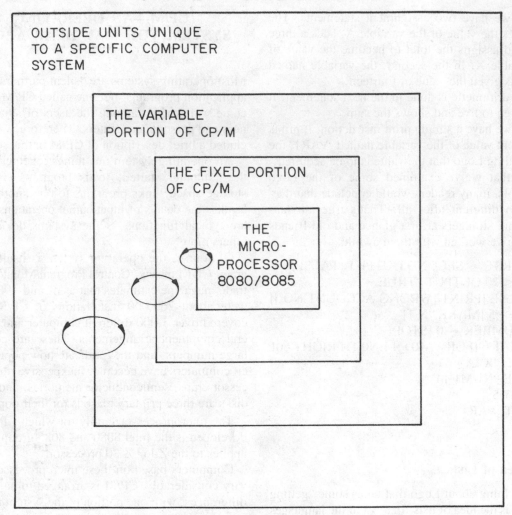

Figure 6-31 The Fixed and Variable Parts of CP/M

CP/M from the diskette to the computer and starts its execution. "Initialization," which means to establish the original operating conditions, then takes place.

The user is first aware that CP/M has taken control of the machine when the operating system display shown in Figure 6-32 appears. At this point, the computer is ready to use. A "ready prompt," the "A>" shown in the figure, signals this.

"Ready" means that CP/M can accept a command from the user. These vary somewhat from one machine to the next, but typical commands are those that call utility programs or programming systems into action.

Certain commands are standard. An example is DIRx:, which acquires a list, a directory, of all the

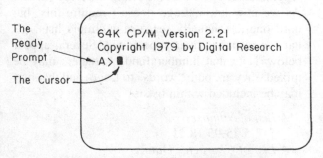

Figure 6-32 The CP/M Ready Display

files on the specified disk number (x) and displays it on the screen.

If the user wishes to call a programming system into action, he types in the name of that system in response to the "ready prompt." The command

"BASIC," for instance, brings in the BASIC system. This allows programs to be written in BASIC, any previously written programs to be run, and any of the BASIC system commands to be executed. In other words, it puts BASIC in control of the computer, under supervision of CP/M.

How to get back to CP/M is the next question, and this is done rather simply. When the CONTROL and C keys are depressed simultaneously, CP/M returns the ready prompt to the screen, showing that it is again ready to accept a command and that the BASIC system, for example, is no longer active.

Why should a computer user or programmer be concerned by whether he will be using CP/M or some other operating system? Its popularity is one very important reason. Since its use is widespread, a great many application programs have been prepared for the computers using it. This makes those programs available to other computers using CP/M and greatly increases the computer's value. In the case of the user, he'll have a greater selection of programs, and the programmer, of course, will have many less that he has to write.

SELF-TEST FOR CHAPTER 6

1. Describe the coordinate system used to organize a display screen for the construction of graphics.
2. Briefly describe what the five following graphics statements in our sample language do:
   COLOR, PAINT, DRAW, LINE, PUT.
3. What does the acronym FORTRAN mean, and what are full FORTRAN and subset FORTRAN?
4. How are comment lines identified in FORTRAN source statements?
5. FORTRAN relational operators are different than those in other languages. Write the relational operators for "equal" and "equal or greater than."
6. How is an assignment statement written in FORTRAN?
7. Compose a statement in FORTRAN to read three variables (A,B,C) from unit 5 and use the format in line 360.
8. FORTRAN has two very unusual rules concerning the names used for integer variables and variables that are real data (having decimal places). What are they?
9. Name the data types handled by full FORTRAN.
10. FORTRAN also has an unusual way of constructing subroutines and user-defined functions. Describe it.
11. RPG, Report Program Generator, is unique among the languages we've covered. What does this system do?
12. The RPG programmer prepares his source program on specifications forms. Name the five primary forms.
13. What information is given on the input specifications?
14. There are three unique terms in RPG that are very important: indicator, detail time, and total time. Describe what each means.
15. RPG limits the size of names, as most of the old languages do. How long may a file name be, a field name?
16. What is a control break?
17. What is the purpose of the calculation specifications?
18. Does RPG use the near-standard operator symbols $(+,-,*,/)$ for arithmetic?
19. What is the purpose of the output specifications?
20. If a programmer wishes to enter the actual headings or other information to be placed in an RPG report, where is this done?

Glossary of Terms

Absolute Value. The value of a number without regard to its sign.

Address. A label, name, or number that identifies a location or unit. A memory address chooses one location to read or store data. A device address chooses a specific functional unit from all others of the same type. Used to select one item with which to operate.

*ALGOL. Algo*rithmic *l*anguage. An older, general-purpose programming language used to express problem-solving formulas. (Algorithm meaning the procedure for the solution of a problem.)

Alphanumeric. A collection of letters and numbers that make up a character set. Also includes special characters such as punctuation and currency signs.

APL. An abbreviation for *a p*rogramming *l*anguage, which was designed primarily for mathematical uses.

Application Program. The program that *applies* the computer to a specific task for which the computer is intended. A program that causes a computer to print bank statements is an application program, but a program that detects and isolates computer faults is not.

Array. A collection of data elements arranged in order. Often used to mean a table of data or a matrix of data items.

*ASCII. A*merican *S*tandard *C*ode for *I*nformation *I*nterchange. A 7- or 8-bit code capable of representing 128 or 256 characters respectively.

Assembler Program. The program that translates statements made in a symbolic language by a programmer into the machine-language program that the computer executes.

Backspace. Associated with magnetic tape units, backspace means to back up one record and stop.

Backup Copy. A second copy of the same data in case the primary copy is destroyed. For example, important information stored on disks for daily operation may also be stored on magnetic tapes, but the tapes would be copied onto the disks only if the original information was lost.

*BASIC. B*eginner's *A*ll-purpose *S*ymbolic *I*nstruction *C*ode. Described in Chapter 3, this programming language is widely used, particularly with small computers.

Batch Processing. The handling of data to be processed in groups of similar items that require the same treatment. Data is collected and processed in a "batch." Contrasted with "transaction processing" in which data is handled as it is available.

BCD (Binary Coded Decimal). An arrangement in which a certain number of bits are intended to be read as a group representing a single decimal digit. Most often four bits are used to represent the decimal digit.

Binary Number System. The number system used by computers. Having only two characters, a 0 and a 1, the binary numbering system is represented within the machines by circuits that have an on and an off condition, usually meaning "1" and "0," respectively.

Bit. The contraction of the words *"bi*nary digi*t,"* but is also used to mean the position that holds a binary digit, such as bit 5, which means bit *position* 5.

Block. Data or storage locations handled as a group. Records are said to be "blocked" when they are recorded on tape without the usual interrecord gap.

Business Applications. Computers and programs devoted to tasks involved in a typical business, such as accounting, payroll, and invoicing. Contrasted with engineering or scientific applications.

Byte. A group of eight bits handled as a unit is the generally accepted meaning of byte.

Calling. To select a program for execution by

stating its name or symbol. The program size varies from a subroutine to a very large program.

Centralized Processing. The processing of data by a machine at one central location. Data may originate at remote locations, be forwarded to the central machine for processing, and then results returned. Contrasted with distributed processing in which there may be many processing stations generally at, or very close to, the source of the data to be processed.

Character. A character is one of the set of symbols handled by a computer. Each letter of the alphabet may be included in the character set, as are numerals, punctuation, and special symbols. There are also control characters included in many character sets; these cause actions and are not shown on display screens and printers. Each character in the character set is represented by a unique binary code.

Character Set. The collection of different characters that a language or computer is capable of representing. See *Character* above.

COBOL—Common Business Oriented Language. Described in Chapter 5, COBOL is one of the older programming languages. Designed to be very English-like in its statements, COBOL is widely used in medium and large business computers.

Codes. Within a computer, a set of binary digits organized so as to represent higher-level functions or symbols; 101111 might always be used to represent an "A," for example, and 00111010 might be the operation code for an ADD instruction.

Coding. Means "writing a program" by giving the words to which a computer will respond and placing them in the order needed to perform a specific task.

Communication Link. The arrangement of equipment needed to transfer data from one location to another, usually over fairly long distances.

Compiler. Similar to an assembler program listed earlier, a compiler program also translates statements made by a programmer into machine language. However, a compiler is usually more powerful than an assembler in that the assembler translates on a one-for-one basis, one programmer statement for one machine instruction, but a compiler is capable of translating one programmer statement into several machine instructions. In other words, the compiler can expand the input while an assembler cannot.

Constant. A quantity that will be used in a program and that is unchanging. Some numeric constants may be named and their values given by the programmer. Some languages have constants already available. PI, for example, is already defined as 3.14 in some languages and may be used by inserting PI into an expression.

Conversational Mode. A computer operating so as to accept English or "near English" statements directly from the user, normally from a keyboard/display unit, and to provide an immediate response that has meaning to the user without translation.

CP/M. Control Program/Monitor. An operating system designed for use with small computers using the 8085 (and related) microprocessor chips as their base.

CPU. The abbreviation for central processor unit. Is not related to centralized processing but rather is the name given to the control unit, arithmetic unit, and often the memory unit of a computer. It may be very small as in the case of a microcomputer or very large as in the case of the "mainframes."

CRT (Cathode-Ray Tube). The display device used in most display screens. A vacuum tube that uses an electron beam to excite an internal coating that glows. A TV picture tube is a CRT.

Cursor. A special indicator placed on a display screen to point out the character or position that is the subject of attention. If the display screen and keyboard are being used by the operator to enter information, the cursor points out the next entry position.

Data Base. Usually a large collection of information maintained permanently, or semipermanently, on which a computer is to operate.

Data Item. Most often a field of information; any named unit of information.

Data Link. A communications link over which computer data is transferred. This may range from voice-grade telephone lines that handle data transfer at low rates to radio links capable of very high rates of transfer.

Debug. To remove the "bugs" from equipment or programs during their initial testing. A "bug" is usually thought of as a design flaw that prevents the equipment or program from fulfilling its intended function rather than a malfunction that occurs after the system has been tested.

Decision Table. A programming design tool that lists alternative conditions that may arise and the action required for each condition or a combination of many conditions. Decision tables, or decision logic tables as they are also called, are often more effective than flowcharts in portraying the problem.

Decrement. (1) To reduce a quantity by a specific number, or (2) the number by which the quantity is reduced.

Desk Checking. The checking of program logic at the programmer's desk before the source program is entered into the computer.

Diagnostic Program. A program intended to test computer equipment and, through a logical process of testing and elimination, isolate failures to small sections of the machine.

Direct Access. Applied to access to data, direct access means that specific data can be reached without reference to previous data. Contrasted with sequential access in which data must be handled in sequence until the desired data is reached.

Directory. A list of items available. A file directory, for example, would list all files available and often their location.

Disk Pack. A removable disk or disks normally enclosed in a case.

Diskette. Also called a "floppy" or flexible disk. A small magnetic disk based on soft plastic material.

Distributed Processing. A computer network in which data is processed near its origins rather than at a central location. (See *Centralized Processing* for contrast.)

Dump. Usually means the copying of memory contents to another storage medium or displaying or printing them for examination. Dump implies the lack of discrimination among the data transferred. In other words, copying is not selective.

EBCDIC (Extended Binary Coded Decimal Interchange Code). A code consisting of eight bits to represent each character. Commonly used to record and communicate data.

Edit. As in writing, to change the content and form of information. Data elements may be reorganized, eliminated, or converted to a different style of presentation by editing tools available.

End of File. A special mark recorded in storage media that designates the end of a group of records that is to be considered a file. Abbreviated EOF.

Executable. Applied to programs, executable means a program that can be performed by the computer rather than a source program that must be assembled or compiled before it can be executed. An executable program is usually called an "object" program. Applied to instructions (statements), it means an active instruction that performs the logic

of the program rather than one that provides information needed by the program.

Execution Time. The most common meaning is the time required for a computer to perform an instruction. A second meaning is a substitute for "run-time" or "object run-time," meaning the time during which a program is being executed to carry out its intended functions.

Executive. The name usually given to a program whose function is to control the jobs to be performed and to select the programs required to perform them. An executive would also manage the storage media as required to provide input data and to store processed data.

External Storage. A storage medium outside the computer memory. Tape units and diskette and disk drives are examples of external storage.

File. A group of records organized so as to be treated as a unit. All the records in a file hold information that is of the same general type.

Firmware. A program or data pattern stored in a device that cannot be changed, usually a ROM, during normal operation of the computer. Some small computers provide their operating systems in firmware to avoid their loss or alteration.

Flowchart. A method by which certain symbols are used to show the functions that a program is to perform and the order in which these functions are to be performed. Decisions to be made, inputs required, outputs produced, and actions to be taken are among the functions shown in program flowcharts.

FORTRAN, Formula Translator. A language originally designed for engineering and scientific use. Described in Chapter 6.

Graphics. The figures other than alphanumeric characters shown on a screen. Computers with the ability to generate graphics in color are now readily available at low cost.

Header. Identifying or labeling information that precedes the data.

High-level Languages. Those near-English languages, such as Pascal, COBOL, and BASIC.

Hollerith Code. A code used in punched cards in which one column of twelve positions each is read as a unit. The combination of punches in these twelve positions is the Hollerith code. Named for Dr. Herman Hollerith.

Identifier. The name given to data or a procedure to distinguish it from all others. Programming systems all have very stringent rules concerning how identifiers are composed.

Impact Printer. A printer that forms characters by contact between the paper, ribbon, and character elements.

Increment. (1) To increase a quantity by a specific number, or (2) the number by which the quantity is increased.

Indexed Sequential Organization. A file in which records are accessible in any order regardless of the previous access. A key, such as social security number, identifies each record. When the record key is given, that record is read. Records are stored in order by value of the key.

Initialize. To establish the initial operating conditions in either equipment or programs.

Interactive. A mode of computer operation in which the user, most often an operator at a computer terminal, and the computer exchange inputs and responses, with one bringing forth the other.

Interrupt. A signal used by other computer units to gain the attention of the control unit. Usually produced in response to important external conditions, an interrupt signal produces a break in the flow of activities. Action taken in response to the interrupt varies according to the programs being executed, but the immediate needs of the external device are normally met before the control unit returns to the point at which it was interrupted. Applied to programs, means the stopping of one activity to pause or to take up a different activity.

Iteration. One performance of a series of steps that are normally performed more than once.

Interpreter. (1) The series of machine language instructions needed to carry out one high-level instruction. (2) The system in which each source statement is converted to machine language instructions as the program is being executed rather than having the conversion done all at one time by a compiler before execution.

Job Control Language. A system of statements used to control the performance of tasks by a computer. This language links the operating system and the application programs to determine what programs are to be performed and in what order.

Key. In access to files and tables, the unique character combination used to locate a specific record or entry.

Line Printer. A printer in which an entire line of characters is accumulated and printed during one cycle of the device.

Loop. (1) A series of steps that are intended to be performed repetitively. (2) One iteration of those steps. Applies to programs, and means a group of instructions that return to the starting point and repeat themselves, usually until a certain event takes place to break the loop.

Low-level Languages. Languages in which the instructions are close to machine-level instructions, often one instruction in a low-level language produces one machine-language instruction.

Machine Language. The binary code for each instruction the computer can execute. It is used directly by the computer without translation.

Main Storage. Generally means the memory that is part of the computer proper, not the storage available in diskettes, disks, and tape units. (That storage is usually called auxiliary storage.)

Menu. A list of programs or functions presented on the display screen. The program causing the menu to be shown accepts operator selections, which are usually made from the keyboard.

Merging. In most programming languages, means the combining of files into one file in a certain order.

Microcomputer or Microprocessor. Usually means a computer on a single integrated circuit chip. Microcomputer most often refers to an entire computer while microprocessor means only the CPU. These terms are frequently used interchangeably.

Network. A group of computers and related equipment that are interconnected, either locally or over long distances.

Nonimpact Printer. A printer that forms characters without having ribbon/print-head/paper contact. Characters may be formed by heat, electrical charges, ink spray, or other means.

Object Computer. The computer that executes the object program, which may not be the same machine that accepted and compiled the source.

Object Program. A program that is in machine language and is executed by the computer. It is the "object" of entering and assembling source statements and represents the final results of the process.

Off-line Operation. An operation that is not in the primary flow of computer activities. For example, data from a magnetic tape may be printed out while a computer is not engaged in or available for its primary task. In this case, the computer is doing off-line printing. Can also mean an operation such as a direct connection between the tape and printer, which bypasses the computer completely and is not under computer control. A peripheral unit that is said to be off line is one that is not immediately accessible to the computer.

On-line Operation. The opposite of the off-line operation above, an on-line operation *is in the primary flow* of computer activities. When applied to the status of a peripheral unit, it means that that unit *is immediately accessible* to the computer.

Operand. Usually considered to be one of two major parts of an instruction, the operation code being the other. An operand is an item to be operated upon or is somehow involved in the operation specified by the operation code. An operand may be a memory address, a number to be added, a parameter of some type, etc.

Operating System. The set of programs that supervises the operations of a computer.

Operation Code. A portion of an instruction or control word that specifies the function that the computer is to perform. Eventually translated into binary-form machine language, the operation code may be any one of several high-level forms when entered by the programmer.

Packing and *Packed*. The process by which data is changed so as to occupy less space. In packed decimal, for example, two decimal digits, each represented by four bits, are placed in one byte (an eight-bit unit). This connects a code that uses eight bits to represent characters to a form that uses only half the storage space.

Parity Checking. As defined in the dictionary, "parity" has to do with maintaining equality. Applied to computer use, it means adding a bit to a unit of information so as to maintain the total number of 1s in that unit always odd or always even, depending upon which method is chosen. The bit added is called the parity bit, and it is a way of checking the accuracy of storage or transfer.

Pascal. A general-purpose language described in Chapter 4. Pascal is the newest of the high-level programming languages.

Peripherals or *Peripheral Equipment*. Units that support the computer. Tape units, disk drives, and printers are peripherals; they do no computing themselves but store and display data.

PL/1 Programming Language 1. A general-purpose language that combines some features of COBOL and FORTRAN. PL/1 is not one of the most popular languages.

Polling. A scheme in which a central unit chooses one remote unit after another and exchanges data with each remote unit that has information ready.

Usually associated with a central computer and many remote terminals.

Program. (1) A collection of computer instructions arranged so as to cause the computer to perform a specific task. (2) The act of selecting and placing in the proper order the instructions required.

Protocol. Most often associated with the exchange of data between two systems separated by considerable distance, protocol means the rules and conventions that will be followed by each system during the exchange.

Pseudocode. The technique of writing out the major steps in a program in a language that is neither English nor the statements of the programming language but which can be converted to statements without difficulty.

Random or *Direct Access*. The ability to gain access to any one storage location among many in an equal amount of time and effort and not depending upon any previous action. Tape units, for example, are serial access rather than random access.

Reading. The retrieval of information from some form of storage.

Read-only Memory (ROM). A storage unit whose contents cannot be changed during normal operation. In other words, data cannot be written into this memory by the computer; it was placed there in advance by a special means, and the computer can only read the memory contents. Read-only memories have the advantage of being very small and requiring a minimum of supporting circuits.

Real-time Processing. The processing of data from an event when the event is actually occurring rather than storing the data for processing later. An example of real-time processing would be a machine tool being operated by a computer in which the progress of the tool was sensed by the computer, and directions given by the computer were based on the tool's progress.

Record. A group of bytes, characters, or words organized and handled as a unit is the narrow definition of "record" used in the computer industry. "Record" is usually applied to the organization of data on magnetic tapes and disks.

RPG (Report Program Generator). A language intended to produce reports from data files. RPG is described in Chapter 6.

Scientific Application. The use of a computer to solve scientific and engineering problems, as opposed to typical business applications.

Sector. An arc-shaped section of a track on a disk or diskette.

Sequential File. A file organized so that information is accessible in the sequence in which it was stored. Data is written at the end of a sequential file.

Software. Very commonly used to mean programs, while hardware means the equipment, but originally meant the programs, programming aids, and the documentation associated with programs.

Source Computer. The computer in which the source program is entered and compiled.

Source Program. The statements originally entered by the programmer before they are assembled, compiled, or interpreted. The program written in the source language.

Structured Programs (Programming). The organization of programs into clearly defined sections or modules using the three basic control structures of sequence, selection, and repetition so that overall program development, testing, and maintenance are simplified.

Subroutine. A small group of instructions intended to perform one specific function. Whenever this function is required by a program, the subroutine is called and executed. This allows several different programs to use the same subroutine and avoids the need to include these instructions in every program.

Supervisor. Part of the operating system that manages the flow of jobs and allocation of resources.

Syntax Error. Improper construction of a statement or entry.

Time Sharing. Generally thought of as the sharing of a large central computer by several parties, usually from remote locations, on the basis of having certain intervals assigned to each party. Sometimes the access is based on demand, and in other cases it is based upon time assignments made in advance.

Translation. The conversion of one form of code to another. For example, source statements are "translated" to machine language by assemblers, compilers, and interpreters. Operation codes are translated into commands by decoders in the control units, and a code such as ASCII held in storage is translated to EBCDIC for transmission to another system.

Variable. A data item whose value is subject to change during program execution and is therefore named rather than provided in a literal form.

Volume. A large collection of files, usually a large physical division such as a reel of magnetic tape.

Word. One of the basic units of information processed by the computer. Most often, a word is considerably larger than a byte. A computer may use a sixteen-bit, thirty-two-bit, or forty-eight-bit word as its basic unit of information.

Writing. The process of placing information in a storage medium.

Answers

ANSWERS TO
SELF-TEST FOR CHAPTER 1

1. A computer program is a set of instructions that makes a computer perform a specific task. Although the instructions may be provided in several programming languages, they are always converted to machine language before being executed.

2. *Application programs* are the programs that cause the computer to perform useful work. *Utility programs* support application programs by performing servicing tasks. *Diagnostic programs* detect and isolate *computer failures*. *Operating systems* manage the computer tasks. *Programming systems* allow programs to be prepared.

3. An operating system is a control program that provides services in order to "tie things together." It manages the loading of programs, controls the use of memory, and schedules jobs.

4. A programmer can control what information is displayed or printed and its position on the screen or paper.

5. OPEN is a common instruction given when a specific file is to be made accessible to other instructions such as READ or WRITE. CLOSE terminates access to a file so that the READ and WRITE instructions cannot reach the file contents.

6. A *field* is a character or group of characters handled as a unit and having meaning as a unit. "Address" may be a field, as may "invoice total," and similar units of information. A *record* is generally a group of fields holding information related to one subject. All the information about one customer would be held in a customer account record,

for example. A *file* is made up of records that are related. Customer account records would be held in a file named CUSTOMER AC-COUNTS, for example.

7. A numeric field is used in calculations and may hold only numbers. Punctuation and related signs may be provided when the field is displayed or printed, however. An alpha-numeric field may hold any of the characters in the character set; it is not used in arithmetic.

8. Sequential access allows a record to be reached only after all the preceding records have been passed. Records are written only at the end of a file and are read in the sequence in which they were recorded.

   Direct access allows a record to be reached without the user having to pass through preceding records.

   Indexed access allows records to be stored in order by their key. Any record can be read immediately when the key is provided, and no preceding records have to be read.

9. A key is a specific field in a record in an indexed sequential access file. Records are stored in order by the value of this field. In order to read from this type file, the program provides a key. The record with the matching key is then read.

10. To eliminate redundant information, which occupies valuable storage space and is costly to update.

11. *Preparation of the program specifications*, which describe what the program must do. *Design of the program*, which lays out the overall logic by which the program will go about meeting the specifications. *Writing the program* in the language required. This involves selecting and placing in order all the steps required to fulfill the program design.

Testing the program first with known information and then in the system of which it will become a part. *Documenting and releasing the program* for all users.

12. A flowchart is used to organize the logic of a program. It shows in a graphic form the processes and decisions needed in the program.

13. A decision is being made at that point in the program logic.

14. Decision tables provide a summary of all possible conditions that may exist at a specific time in a program and show the action to be taken for each condition.

15. An English or near-English statement of the program logic. It is used in program design to lay out the functions to be performed and decisions to be made.

ANSWERS TO
SELF-TEST FOR CHAPTER 2

1. During the *entry* phase, the program source statements are provided to the programming system. During the *compilation* phase, the source statements are processed into a form that can be executed by the computer. And, during the *execution* phase, the program is performed.

2. A high-level language provides instructions that produce recognizable operations such as OPEN, READ, PRINT, PERFORM.

3. A compiler is a program that translates the source statements into the form needed by the run-time system for the execution phase. It produces an object program and a list of any errors found in the source program.

4. The source program is the set of source statements provided by the programmer. A source list is a list of those statements after they have been entered into the compiler and processed by the compiler. A source file is the file in which the source program is stored after it has been entered into the computer. An object program is the final (finished) program ready to be executed.

5. A syntax diagram shows how the body of a source statement may be constructed. It is needed as a guide to construct a statement correctly in the programming language. A

great many combinations are possible in the construction of most statements.

6. To show the proper position of the components of each source statement.

7. Arithmetic operators included $+$, $-$, $*$, $/$, and $**$. Relational operators included: $=$, $<>$, $>$, $<$, $>=$, and $<=$. Answers are:

   A*B/C

   (A**2)**B

   A<B

   B<>A

8.

Operators	Order
+ (Add)	4
*	3
/	3
− (Sub)	4
**	2
+ (Make positive)	1
− (Make negative)	1

9. A one-dimension array has a series of entries in the form of a list. Each item in the list is chosen by a single subscript. A two-dimension array has rows and columns, as in a table or matrix. Each item (element) is identified by a double subscript (2, 2) that selects an element at the intersection of the row and column number given.

10. A function is a preprogrammed calculation. When the function's name is given in an expression, the function is performed and the result entered into the expression at the point at which the function name and its argument (the quantity named within the parentheses following the function name) appear.

11. "Evaluated" means that all the components of the expression have been fully processed (resolved) and that the final result, whether "yes" or "no" or a number, is available.

12. This question could be answered in a variety of ways, but the greatest effect on the programmer is that he must learn a new way to write mathematical expressions.

13. A procedure is a section of an overall program that is handled as a unit. It is named in some manner and has a definite beginning and end. A procedure is "called" by the overall program when the specific task the procedure performs is needed.

14. Structured programming allows the parts of

a program to be clearly identified and separated. This makes it easier to write a program in sections and to test and maintain it.

15. They make it possible to use structured programming. Without these control structures, the programmer must construct his own structures to obtain the same results.

16. The programmer is responsible for arranging for the return; it is not automatic. Of course, the return can be provided by another GOTO instruction.

ANSWERS TO
SELF-TEST FOR CHAPTER 3

1. c. A3. String variables are named with a letter (A–Z) followed by a $.

2. Numeric variables may have one- or two-character names. The first character must be a letter (A–Z) and the second character, if used, must be a number.

3. String constants are enclosed in quotation marks; numeric constants are not.

4. a. Establishes a numeric array, named A, of 10 rows and 25 columns.
   b. Adds A and B, divides the total by 2, and puts the result in numeric variable S.
   c. Prints the words PROGRAM COMPLETE, beginning at wherever the current printing position is. Then goes to the beginning of the next line.
   d. Enters HARRIS, GILMAN, and WILLIAMS in a string data table. Enters 70, 90, and 75 in a numeric data table.

5. a. Six.
   b. It is labeled as if it were a numeric variable; it is a string variable and should be named E$.
   c. GET #2 31 = H1
   d. PUT #2 36 = G

6. *Beginner's All-purpose Symbolic Instruction Code.*

7. The symbols used to indicate the arithmetic operations to be performed: + means add or make positive, − means subtract or make negative, * means multiply, / means divide, ↑ or ** means raise to the specified power.

8. The symbols used to show relationships between expressions that are to be tested.

9. All are. A string constant can include any character, including numbers, but string constants are not processed as if they have numeric value.

10. It establishes the format (and sometimes part of the contents) for data that is variable and can be set up only once for many items to be handled.

11. BASIC form:
    a. LET A = (B*H)/2
    b. P = X**3 + 78*X + A
    c. C = SQR(3*X + N)
    d. A = (T + I)/M

12. To establish a new file of data and allow computer access to that file.
    To allow computer access to an existing file.

13. DATA "CHAIR", 99.95, 3, "CLIPBOARD", 2.50, 14, "PAPER PAD", 0.90, 40

14. READ T$,P,Q

15. DISPLAY (or PRINT) "TYPE OF PRODUCT", "PRICE EA.", "QUANTITY"

16. INPUT T$,P,Q

17. PRINT #1 "TYPE OF PRODUCT", "PRICE EA.", "QUANTITY"

18. PRINT #1 T$,P,Q

19. LET B1 = B − C

20. LET T = L*W*D

21. FOR X = 1 TO 10

22. IF A > = 40 THEN 500

23. GOSUB 700

24. A = 10, B = 20, and C = 30 after the READ statement. A is raised to the power of 2 (squared) first, placing 100 in the expression, B is multiplied by 3 next, placing 60 in the expression. Then B (60) is added to A (100) to total 160. Finally, C (30) is subtracted, producing a factor of 130 to be assigned to X.

25. First Program: Three variables (X,Y,Z) are to be read from the numeric data table but only two (5,10) are provided by the DATA statement.

    Second Program: The relationship in line 30 is true if A is greater than 3, but the branch to line 60 prints the opposite message. The messages are reversed or the logic in line 20 is wrong.

    Third Program: There is an error in the expression in line 20. The multiplication operator is missing from 2Z.

    Fourth Program: The FOR/NEXT Loop A crosses over the FOR/NEXT Loop B. B's action must be within A's, so lines 50 and

60 have to be reversed to make this a legal use of nested loops.

ANSWERS TO
SELF-TEST FOR CHAPTER 4

1. Declarations section and main body (or main block).
2. Labels, constants, data types, variables, procedures, and functions.
3. 2
   4
   1
   3
4. a. Invalid because it begins with a number and includes a hyphen.
   b. Valid. Identifiers may include digits, but may not begin with a number.
   c. Valid. Identifiers may be of any length.
   d. Invalid. Includes a reserved word (LABEL).
   e. Invalid. Identifiers must start with a letter and only include letters and digits.
5. Either of two ways.
   (1) Enclosed within (*....*) and (2) enclosed within { }.
6. Integer, real, character, and Boolean.
7. Arrays, records, strings, files, sets, and lists.
8. A value of 49 is placed in the expression at the point where this function (square) and its argument (X) appear.
9. ARCTAN (arctangent) and ABS (absolute value) are arithmetic. PRED (predecessor) and SUCC (successor) are character.
10. Truncate "chops off" the number at the decimal point; therefore, A has a value of 2.
11. a. Legal.
    b. Legal.
    c. Not legal because commas are not allowed.
    d. This is a real data type, not an integer.
12. a. Legal.
    b. Missing zero to left of point.
    c. Legal.
13. ( ) parentheses would be removed first.
    −, + are equal in precedence. Whichever is on left would be applied first.
    > is a relational operator; it is applied last.
14. 2 times 3 is 6. 6 divided by 5 is 1.2. 4 plus 1.2 is 5.2.

15. DIV is used with integers only. The result here could be (and is) a real number.
16. Prints or displays the words GOOD MORNING on a printer or screen.
17. Use WRITE ('GOOD MORNING'); This statement produces the same words but remains on the same line for additional entries.
18. AVGRADE: = (ENGLISH + MATH)/2;
19. VAR INTERESTRATE, PERCNTPAID, BALDUE: REAL;
20. BEGIN and END;
21. The REPEAT/UNTIL loop will perform the enclosed statement at least once because it checks the condition at the end of the loop. WHILE/DO checks the condition at the beginning of the loop.
22. a. PRED (BLUE)   a. RED
    b. PRED (RED)   b. None (Error)
    c. SUCC (BLUE)   c. YELLOW
    d. ORD (RED)   d. 0
    e. ORD (BLUE)   e. 1
23. a. Declares the variable J to be of the INTEGER data type.
    b. Opens NEWFILE for writing.
    c. Opens OLDFILE for reading.
    d. Terminates the main body of the program.
    e. Provides a comment.
    f. Creates a blank line on the printer or display.
    g. Assigns the value of 5 to the variable ITEM.
    h. Performs procedures INITIALIZEACCOUNTS and REVISEACCOUNTS, then ends the program.
    i. Adds the current value of CHARGES to the current contents of an element of the array COSTS selected by (indexed by) DEPT and then returns the sum to that same array element.
24. a. WRITELN;WRITELN;WRITELN;
    b. WRITE ('MY NAME');
    c. VAR DEDUCTIONS: REAL;
           EMPNO: INTEGER;
           JOBCODE: CHAR;
    d. READ (EMPNO [1]);
    e. BALANCE: = BALANCE + DEPOSIT;
    f. MONTHPAY: = AMTOWED/36;
    g. VAR EXPENSES:ARRAY[1..50] OF INTEGER;
    h. IF APPAGE > MINAGE THEN WRITE ('AGE OK');

ANSWERS TO
SELF-TEST FOR CHAPTER 5

1. Identification provides the program name and information concerning the program origin. Environment relates the program to the equipment and system it will be working with. Data defines and describes all data the program will process, including the forms of inputs and outputs. Procedure provides the executable statements that carry out the logic of the program.

2. Column 7 defines the type of statement on a specific line, as follows: A blank indicates a normal statement, a hyphen (-) the continuation of a word or number from the previous line, and an asterisk (*) means the line is only a comment.

3. Invalid identifiers are:
   TOTAL OF FIRST includes blanks
   CUSTOMER'S-ACCOUNT includes punctuation (apostrophe)
   ACCEPT uses a reserved word.
   4TH GRADE STUDENT AVG includes blanks.

4. 30 characters.

5. A Only alphabetic characters may appear in the position.
   X Alphanumeric. Any character in the character set may appear in the position.
   9 Numeric. Only numbers may appear in the position.

6. 01 CUST-ORDER
   03 ORDER-NO   PIC X(10).
   03 FILLER   PIC X(2).
   03 CUST-NAME   PIC X(28).
   03 ORD-DATE   PIC X(6).
   03 TOT-AMT   PIC 999V99.
   03 FILLER   PIC X(9).

7. DISPLAY 'ENTER EMPLOYEE NAME.'

8. 01 An overall data group, such as a record or a table.
   02–49 Items within a data group and subsequent subdivisions of the data.
   77 An independent data item, which is not part of a data group.

9. a. PIC 99V99 A four-place number with two decimal places.
   b. PIC X(7) A seven-place field that may hold any characters.
   c. PIC A(20) An alphabetic field (letters only) of twenty positions.
   d. PIC 999 A three-place integer.
   e. PIC XXXXX A five-place alphanumeric field.
   f. PIC 9(5)V9(2) A seven-place number with five integer positions and two decimal positions.

10. PIC 999 becomes PIC S999.

11. To move either a literal or the contents of a variable into another variable. Often used to construct output records and printer or display lines. (MOVE CUST-TOTAL TO BAL-DUE.)

12. a. ADD DEPOSIT TO BALANCE.
    b. ADD DEPOSIT TO BALANCE GIVING NEW-BALANCE.
    c. SUBTRACT PAYMENT FROM AMT-DUE.
    d. MULTIPLY AMT-BORROWED BY INT-RATE GIVING INT-CHGS ROUNDED.
    e. ADD INT-CHGS TO AMT-BORROWED GIVING TOTAL-DUE.
    f. DIVIDE TOTAL-DUE BY REPAY-PERIOD GIVING MONTHLY-PAYMENT ROUNDED.
    g. COMPUTE A = B*H/2.

13. a. Words that may be used to improve the clarity of a statement but which are optional.
    b. Words that are mandatory if a specific statement and feature is to be used.
    c. Square brackets show optional material.
    d. Braces show a choice that must be made.
    e. Lowercase words are the generic names for variables, records, literals, etc.
    f. Ellipsis points show that the previous option may be repeated.

14. IS NOT EQUAL TO is the same as NOT =.
    IS GREATER THAN is the same as >.
    IS NOT LESS THAN is the same as NOT <.

15. Add, subtract, multiply, divide, and raise to a power are the actions of +, −, *, /, and **, respectively. First applied: **. Second applied: * and /. Last applied: + and −

16. ACCEPT and DISPLAY are most often used for low-volume inputs and outputs, respectively. Installations differ, but ACCEPT could be used for keyboard or card reader inputs while DISPLAY could be applied to the display screen or printer. READ and WRITE,

on the other hand, would be used for high-volume inputs and outputs, which could include some card readers and printers as well as tape and disk files.

17. GO TO, PERFORM, and IF/THEN/ELSE.
18. IF CURRENT-BALANCE IS LESS THAN MIN-ACC-BAL DISPLAY 'BALANCE TOO LOW.' ELSE NEXT SENTENCE.
19. The value of the data item whose name appears in the DEPENDING ON phrase is determined and it chooses one of the procedures listed in the GO TO statement. If the data item value is two, for example, it causes the GO TO statement to branch to the second procedure listed.
20. PERFORM FINISH-CHECK-PAYMENTS.
21. PERFORM SALESMAN-COMM-CALC 7 TIMES.
22. The environment division names each file, assigns it to a specific unit, and declares the access method. In the data division, the file is further described, giving the format of records used.
23. ENVIRONMENT DIVISION, INPUT-OUTPUT SECTION, and FILE-CONTROL paragraph.
24. DATA DIVISION, FILE SECTION, and FD (file description) paragraph.
25. OPEN, READ, CLOSE.
26. *One record* is read; *one record* is written.
27. OPEN INPUT FORMER-EMPLOYEES. OPEN I-O FORMER-EMPLOYEES.
28. Provided in the data division, loaded from an external source, and results from computations.
29. OCCURS clause. DATA DIVISION, WORKING-STORAGE SECTION, description entry paragraphs.

ANSWERS TO
SELF-TEST FOR CHAPTER 6

1. The display area is organized into a grid pattern. Any point on the grid can be selected by giving the number of a column (X coordinate) and a row (Y coordinate). The point chosen is at the intersection of the selected row and column. Movement is described in terms of direction and number of grid squares to be moved, such as RIGHT 10.

2. COLOR chooses the background color and a palette of colors from which foreground graphics may be constructed. PAINT chooses the color to fill a specific area, such as a square or triangle. DRAW constructs a shape; part of the statement is a list of movements necessary to draw the shape. LINE produces a straight line from the current point to a point specified in the statement. It can also draw a line between any two points specified. PUT acquires a rectangular display section that was stored and places it on the screen at the position specified.

3. The acronym FORTRAN is composed from sections of the words *"for*mula" and "*trans*lator." Full FORTRAN is the language incorporating all features set out in the 1977 standard. Subset FORTRAN, while fully compatible with full FORTRAN, lacks certain features such as complex data types.

4. An asterisk in column 1 of the coding form.

5. .EQ. means equal, and .GE. means equal or greater than.

6. It appears: *variable = expression* and is thus like BASIC and COBOL but different than Pascal, which uses : = in place of the equal sign.

7. READ (5,360) A,B,C

8. Names for integer variables must begin with I, J, K, L, M, or N unless declared otherwise, while real data names can begin only with A through H and O through Z unless declared otherwise.

9. Integer, real, character, double precision, complex, logical.

10. Subroutines and functions are handled as separate programs, entered and compiled individually outside the main program.

11. It produces programs that are primarily used to generate reports from data held in existing files, although more powerful programs can be prepared by RPG.

12. Control card specifications, file description specifications, input specifications, calculation specjfications, and output format specifications.

13. Primarily the description of records in each input file handled by the program.

14. An indicator is an on/off device that shows what conditions exist. Indicators are each identified by a two-character code. Detail time is the time during which the sections of

the program dealing with the detailed lines of data are performed. Total time is the time during which the "total" logic sections of the program are performed to provide total and subtotal lines in a report.

15. File names may be eight characters, but only seven are used in some cases. Field names, table names, and array names (including references to elements in arrays) may be only six characters long.

16. A condition in which a record is read that differs from the previous record in ways specified by the programmer. Special action involving the "total" logic must be taken.

17. It provides the source statements involved in the arithmetic and related data manipulation to be done.

18. No. It uses ADD, SUB, MULT, and DIV, which is similar to low-level languages.

19. It describes the format of the output records.

20. On the right side of the output specifications. Editing words also appear in this area.